SURVIVING TO TELL THE TALE

D1596209

SURVIVING
TO TELL
THE TALE

A Time To Forgive

RICHARD A. VINCENT

First Edition

Hardback ISBN: 979-8-9878730-3-8
Paperback ISBN: 979-8-9878730-0-7
eBook ISBN: 979-8-9878730-1-4

Dedicated To
Tyler, Ben and Elizabeth Vincent

A journey into hell, following the devil's bidding, with no way out. A good Catholic kid's journey from a small quiet Indiana town, Noblesville, into the horrid bowels of the Vietnam war, and his thirty-year battle to forgive himself and come home, leaving booze and the devil's bidding behind.

NOVEMBER 15, 2022

Table of Contents

Introduction   xiii

SECTION 1--CHILD AS FATHER OF MAN   1
Chapter 1--Earliest Memories   3
Chapter 2--Just A Kid Growing Up In Noblesville   6
Chapter 3--Ice Hockey -- Not A Game For Wimps   15
Chapter 4--Mass With Father Gilman   19
Chapter 5--Sister Concepta's Wrath   22
Chapter 6--Slowly, Things Turned   25
Chapter 7--I Told You   27
Chapter 8--Mr. Lieber   31
Chapter 9--The Courage To Get It Done   39
Chapter 10--Like A Speeding Rocket   43
Chapter 11--Life Was Good   47
Chapter 12--Changes   50
Chapter 13--Moving On   53
Chapter 14--Doing My Dut   55y

SECTION 2--GO WEST YOUNG MAN   61
Chapter 1--Careful What You Ask For   63
Chapter 2--SERE Survival Escape Resistance Evasion   68
Chapter 3--Last Task Before Leaving   72
Chapter 4--Last Liberty   75
Chapter 5--Take A Trip   77

SECTION 3--ANOTHER WORLD--THAILAND   81
Chapter 1--A Whole New World   83
Chapter 2--Getting Ready   85
Chapter 3--Low And Slow   87
Chapter 4--Covering Air Force Ass   89
Chapter 5--Getting Shot At   93
Chapter 6--Free Time in Villages And Town   95
Chapter 7--Helping Hand   98
Chapter 8--Beer Hall   101

Chapter 9--Deal With The Devil   104
Chapter 10--The Deal   106
Chapter 11--Sympathy For The Devil   107
Chapter 12--Devil's Payment Now Due   109
Chapter 13--Just Keep Trucking   112
Chapter 14--Time To Reflect   115

SECTION 4--FLYING DEAD SUICIDE MISSIONS   121
Chapter 1--Like A Zombie   123
Chapter 2--Going Across The Fence   127
Chapter 3--Death And Evil   131

SECTION 5--ACROSS THE FENCE--FLYING INTO DEATH 137
Chapter 1--Just Another Day in Paradise   139
Chapter 2--Reality   141
Chapter 3--Popcorn, Ice Cold Beer, And Mary Poppins   142
Chapter 4--Keep On Keeping On   144
Chapter 5--Just Keep On Trucking   147

SECTION 6-1968--TET OFFENSIVE   151
Chapter 1--The Lying Never Stops   153
Chapter 2--No Time For Celebration   154
Chapter 3-- Marine Base Khe Sanh-Help Is Coming   157
Chapter 4--The Marines Needed Help   160
Chapter 5--Put It All In The Air   163
Chapter 6--VO67 THE GHOST SQUADRON   165
Chapter 7--Just Get It Done Right   167
Chapter 8-- My Friend Baat The Monk   167
Chapter 9--Vince And Bence   171
Chapter 10--Bang-Bang, Not Coming Home   175
Chapter 11--What's The Point   177
Chapter 12--Certifiably Crazy   180
Chapter 13--Thank God, Springtime   184
Chapter 14--Now What   186
Chapter 15--Home And Change   189
Chapter 16--Sleep   193

SECTION 7--DISORIENTATION AND WITHDRAWAL   199
Chapter 1--Dreams Sometimes Do Come True   201
Chapter 2--My Last Duty Station   204
Chapter 3--Reporting   206

Chapter 3--Getting Started   209

Chapter 5--The New Dream Japan   213

Chapter 6--Photographs My First Love   216

SECTION 8--LIVING THE DREAM   **219**

Chapter 1--USS Pueblo   221

Chapter 2--First Mission North Korea   223

Chapter 3--Waiting   225

Chapter 4--Getting Off The Carrier   227

Chapter 5--Saigon -- A Beauty   230

Chapter 6--The Job At Hand   232

Chapter 7--Finally, A Real Job   235

Chapter 8--The Coroner   237

Chapter 9--Give Love A Chance   241

Chapter 10--Helpful Kids   245

Chapter 11--A Good Piece Of Bullshit   249

Chapter 12--Red Light Kaz   253

Chapter 13--Junco Can Go   255

Chapter 14--Kazue & Sister   256

Chapter 15--Booze & Baths   259

Chapter 16--Quiet   263

Chapter 17--Summit Stamps   265

Chapter 18-- Photographing The Secretary   267

SECTION 9--GOODBYE VIETNAM   **273**

Chapter 1--Final Answer   275

Chapter 2--One Last Time   277

Chapter 3--Always Love a SEAL   281

Chapter 4--Goodbye Saigon   285

Chapter 5--Keep Moving   288

Chapter 6--The Folks Hanging Around   290

Chapter 7--Last Gig   292

Chapter 8--Last Stay Yokosuka   300

Chapter 9--Pack Up, Time To Return   302

Chapter 10--Home, North Island   303

Chapter 11--Man Animals At The Zoo   305

Chapter 12--John Wayne, The Duke   310

SECTION 10--HEADING HOME   **315**

Chapter 1--Going Home   317

Chapter 2--My God Still Alive   319

Chapter 3--Another World Home   321
Chapter 4--Trying, Failing, Trying, To Get It Right   323
Chapter 5--The Weekend   327
Chapter 6--Mrs. House Saves The Day   329
Chapter 7---What's Wrong With This Picture   333

SECTION 11--FULL CIRCLE   **335**
Chapter 1--Now What   337
Chapter 2--Plans Changed-- Do Over   339
Chapter 3--Now What   341
Chapter 4--Blaine Newcomb, Master Chef   344
Chapter 5--The Job   349
Chapter 6--The Golden Girl   349
Chapter 7--Summer Dreams   351
Chapter 8--Limestone Pits   353
Chapter 9--Mike   356
Chapter 10--My Last Photo Shoot--Late spring 1974   358
Chapter 11--Baby Killer   361
Chapter 12--Going Round And Round With The Devil   364
Chapter 13--Marriage   366
Chapter 14--On My Own   368

SECTION 12--DEMONS TO REST   **371**
Chapter 1--Help Please Help   373
Chapter 2--Reunion   376
Chapter 3--This Is The End, My Friend, The End   378
Chapter 4--Start Over and Put It To bed   385
Chapter 5--Start Of The End   391
Epilogue --The End, Naw, Just The Beginning   395

Acknowledgments   399

Introduction

W ell, this has taken me a long time to complete. It was started about 20 years ago but didn't go much farther than some disjointed thoughts and remembrances but I soon gave up on the idea that I could produce a story of my childhood and the events of Vietnam. For many years, I just didn't want to relive the trauma of the war.

But after a while, I began to contemplate the tragedy of it all. Eventually it became my obsession. I felt that my children should know about how for some the tragedy that was often left to endure after Vietnam, effected their lives for years after the war was over. Many, like me, eventually worked through it all. However, there were a lot of guys that just didn't find the path to redemption.

It was a very hot summer day as I recall, when by best school hood friend, Sergio Kornov stopped by, The sun was on the western horizon, if I remember correctly. It was certainly a great joy for me to have the opportunity to catch up on both of our lives. When he passed away, not very long after that visit I knew that some of us needed to talk about the Vietnam war, to find forgiveness. There was no question it affected everyone that went to war, served their time, and then came home and found it was needed to forget everything that happened. Society at that time, just didn't want to hear about it, politicians in particular felt compelled to disparage a lot of the men that served.

This was a time when a great percentage of society had great disdain for the veteran. It went on for years after Vietnam was over. Those were sad and tragic days, months and years for the guys coming home. Just about everybody forgot to say, Thank You, to all the guys that offered their lives willingly for their country.

It happened to a great deal of Vets. The loneliness and despair the war left us with. For a lot of those Vets, it was much harder to just put it behind us.

While I can't say with certainty that I always got the names exactly correct, I can say I spent a great deal of effort to make the story as accurate as was possible. In a few instances, I've deliberately changed a name hear and there. In some cases, I've left names out, but kept there position intact. (President, General, Secretary, etc.)

In a few cases, a name was omitted because they are still in government service. But every effort has been made to actually portray the event, and the person as accurately as was possible. The story has been constructed as accurately as I can remember or researched.

It has taken me over two years to complete writing this book for my children. And I guess, over thirty years to complete the story.

SECTION 1

Child as Father of Man

Do not follow the idea of others, but learn to listen to the voice within yourself.

Dogen Zenji

CHAPTER 1

Earliest Memories

SURE, I CAN DO THAT.
WHILE I MIGHT NOT HAVE A CLUE, MY MANTRA IS: SURE, I
CAN DO THAT. NO EXCEPTIONS, NO EXCUSES, JUST JUMP
RIGHT IN, AND WING IT IF NEEDED. IT'S AMAZING WHAT
GOOD THINGS CAN HAPPEN, IF YOU JUST JUMP RIGHT IN, TELL
YOURSELF THAT YES, I CAN DO THAT.
JUST KEEP TRYING, JUST KEEP GOING, JUMP RIGHT IN, YOU
NEVER KNOW, IT MIGHT BE FUN.
AND IF IT TURNS OUT YOU ARE UP TO YOUR ASS IN
ALLIGATORS, IT'S OK. AT LEAST YOU DOVE IN AND TRIED,
WHICH PUTS YOU WAY AHEAD OF THE CROWD.
TRY IT, JUST TRY....

That's what I learned growing up in a small town. My first clear memory was when I was three or four years old, and it's always stuck with me. It was springtime, and I remember crying in my bed. Mom came to me and picked me up, taking me to the rocking chair and holding me closely. I had a fever, and really was not doing well at all. Mom, I remember, began to read to me and after a while asked what book I would like to hear next. I remember it was "Little Black Sambo" that at the time was my favorite, and so that is what we read.

Political correctness hadn't arrived just yet, and "Little Black Sambo" wasn't considered racist or bad. For me, it was just a book I liked to have read to me, because it was a about a child and his determination.

At five I was sent to kindergarten at the First Ward school, right down the street from where we lived at the time. Between the school and our home on Evans Avenue, there was a giant field, with grass about eighteen inches high. Well, from the start, kindergarten just didn't seem like much fun to me. So, after a few days of sitting there trying to behave, which was not an easy task for me, I decided to leave, just call it quits. Around ten that morning I got up, walked out the door, and started home.

First, I had to cross the field with the tall grass. It was a beautiful sunny day and the grass seemed mighty inviting. So, I lay down and looked curiously at all the nature around me. Of course, I quickly drifted off to sleep, dreaming about the strange place I was in.

When the school eventually figured out that I was gone, they called my mother, wondering if I was home. Nope, I wasn't. In fact, I was nowhere to be found. Soon everyone began to freak out, mom, dad, the school, and the police. After a nice nap, maybe an hour or two, I finally awakened to the sound of police sirens, and people yelling my name. Of course, I found this quite distressing, and I jumped up and ran home as quickly as I could.

When I arrived, Dad was there to meet me at the door. He scooped me up and asked where I had been. I told him that I decided to leave school because it really wasn't very much fun.

And on the way home, I lay down in the tall grass by the school, just to see what it felt like, and fell asleep.

I remember he just looked at me, chuckled, and said, "Sounds like you had quite the adventure."

You better believe I did.

It was also the first time I understood the concept of trust. Dad would remain my most trustworthy of friends. He passed away when I was 17 years old. But even today when I have something really important to decide, Dad is always there, sitting on my right shoulder, ready to give advice, if I need it.

CHAPTER 2

Just A Kid Growing Up In Noblesville

My Roman Catholic family consisted of six brothers and three sisters, and of course, most of us went to the little parochial school on North 11ᵗʰ Street. Our Lady of Grace School was a small brick building, with three classrooms. Each room held three classes, except the room in front of the school, which only had the seventh and eighth grades. I started in the First, Second and Third Grade classroom.

The first day of school, we were taught how to tidy our desks. I glanced over at the other desks and quickly noticed a difference. One of the Craig boys had a deskful of new supplies. He had six new pencils, a new tablet with lines on each page, even a new box of crayons. I wondered what in the world did we need all this stuff for. Even though I hadn't a clue why we needed all this, I did know that I had nothing new. My pencils were all about three or four inches long with the erasers mostly worn off, and my tablet was just a pile of lined paper. It soon became clear that as a member of a big family, nothing I had was new, darn it.

Even though I was now suffering from a serious case of envy, my first day went comparatively well, with recess being the main event. Quickly I learned that there was a lot more parity outside on the playground. For the first fifteen years of my life, if size mattered, I had that in abundance.

But I soon learned that there was no parity when it came to anything costing money. New anything was not going to be in the cards for me for a long time. I had to accept that a pencil stub worked just as well as a brand new one did. I was beginning to think that having new stuff sometimes did matter. But it took a lot longer to learn that the 'new stuff ' really didn't matter so much after all.

At the start of grade school, most of the kids were excited to be there, but not me. I was ready to go into the world and begin running something. I'm not sure what, but I definitely should be running something. And for that, no schooling would be needed. With an attitude like this, I was often in trouble with the nuns at school, because virtually all the time, they insisted I still had things to learn. When I joined the first grade, the nuns started by putting me in the first row, but at the rear. Perfect for me, as I had a whole row of kids in front that I felt always needed to be pestered.

Otherwise, I was just plain bored. I suppose all kids have their difficulties, as they traverse that grey area between early childhood and teenage years. In my case, it seemed to be a hard, slow ride. I never felt quite on the same page as everyone else as they studied and did homework. I wanted to get moving, to do something, to prove my worth to my friends and classmates. Instead, I was always running to catch up to everyone else.

In hindsight, I was doing fine in school, learning to read and write. But I never felt fine. To me the world needed to be conquered, and I wasn't able to do that yet. I know I came across to classmates as a loner with a desire to prove that I was a lot better than they could possibly imagine. I always felt it imperative that I prove to all that I was the best, that I could do anything they could do, but way better.

In the playground at recess, we played a kind of kick ball. The playground's principal purpose was as a parking lot for church on Sunday, and it was covered in the limestone gravel used to pave roads and alleys. Most of the gravel pieces had sharp edges. Whoever had the ball was subject to being gang tackled, and so it was not a game for wimps. When my friends and I were playing, clothes got ripped, torn, and dirty from the first tackle, not to mention the cuts, scrapes and bruises also inflicted. While this was largely because of the gravel playing field, it was also because we were Catholic boys, and the Catholic kids always played rough.

Sometimes the priests staying at the rectory would come over and play with us. We extended no mercy and would tackle them just as hard. Sometimes visiting priests would join the fun with nice clean hassocks on, only to leave a half hour later, covered with scrapes and tears from the rocks we had to play on. It was great fun for all of us. Even the senior pastor for the parish would put a round or two in from time to time. He was a tough Canadian who had played hockey in his youth, so he treated us with no mercy. We loved that to him wounds simply meant you had done your duty and survived, even if your shirt or pants didn't. But he was smarter than the visiting priests. He would come over to play with his already torn and battered pants.

The school, on the other hand, was run by the nuns and governed by different church authorities. But it was clear that outside the classroom, Father Gilman was always given preference. This was important to me, because I got into about as much trouble on the playground as I did in class. And when Sister Concepta, the school principal, came to rebuke me, Father Gilman often took over. He was often around to help adjudicate my behavior on the playground. When I needed an attitude adjustment, he would not take much nonsense, but he was always fair and to the point. I liked his straightforward brand of discipline.

Unfortunately, I knew that when recess was over and we all went back inside, I belonged to Sister Concepta, and she never neglected to deal out justice as she saw fit. As Catholic nuns went, she was one of the sternest. She was a tall, slim, and much older than the other nuns. When she spoke, even the other nuns would stand, giving her all the attention, she demanded.

Her favorite punishment was the metal edge of a ruler, which she wielded with a vicious swipe across the knuckles. At least every other day, I got a good whack across the knuckles, with the sharp metal edge of her weapon. There were times when both of my hands were black and blue with her knuckle punishment, and sometimes it went on for weeks at a time.

Although I deserved all the punishment she dealt out, she had a way of shaming kids as well. I tried my best not to let dad know about the punishment. I never told him about it, and never showed him my knuckles.

My best friend at that time and later in life as well was a great guy named Sergio Kornov. We were friends all the way through our school days and beyond, and even after the war in Vietnam we remained close. His parents had come to America as refugees after WW-2. I remember his dad as a great man, and I had a lot of respect for him. Sergio told me he was an Italian tank commander during the war. When the Americans got close to him, he surrendered his tank, and was grateful to be taken prisoner by US forces.

When Sergio and I were both Boy Scouts, we went to summer camp together. One of those scouting excursions was quite memorable for both of us. That first day, we sat around the campfire listening to the camp counselors tell us scary stories about adventures in the woods. It started to get late, and we were all tuckered out from the day's activities, so we headed for our bunks still a little spooked.

Naturally Sergio and I shared a tent, and we crawled into our adjacent bunks. Now Sergio's momma was sweet enough to make Sergio a large box of peanut brittle, which we felt we should try out. Sergio's momma was a really good cook, and she made the best candy in the world. As we lay there crunching on the delicious peanut brittle, Sergio whispered, "What was that?" At first, I heard nothing, then I heard something inside our tent. It was a giant raccoon, and after those scary stories, it looked like a monster. The camp counselor had already warned us about raccoons: "Leave them alone! They look friendly but they're actually quite mean, so avoid them at all costs."

I said, "Sergio, I think it's a raccoon, don't move." Then the raccoon jumped onto Sergio's stomach and proceeded to eat the entire box of peanut brittle, spitting peanuts all over both of us. Naturally we were both scared absolutely out of our minds and didn't move a muscle until the darned thing was finished and left.

I finally whispered, "Sergio, is it gone?"

"Yea, I think so."

I whispered back, "Do you think we should get one of the counselors?"

At first Sergio and I were both silent, then Sergio said, "Nah, I think he's gone, no peanut brittle left. Let's just go to bed.

Good night, Rickey." I thought that was a mighty fine idea, so we waited until morning to tell the counselor about our visitor.

Later, that morning, our counselor complimented both of us for not moving until the coon had left, and then told us about another boy's encounter. This Scout didn't believe the counselors and tried to climb up a tree after one of the critters. His reward was a very severe wound and a series of rabies shots. He of course, told us in great detail about the pain he had to go through with each of the rabies shots, and the size of the needle used.

That fall we told Father Gilman about our Scout trip, and his comment was, "Well, you boys really did have quite the adventure." Quite shyly I replied that we sure did.

Back in school, both Sergio and I got into a bit of mischief and were given the ruler across the knuckle's punishment. The next day, Mr. Kornov came to school with Sergio in tow. He was Italian and spoke little English just yet. I could not understand a word he said, but I could tell he was unloading on dear Sister Concepta. During this beautiful tirade, I whispered to Sergio, "What's your dad saying?" He got a huge grin on his face and said he couldn't repeat exactly what his dad said after that, but the Italian words for *dirty* and *bitch* were used a lot. Of course, I had no idea what bitch meant at the time, but it was not hard to guess. "Wow" was all I could say. What Mr. Kornov said in Italian was something to the effect that he was not going to have anyone, especially a nun, touch his child, ever again. If corporal punishment was needed, it would be dealt out by him. We laughingly reminded each other of that time on many occasions through the years. I finally got Sergio to tell me how to say the words in Italian. You never know when you might need them!

My school years opened me up to these new experiences, but my personality was still shaped mostly by my parents. Mom and Dad were very different. While Dad was kind of an optimist, Mom was always telling us that life was a struggle. And her life was really quiet a struggle I guess, starting when she was just a child. Then she was given charge of her smaller sister, Goldie, who was totally blind from birth. Instead of enjoying her teen years, she always had to take care of Goldie, so she never had the chance for relationships with other girls and boys.

Everything revolved around taking care of her sister, until she reached the age of eighteen and left home, never to return. When she looked back on her childhood, she remembered only the struggle of taking care of a blind sister. This fatalism never left Mom, that life was always a struggle, there would be little to be thankful for, just work, struggle, toil, and maybe on rare occasions a little time to rest. Mom saw the dark side of everything, and that led her to warn me about all the difficulties she assumed were ahead in my life.

On the other hand, Dad was always chipper. He loved life, and every day was the beginning of a new adventure. He was always onto the next adventure, the next dream. This served him well most of the time, but he had no middle ground, no way to stay focused on the daily tasks at hand. On occasion this tendency would leave him with projects unfinished, with work to do that just didn't get done.

I remember that in the late 1950s, Dad really got excited about water softeners, and began to sell them, lots of them. He sold the Pilgrim softener, which was made in a town about the same size as Noblesville. Quickly Dad discovered that water softeners were usually only purchased by the wealthy who could afford to replace them when necessary. They were all made of metal, both the softener itself and the salt tank, which was needed to clean the softener mineral. Because of the steel used to make them, they would rust out within a few years.

Soon Dad began to experiment with fiberglass and invented a method to make the tanks with this material. He could sell them as softeners that would never rust, so they could last a lifetime.

Suddenly, our family went from just getting by, to one that had a little wealth. Dad had his tanks patented, and for a year or so, we were all set. But then he was off to invent other ways to use fiberglass, none of which were as successful as the tanks. They slowly strangled his company in development costs. When he passed away at the age of forty-eight, we were out of money.

Dad lived his life as if anything were possible if he could just get up and give it a try. He was always full of excitement, and it was contagious. He was a dreamer, and such a sweet man.

Mom and Dad were quite the combination: One always full of sadness, the other always ready for the next adventure. I guess I was lucky to have them both. Dad's excitement for life inspired me, but Mom's caution always kept me from dreaming too far out there.

The combination of viewpoints was an important lesson for me to learn. Yes, life could be fun, but it must also have rhythm. I needed to learn, stay on task, and never give up. I decided to go in a straight line and have fun. When I got sidetracked, I always came back to the line I was following, something Dad just couldn't do. There is a yin and yang, a good and bad, a right and wrong, to everything. I learned this early on, from both Mom and Dad. Both light and dark have purpose if you just look for both and recognize their intent.

CHAPTER 3

Ice Hockey—Not A Game For Wimps

Later that fall, the Indianapolis Chiefs hockey season began. Father Gilman was a hockey player in his youth, and as he came from Canada, hockey love was built into him. When my dad asked Father if he would like to attend a game with him, of course the answer was, "You bet I do."

Dad was from Concord, New Hampshire, and he had been in love with hockey since he was old enough to skate. He loved hockey just as much as Father Gillman did. They both got just downright crazy when watching a hockey game.

That day, my brothers and I piled into Dad's car with Ft. Gilman, and headed for the Indiana State Fairgrounds, where the Chiefs played. In the Indianapolis Field House, Dad had a pair of seats right behind the scorer's table and the Chiefs home bench. This way, he could extend his wisdom to the team on just how to play.

At that time, the Chiefs were the farm club for the Detroit Redwings, where the really big boys played. Most fans will tell you that the greatest hockey player ever was Gordie Howe, and I think he probably was. However, the Chiefs also had a great player, Armand "Bep" Guidolin. At the age of eighteen, he would soon be moving up to be the youngest player in the NHL. But this game, in the 1960-61 season, he was playing left wing for the Chiefs.

To have seats right behind the players was pretty special, even with a farm club team. On this particular day, Dad and Father Gillman were both excited to help out the team. They didn't hesitate to give the boys all the encouragement they could possibly give. Finally, Bep had had enough of their coaching and angrily skated up to their seats.

Now Father Gillman was usually dressed in such a way that you would know that you were talking to a priest, but not today. He was just wearing a black turtleneck, and nothing to show he was a priest. So, the unwitting Bep showed him no respect. "Now you folks have been giving me advice all day, and I've finally had enough. So, if you shitheads can just keep your mouths shut for the rest of the period, I'll win this game for you. Please, can you two assholes manage that?"

Both Father Gillman and Dad looked at each other, then up at the game clock, and saw that there was only about two minutes left and we were behind 0-2. If Bep did this feat, he would not only have a "hat trick," but we would win the game. Now to get a hat trick, a player had to score at least three goals in one game, and that was very, very hard to do. Father Gillman doubted it was possible, but being a good sport, he promised to be good for the rest of the game, just two minutes. I remember Dad asking Father Gillman if he thought there was even a prayer of a chance. They both looked at each other and laughed.

Well, the first thing Guidolon did was have a conversation with the coach, which we could not hear. All he wanted was the coach to leave him on the ice until the game was over. Of course, Coach agreed, because Bep was the best player on the team. Within a matter of seconds, Bep had scored a goal. That was wonderful but still a long way off to a win. Then within another half minute, he stole the puck, and charged to the other end, scoring another goal.

This was incredible, two goals in one minute. But now the puck would have to be won when the referees dropped the puck at center ice to begin play. Incredibly, we ended up with the puck with about 45 seconds left. Quickly Bep took the puck and began to move down the right side against the boards. Out of nowhere a defenseman checked him hard against the boards. Bep wasn't going to have any of that, and somehow managed to hold onto the puck. Incredible, just an incredible move.

Incredible wasn't over with just yet. He skated half the length of the ice, avoiding two defensemen, and scored the winning goal. To top it all off, Bep had gotten his hat trick, which meant he would be rewarded at center ice with a large fresh turkey, ready to pop into the oven.

Finally, after watching one of the best two minutes of hockey we had ever seen, the crowd started to come back to earth. Then Bep skated over to my dad and Father Gillman and then away to center ice. All of a sudden, Father Gillman became a priest again, rising and beginning to give a blessing to all the team members on the bench. Of course, the team was mostly Catholic Canadians, and they all crossed themselves and genuflected.

All but Bep, that is. He had no idea that he had been cursing a priest, and worse yet ordering him to behave. Quickly he came to his senses and genuflected at mid ice, red-faced and holding that enormous turkey. But no matter, the team came onto the ice, and as he stayed on one knee, pushed him right over to Father Gillman. Of course, the crowd was now in hysterics, but nonetheless the imperturbable Father gave him another blessing and then congratulated him.

Then, realizing that he was still holding a fresh turkey, Bep stood and handed Father Gillman the turkey. While Guidolin was clearly embarrassed for speaking harshly to Father, he was quickly forgiven, and thanked again for the game and the turkey. Actually, that was only fair. As I remember during that game, there was a lot of pretty salty language coming from both my Dad and Ft. Gillman.

Both Dad and Father Gillman really wanted the very best for the team, and they both truly cared. The best part was that on that day, I began to learn what belief really meant. With the game score at 0 to 2, with only two minutes left, it was going to take a miracle or at least a tremendous feat by Bep. Because of the attitude of Dad and Father Gillman, I began to realize that with faith, almost anything could happen. Just believe and with that you never know, anything was possible.

CHAPTER 4

Mass With Father Gilman

In our church, service for Sunday mass often had a shortfall of an altar boy, and sometimes two. On this particularly early morning mass, I was asked to help as one of the altar boys, and of course I was happy to oblige. It was a sweltering summer day, and the church was hotter than blue blazes. Of course, this little, white-framed church on North 11th Street had never been air-conditioned, and it could become quite warm in summer months.

The sacristy, which was found right behind the altar, had two areas. One was for the altar boys, where they dressed and kept the equipment for lighting the candles and preparing the incense. On the other side, the priest would be saying his Mass preparation prayers as he dressed in his vestments. Between these two areas was a narrow pass-through, where my dad had installed two enormous exhaust fans in the windows there, to at least get some air moving through the church.

Naturally, the altar boy side would get a little noisy from time to time, as it was on this Sunday. Father Gilman was comparatively tolerant of our mischievous ways, but on this Sunday,

Sister Concepta happened to be praying in the first pew of the church. She could easily hear our mischief and became so enraged that she stomped out of the church and around to the outside door to the sacristy. In she stormed, a nun prepared to do battle.

She blasted through the door and tromped right past Father Gilman as he said his prayers and prepared for mass. Down the hall she stormed, with a righteous blast of hell to be distributed to those little heathens. She got me by the ear and jerked me around, right into her face. As she was preparing to storm right down my throat, Father Gilman appeared. This sweet, kind, always peaceful man had transformed into a Wild West sheriff. He was not in the mood for taking prisoners. An invading nun had just interrupted him, and he was not going to stand still for this. Women in general were not supposed to be in the sacristy before or during mass, as decreed by the Pope in Rome.

He grabbed her shoulder and spun her around, right into his face. "Get moving, Sister," was all we heard him say as he began to back her down the hall. We all looked at each other and at the same time said, "Exhaust fans, Sister's veil, oh dang."

We all hustled into the hall to see what was going on, and there she was. The exhaust fans had sucked up her veil and wound it up so tightly she appeared to have been nailed to the wall. At this point, Father Gilman told us to line up for our exit to the altar. As we left for the altar, he whispered to us with a mighty big grin, "Let us not forget to pray for a safe extraction of Sister's garments."

Can I have an amen? Another lesson learned: Always stand firm and never get flustered. If you're right, you're right, and if you're wrong, you're wrong. In any case, it is no reason to fear the consequence. Father Gilman saved us from Sister's rant and anger, just when we thought we were all guilty of a punishable offence, having a good laugh, and being, well, boys. Always accept what you are and keep going, and never, never back away. Sister Concepta was standing there, ready to tear our heads off, but then our real boss showed us to stand firm, after all, he was in charge, she was in his domain, and so was banished. Indeed, can I have an amen.

CHAPTER 5

Sister Concepta's Wrath

I do remember I tried, and tried some more, to keep Sister Concepta happy with me. But there was a point she finally had had enough of miscreant behavior from little Ricky and called both of my parents to an after-school meeting. Of course, during the meeting with Mom and Dad, I was told to leave the room.

I knew they were going to be talking about me. As soon as I was out of the room and into the hall, I parked myself right against the crack at the bottom of the door. There I had an easy time listening to the entire conversation. Sister began the conversation in her typical blunt way, "As you know, for the entire semester, Ricky has been in trouble, disturbing the class, not paying attention, and not doing his assignments well. Really, at first, I thought it was just childish rebellion. However, I think his problem is much graver than that. He is just not as bright a child as others. Therefore he covers this inadequacy with childish, disturbing behavior."

My mother commented, "Well, I thought the same, but I just did not want to admit it. He behaves just the same at home, always the one in trouble. If there is a fight, if there is a disagreement among the neighborhood kids, I do not have to look far to find the culprit."

"But just a minute," Dad chimed in, "just because he is a bit mischievous at times does not mean there always is something wrong, does there? He is a kid. Kids are full of mischief. I was full of mischief. How do you know he is so slow?"

"Well," Sister said, "look at his work and his behavior on the playground, look at these recent test papers, homework papers. The best we can hope for here is a C student, and that is only if he begins to apply himself. He has not shown us he is capable of much more, and frankly, I do not think we can expect much more. Unless we see a marked improvement, what we should be striving for is to see to it that he gets a good basic education, so that he can become a good garage mechanic, or something of that order. Of course, we all need to keep Ricky in our prayers, which I assure you we do."

Hearing this conversation was crushing. It was the beginning of a very lonely ride through my youth. I was hearing that at best, I was just going to be a garage mechanic. I wouldn't even own the garage. I would never succeed on my own. It was absolutely crushing to me.

Naturally I immediately thought of myself as being a loser, one of those dumb kids. It was crushing and the worst thing you could have said about me. But worse yet, Mom was in complete agreement. Fortunately, Dad's words kept me from spinning completely out of control. When we got home after the meeting, Dad grabbed me and asked me to help him for a few minutes. We went to his shop, the now-converted garage, and started to move some stuff when he said, "If you want something, Ricky, all you need to do is believe, no matter what, just believe. If you do, you'll be amazed at what can happen. Don't let anyone dare tell you that you aren't smart enough. In the end, only you know who you are. The only judge is you. If you think it can be done, all you need do is begin. God has already given you the brains, just use them."

With that little sermon, I once again knew he was right. But still, that conversation with Sister Concepta and my parents would stick with me for a long time, a very long time. In the end, I knew dad was right, I knew all I had to do was believe. Little did I know at the time, that Dad's little message would serve me well and save me from a very dark period, coming right around the corner.

CHAPTER 6

Slowly, Things Turned

Both Sister Concepta and my mother were in perfect agreement with what they thought was my future. My dad, however, never agreed, never allowed me to think that I could not do anything I wanted. As far as he was concerned, my only challenge was finding something I wanted enough, to work for it. If I did, as far as he could see, everything was within my grasp.

But the damage was done. I'd heard their opinion that I was not the sharpest knife in the drawer by a long shot. Or so I thought at the time. But soon, I would know better, and take off like the rocket I was beginning to feel like, and felt I was perfectly capable of becoming.

When I got to junior high school, my prospects did not seem to improve much. I just didn't like school. But I soon realized that I loved learning. I loved books, and I liked to write stories just for my own fun. I liked to write about myself as some of the kid heroes at that time, like GI Joe, Superman, Rawhide Kid, or my favorite, the Lone Ranger. I never thought of my writing as anything more than fun, a way to exercise my imagination.

It was about this time that I also began to take interest in photography. As usual, I tried to read every book the local library had on the subject. I decided that photography was the perfect form of expression for me. With a camera, I could express myself and let my love of life show. It became the perfect metaphor for life. The visual image could say so much more than I knew how to express in words. It could say love, or death, or living. Suddenly I could make even a leaf tell an entire story.

When I discovered this miracle, I became engrossed. Photography captured me and held me for many years to come. There was a comfort it gave me that I couldn't get any other way. Soon I began to understand the power of an image. One image, one picture could tell a story, and do it eloquently. But I still hadn't figured out all I could do with my new skill.

By the time I got to high school, I still was not sure what I was going to do with this new interest. But I felt there must be some way to use my photography skill productively. Eventually I realized I wanted to take pictures for the local paper, the *Noblesville Daily Ledger*.

The *Ledger* was owned by the Neal family. Jim Neal was the editor, and his brother John ran the business end of things. I knew John Neal well, as he had been my Sunday school teacher. As time went on, I became very interested in any advice that Jim Neal would give me, especially as pertained to photography.

But I held back from offering my services to the *Ledger*. I thought I was not prepared to take on such an exalted role of newspaper photographer. Unfortunately, I did not yet own a decent camera. Also, I knew nothing about how to use a darkroom where I would be able to develop my film and enlarge pictures from the negatives. But fortunately, that was all going to change in the next year or so. Dad was right all along, "If you want it bad enough, anything is possible, anything."

CHAPTER 7

I Told You

At the start of my sophomore year of high school, the school paper put a notice out that they were looking for a photographer. Well, I thought this might be just the opening I was looking for. Unfortunately, they required a short-written piece along with a portfolio of pictures. Of course, I had no portfolio or written work. But I did have a lot of snapshots that I had been taking for the last few years with my trusty Brownie Star Mite. I bought a piece of black poster board, and started what I hoped would be a masterpiece. I took my best pictures and arranged them into one large picture by cutting the white border from each of them and mounting them all end to end and side by side, creating a giant picture. It turned out to be a winning idea.

It was hard to believe how my prospects had changed. On Monday, I was just a kid dreaming about someday being a photojournalist. By the middle of the week, I had managed to get the job as school photographer. That meant I would be doing all the photo work for the school paper and the school's yearbook. Unfortunately, I had no clue how I was going to get a camera and the other necessary equipment.

I also needed a darkroom to process the phenomenal pictures I was going to take with the new camera. Fortunately, the art teacher Mr. Morrison told me that the school did have a darkroom, but it had been shut down for several years. Of course, Mr. Morrison was delighted that someone had interest in using the darkroom as it was intended. However, it had long since been converted to a broom closet, and all the equipment was missing. Mr. Morrison would be no help as he knew little about darkrooms, although he did think of photography as a legitimate art form.

So, I had a darkroom but still needed to furnish it with equipment. Mr. Morrison suggested that I ask the school for permission to replace all the missing equipment. "You'll probably need to go see the school superintendent, Mr. Swinford, to get that kind of authorization."

I was going to have to con that high authority figure, the superintendent, to get the permission to furnish a darkroom lab. And then I still had to learn how to process film, enlarge, and print the film. I was just a high school sophomore!

But then I reminded myself that I had managed to get hired into a job that I had no idea how to carry out. I told myself, "Sure, I can do that." But how was I going to learn? I knew nothing about how to use a real camera, or a darkroom, and I knew no one that could help or give me advice.

This was not the first time, and would not be the last, that I had committed to something I knew nothing about. For me, half the fun of life was jumping into the water, then figure out how to swim. But, in the moment, this new job was more challenging than I had taken on before, and I was more than a little concerned. I will admit that I was in this way over my head, and could easily drown, unless I acted fast and learned enough to make a credible effort.

But what should I do first? Maybe, I needed a plan. By Friday I had gathered most of the information I needed to buy a camera and whatever other equipment was needed. Still, I had no idea what to do about the empty darkroom.

The next morning, Saturday, I got up and put all the money I had in a big pile on my bed. I had about forty-nine dollars and change. I knew this was not nearly enough to buy a camera, but then I had no idea what a camera cost either. At least it would be enough to get me a round trip bus ticket to downtown Indianapolis. The largest photo store in the state, one of the largest in the Midwest, H. Lieber Company, was only a few blocks from the bus station.

In 1962, the bus station in Noblesville was a block off the town square. I had never been on the bus, but I knew a lot of people used this to go to downtown Indy on Saturday to shop. The round-trip ticket cost me $1.05, which at the time seemed exorbitant, but I told myself it was either that or hitch hike. Because I was on a mission of the highest importance, it was imperative I make the trip.

Taking the bus to downtown Indianapolis, I was mesmerized by the sights along the way. But I kept focused on my mission. When I arrived at the downtown bus station, I realize I had no idea exactly where H. Lieber Co. was. All I knew was it was supposed to be the largest photo supplies store in the state, and I figured big was good.

People were going every direction from the station, as it was right next to the center of town, the Circle, and all the big stores were close by. Finally, I asked a woman, who was walking amazingly fast from the station, and was clearly on a mission, "Would you happen to know where the H. Lieber store is, Madame?"

She looked at me, said she had not a clue, and pointed to a phone booth. "Why don't you look it up?" Oh, good idea, I thought, going into the booth, and checking the phone book. I discovered the store was on Washington Street, only a block from the bus station.

As I entered H. Lieber's, my mouth was open, and my eyes were bulging. This was the largest store I had ever seen, much larger than Craycraft's, the department store in Noblesville. It was several stories high and dominated a good half of the block. Man, I had no idea they had a photo store as big as this. It was a monster of a store. For at least an hour, I stood in front of the store windows looking at all the equipment for sale. Some of it I recognized at once, but with other items, I had no idea what their purpose was. At first, I just stood there trying to decide if I should even go through the doors. Maybe they had a "no kids allowed" policy and I was too young. Or even in my Sunday church clothes, I was not dressed up nice enough to go into such a fine store. So, for a long time, I just stood there and watched people come and go through the front doors.

Finally, I realized I had spent a lot of my money, one dollar and five cents, just to get me here, and I had an important mission. In I went and as I looked around, I marveled to see aisle after aisle of products that had to do with taking a picture. There was darkroom equipment, lighting supplies, and one exceptionally long counter with what had to be at least a bazillion cameras. Man, oh man, now what do I do?

I decided this was a time when I would just have to let fate take over. I wasn't about to turn back, not now.

CHAPTER 8

Mr. Lieber

As I suspected, there were not very many kids my age on the premises, so I tried to look asßtute and with profound knowledge of all I was seeing. Of course, I had not a clue what all this equipment was for, but man, did they have a lot of it. One aisle had all kinds of chemicals and photo paper, another had enlargers, and another had timers and other mechanical items I couldn't identify. I became engrossed in this photo equipment heaven.

Slowly, I walked up and down each aisle, reading both front and back as many of the packages as I could, hoping I would not be discovered as an impostor and thrown out. This store was magical, amazing, and more than a bit confusing. Up and down each aisle I traveled. Soon I concluded that I was not just over my head, I was in a new world, without a map, without a compass. At this point I thought I should just leave, go to the library, and try to learn about all this stuff.

But I knew I needed to at least look at cameras and hopefully find a good used one. I just hoped that they would not take one look and toss me out, especially if they found out I was not exactly a legit customer.

It must have taken me a least an hour to navigate my way to a position about thirty feet away from the cameras. I knew it was getting late and I would have to be hopping on a bus within an hour or so. But I just could not belly up to the counter, where they had dozens of stools for customers to examine various pieces of equipment. I just felt like I had no right to be there, that I was somehow intruding, even though at this point there were very few customers left in this photo heaven.

Suddenly a giant man, at least six and a half feet tall, approached me and asked if he could help. He was dressed in a suit that was badly rumpled and a shirt that had more wrinkles than I had ever seen. His tie was sort of tied, but it had a big stain that looked like ketchup. And his hair was more like a giant glob of un-cut grass. But besides all that, he had the kindest way about him. "Well, what brings you in today?" he asked. His voice was soft but firm, and I instantly felt a sense of comfort.

"Sir, I do not want to be a bother, I was just looking at your darkroom equipment, and someday I want to buy a camera. But I do not know what I should do about it all."

The salesman said, "Well, young man, let us see if we can begin to fix that. You are interested in darkroom equipment, someday, and a camera as well, someday. Is that about right, or is it darkroom someday, but you need a camera right away?" Then he started laughing, and the more he laughed, the more comfortable I became with him.

I admitted, "Yes sir, that is pretty close, but I do not have much money today, and I sure don't want to be a bother. My school, Noblesville High School, just made me the photographer for the school paper and yearbook. But the school's darkroom does not have any equipment, and I just have a Brownie Star Mite and know that will not be sufficient."

"OK, let me see if I have this straight, you have a darkroom to use, but no equipment and do not know how to use it even if you did. In addition to that, you need a camera. Is that about, right?"

I replied, "Yes sir, I guess so."

"Let's start where we are at and look at darkroom first. But wait just a minute, I need to retrieve an invoice book so we can keep track how much this will cost you, or somebody. Be right back."

He was only gone a minute, and when he reappeared, he had a clip board with a blank invoice on it. "Now, the first thing you are going to need is an enlarger, so let us start there. Then you are going to need a good timer, trays, beakers, forceps, couple of special bulbs for the lights, and of course photo paper and chemicals, and a device or container to develop film."

As we walked up and down the aisles, he explained to me what each piece of equipment was for, and how to use it. Man, I thought, he has great knowledge of all this stuff. I am not sure how long this educational process took, but he had to have spent at least an hour with me. I began to worry that I was taking too much of his time, when I could not buy any of these products, even if I wanted to. And boy, did I want to.

Suddenly, he spun around and said, "I'm Kurt by the way, and your name is?" He extended his hand, again with that giant smile.

"Rick Vincent, sir, and I really appreciate all the help you have given me."

"Not to worry, Rick. We're just getting started, hope you're having fun."

"Oh, this is swell, really swell, I didn't know photography involved so much stuff."

He nodded. "Let's look at cameras, shall we."

Off we went to the long counters, the really magical area, with cameras of all sizes and kinds. By this time, we were about the only people left in the store. Again, I apologized for taking so much of his time and asked if they were about to close. He said yes, but that did not matter, we could spend as much time as we wanted. At this point, one of the clerks came up to us and asked Kurt if he needed help to close out the sale.

"No, we don't need your help just right now. But in a few minutes, I'll need somebody to go upstairs and retrieve a camera for me."

The clerk said very politely, "Yes sir, happy to oblige."

Then Mr. Kurt looked at me and said, "Okay, what are we looking for, do you think? This being your first camera beyond your Brownie Star Mite, maybe we should look at some of the cameras over here."

He put on the counter a beautiful camera, with lots of chrome and a real glass lens. It was a Hasselblad, I knew from looking at all the ads in the photo magazines, an exceptionally fine, and awfully expensive camera. After showing me a little about how it worked, how to focus it and hold it, he handed it to me and said, "Try it out." Suddenly, I found myself holding one of the crown jewels of cameras. I was shaking. It could not be true, but here I was holding and looking at the most beautiful camera I had ever seen.

"Next," he said with that big smile, "let us look at a more practical camera for a hot-shot photojournalist."

"Yes sir, yes sir, I agree." Thank God he took back the Hasselblad camera. It had a price tag of almost a thousand dollars, and I knew you could buy a really nice car for that.

Then he took me down the counter to a section with dozens of cameras he called "twin lens reflex cameras." Soon he found the camera he was looking for, a real beauty, a Yashica D, twin lens reflex. I had seen these in the photography magazines but had never held one before. It was like holding a rare piece of art.

After letting me enjoy it for a few moments Kurt said, "This is a great camera for a young photojournalist. It's durable. It has a particularly good lens and can be used with other lens attachments if desired. In addition, it comes with a few other items you might need as well." He explained that I would need a light meter, film, instruction manuals, and a few other things.

Suddenly I returned to reality. How would I ever be able to afford all this? It would take me a good long time to make enough, weeks or months maybe. Then Kurt asked me how much money I had brought with me today. I reached into my pants pocket and pulled out all the nickels, dimes, quarters, pennies, and dollar bills, and put the entire cache on the counter. It was just a little over forty-six dollars and change. I told him he could have all my money as a deposit, and I would be working ridiculously hard to get the additional money to complete the sale soon.

He looked at my pile of money, and back at me. Then he looked again at the money in deep contemplation and said, "Just sit tight, while I tally up the costs for you, and then we need to talk."

"Yes, sir," I said. "That's all the money I have now. But I do work after school almost every day and on weekends as well."

Kurt replied, "Be right back, just give me a couple minutes."

Then he asked the clerk to go upstairs. I could not hear what was being said, but I noticed that the clerk took off at once. After a short while, Kurt returned and put a neatly typed invoice in front of me. It was addressed to Noblesville Schools, and I thought, looked very official. At the bottom of the invoice was a line that said, "All questions should be brought to the attention of Mr. Kurt Lieber."

I realized Kurt was related to the H. Lieber family but did not mention it. He was continuing, "Okay, that should take care of the darkroom for the moment. Just tell them that we deal with a lot of the school systems in the state and will treat them with fairness. Now, let's you and I go over to the book area."

I had not before noticed their entire section with books about photography. Kurt pulled out a couple books. "Now you are going to need a few basic instruction manuals. This book here, *Kodak Darkroom Procedures*, and you will also need this book, *Basics of Photography*. These two books should give you, for now, all the info you need to take pictures, develop the negatives, and print them. At some point you will probably need more detailed books, but that is down the road a far piece, for now these will do nicely."

I said eagerly, "Yes, sir, I'm sure it would. But the money I have is not near enough, and I don't have any more. I'll have to work for it and that is going to take a little time. But I promise, when I have enough, I'll be right back and buy everything, just as you suggest. You can keep all the money I brought with me today as a deposit. I promise, I will be back soon with more money."

He looked at me and just started to laugh. "Son, here is what I am willing to do. You take all this stuff home, get started taking pictures for your school, and do not forget to remind people where you buy your equipment and film. I expect you to send me what you can, every week until the bill is paid. The bill totals out to sixty dollars with the camera and accessories. And the deposit you will make today, forty dollars even, will be more than enough. Does this sound agreeable to you?"

I took a deep breath. "Yes, sir, but--"

"I expect you to send me a payment every week, directly to me. Here is my card. Also, here is a second card which you may need to give to the school. If not, just keep it handy, in case you have any questions. Now if you don't make all the payments, I'll send a bill for the remaining balance to your school principal. But I don't think that's going to be a problem for you. Also just send the invoice for the darkroom equipment when it has been approved, or call if you want, so we can get your darkroom up and running. Now I've also put a few more essentials in this shopping bag. You will need a light meter and a dozen rolls of film to get started."

"Yes, sir," I stammered. "But are you sure? I mean, thank you, I will do my best to pay you as quickly as possible. I will work every day after school and the weekends to." I was still thanking him as I left the store to catch the bus home.

That was how my photography career started, like a dream. Because of one man's kindness, I began a chapter of my life that was going to be full of adventure, challenge, and excitement. Due to this man's generosity, my photography would take me all over Southeast Asia, meeting presidents and peasants, admirals, generals, and dignitaries. It would cause me work for PBS while attending college, and let me work with basketball great Bobby Knight, and Bill Monroe, the inventor of bluegrass music. It would keep me alive when everything else seemed impossible. It was the beginning of a wild ride; it would be the perfect response to my grade school sadness. Suddenly I could go as high and as fast as I wanted to go. Suddenly there was nothing in front of me to hold me back. I could fly.

It was the biggest turning point in my young life. Suddenly I could do about anything if I just wanted it bad enough. Dad was right all along when he said, "Just tell yourself where you want to go, then do it. Don't worry about anything else."

"Now, this is the invoice to give to whoever you are working with at school. Do not forget this. I am sure you will need it." It was not until later that day, when I was sitting on the bus, heading home, that I really looked at the card, it said, *H. Lieber Company, Mr. Kurt Lieber, President.* I must have gone to photographers' heaven. Could this be real? I guess it was.

As I sat on the bus to take me home, I began to think about the day's events. I'll be darned if Dad wasn't right all along, all I really needed was to want it bad enough. Always look forward, never back. And trust in the kindness of others.

CHAPTER 9

The Courage To Get It Done

All I had left to do was persuade the school superintendent to equip the empty darkroom with new equipment. But when I looked at the paperwork that Kurt had given to me, I freaked out. The darkroom equipment was really expensive, holy mackerel. I figured I would never get this approved.

What now? Well, I decided, I might as well have them tell me no. Maybe I should trust in the kindness of others—that worked with Mr. Kurl Lieber, after all. Maybe the school superintendent was not the ogre that I imagined. I asked the art teacher, Mr. Morrison, what would be the best way to approach the superintendent. He suggested I call and make an appointment, but only after speaking with Mr. Wolfe, the school principal.

Fortunately, Mr. Wolfe was known as a cool guy, who would listen to your problems. But at the principal's office, the secretary, Mrs. Wyman, told me he was not in and asked why I needed to see him. After I gave her the information in the most desperate manner I could conjure up, she looked at me and said, "Well, this really is quite the issue. Come back after your next class and I'll see if I can get an appointment for you."

As I walked to my next class I thought, "Wait? I hate 'wait.' They should remove that word from our vocabulary." It was not fair to put me in this waiting hell. But I really had no choice, so waiting hell was where I spent the next hour.

After class, I hustled my butt back to the principal's office. Mrs. Wyman announced as I walked into the outer office, "He'll see you tomorrow morning, before classes begin, at 7:30 a.m. Please be on time." More waiting!

But the next morning, I arrived at 7 a.m., ready to see Mr. Wolfe. I did not want to chance being late. About 15 minutes later, Mrs. Wyman walked in and smiled. "Good to see you're on time, I'll tell Mr. Wolfe you are here." After a few minutes she told me to go on in his office.

The principal, Mr. Wolfe, was a tall, skinny guy, with teeth that protruded when he smiled. It was sure impressive. Of course, Mr. Wolfe was a natural, constant smiler. As I entered, he asked me to sit in a tall wing chair, and he got up and moved to the sofa next to the chair. Mr. Wolfe was the kind of guy who made everyone feel right at home. He was genuinely one of the kindest men I had ever met.

Later the next year I took a picture of Mr. Wolfe sitting on the baseball teams bench waiting his turn to get up to bat. It was one of the winning photos submitted to Wm. H. Block Department Store and helped me win the contest as the best photographer's work submitted that year. His smile just couldn't be beat.

Mr. Wolfe said, "As I understand from Mrs. Wyman, you want to spend a whole lot of the school's money. Is that correct?"

"Yes, sir, I would like to see if we can re-equip the school darkroom."

"Darkroom, I didn't know we had a darkroom. Are you sure we really do have a darkroom?"

"It is a giant storage room, really, just where people have been sticking stuff. But Mr. Morrison said it should be restored to its original use. He thinks it was used properly until just a few years ago, before he started to teach here."

Mr. Wolfe asked, "Do you happen to know what equipment is needed, and what happened to the equipment to begin with?"

"I do not, sir, but maybe Mr. Morrison will know. I think this is the way he found it. I went to H. Lieber's, downtown Indianapolis, and they put together a list, an invoice, of what a darkroom needs."

At this, I handed Mr. Wolfe the paper that Mr. Kurt had given me. He read it over, and observed, "My, young man, this is quite the list. Just how soon would we need to equip this darkroom?"

I straightened up in the chair. "Well, sir, the school just hired me to take pictures for the school paper and the yearbook. I have the camera I need, but I do not have a darkroom to process the film and then make pictures."

"All right, Mr. Vincent, let me talk to Mr. Morrison about this issue and then see what we can do. Why don't you come back tomorrow, same time, and let us talk some more about your *dilemma?*"

"Yes, sir," I replied, but I was thinking, darn it, I must wait another day. This was beginning to give me a case of the jitters.

The next morning, Mrs. Wyman was already there, and she ushered me in. As I sat down in a chair in front of Mr. Wolfe's desk, he said, "Well, I have looked at our darkroom that apparently nobody knew we had. Also, I had a nice talk with Mr.

Morrison and Mrs. Kennedy. They both spoke highly of your eagerness to be a good school photographer, and they both said that re-equipping the present school darkroom was entirely proper and, in their opinion, needed." He frowned at me. "But an expenditure like this will need the school superintendent's authorization. I will recommend to Mr. Swinford that your request is in line with school needs. And Mr. Morrison and Mrs. Kennedy both said they would also endorse the need. Here is Mr. Swinford's office telephone number. You will need to call his office and ask for an appointment to see him, but you have the high school's approval and agreement that we need to refurnish the school darkroom."

I was excited and terribly disappointed all at once. It was great to know that I had the school's approval, but I still needed the school superintendent's agreement. I had no choice but to make another phone call and again present the invoice.

CHAPTER 10

Like A Speeding Rocket

Within an hour I was on the phone to Mr. Swinford's office. This time they were expecting the call. His secretary, Mrs. Alexander, told me to come to the office right after school.

Directly after the last class, like a speeding rocket, I was on my way to the school's superintendent office. They had recently converted the old junior high school building into the offices of Noblesville Schools. It was only four blocks away on Conner Street, the main east-west street through Noblesville. I was so excited that I forgot the invoice, so I hustled back to school, got the invoice, turned around, and ran back to the superintendent's office.

After entering the lobby, I realized I had no idea where to go in this big building. I had to maddeningly take the time to read the building directory to find the right office. While this did not take long, it just seemed to this fifteen-year-old kid that I was losing time. Up the stairs, down the hall, around the corner, I dashed.

As I entered Mr. Swinford's office, his secretary Mrs. Alexander told me to have a seat. So, I sat and sat, waiting. Maybe they were annoyed that I had taken too long when I had to return to get the invoice. Finally, Mr. Swinford came to his door with an expression that could have been used to pound nails into my carcass. He had long grey hair, swept back in such a way as to give him the distinct look of the man in charge, a man of brilliance. He was always very well dressed and distinguished looking.

He just pointed at a chair off to the side of his desk. Without saying a word, he turned and walked back to his desk. While I had never met this man before, suddenly I had the feeling I was about to be verbally whipped into submission. Carefully he sat at his desk and looked at me with great distinction but said nothing. I began to sweat. I thought, this is not good, not a clever way to start, he is going to eat me alive. Then, all at once, his expression changed into a huge grin, and he began to laugh.

Suddenly he jumped out of his chair, extended his hand, and introduced himself. It was all I could do to keep from peeing myself. He began to laugh, saying, "Well, I have wanted to try this act on one of my students for a long time. You sure passed with glowing colors. Obviously, a school superintendent does not scare you." Little did he know, but I was not about to correct him.

I began to relax just a little, but still I was a bit cautious. Maybe he was just tricking me to relax, then he would bite. But he continued genially, "Well, son, what brings you to see me today? You will have to be quick. I have a student that was supposed to be here right after school to try and get me to spend a whole bunch of money. Or maybe that is what you're here for."

I realized that he was a big kidder, and he had indeed tricked me with his clever performance. I started to like the distinguished gentleman because he was in fact a kind man. Wow, just like Dad said, most people were indeed kind.

All I had to do was ask for what was reasonable. So, I handed the photo equipment invoice to him. "Sir, Mr. Wolfe told me I would have to have your approval for this invoice."

He commented that he had heard about an invoice but wanted me to tell him more about its purpose. As it turned out, Mr. Wolfe had already explained the need to re-establish the high school darkroom and given his wholehearted approval.

I replied, "Well, you see, sir, Noblesville High School has a complete darkroom, but all the equipment is missing. I am not sure why, but Mr. Morrison seems to think that it was furnished at one time. I was just given the chance to be the school newspaper's photographer and help with the yearbook. I have a camera, but I need a darkroom, and Mr. Morrison said he would be fine with my using the darkroom the school already has. If that is all right with you, I mean."

At this, he began to inspect the invoice that Mr. Kurt had made for me. His eyebrows rose at one point, and he whistled. "This is quite a lot of money you are asking us to spend. When do you suppose you will need all this equipment? Have you looked at all this equipment, is it the right equipment for us, or do you even know?"

I took a deep breath. "Well, sir, I took the bus to downtown Indianapolis last weekend and went to H. Lieber Company. The man who helped me, Mr. Kurt Lieber, said this is all essential equipment and that he would make sure that the prices were very fair. He said they work with a lot of the school systems in Indiana, sir. He suggested you call him if you have questions, and that he would be happy to help with any questions you might have. He was really a swell guy, and he was a huge help to me."

Mr. Swinford said, "As I am sure you know, this is quite a lot of money that you are suggesting we spend. While I can appreciate your eagerness to get started, I am going to have to bring this to the school board's attention, or at least run it by the president of the school board, Mr. Dorman."

I realized there was still hope of success.

He added, "Frankly, I think I must agree with not only you, but the school principal, the art teacher, and the yearbook and newspaper teacher. I will do my best to have an answer by the end of the week. Does that work for you?"

"Yes, sir, and thank you for letting me speak to you, sir." I did not know what else to say, so I just sat there and tried not to look too dumb. Here I was, discussing expenditures with the school superintendent. At this point, I was really starting to believe in myself. Finally, I was proving Sister Concepta wrong, and validating my father's belief in me.

Mr. Swinford chuckled again. "You have made an exceptionally good and forceful presentation today." Then he stuck out his hand and thanked me for bringing this issue to his attention. I could not believe that he wanted to shake my hand, like I was a grownup and not just a student.

By the end of the week, the approval had been made. All that was left to do was take the paperwork back to H. Lieber and get the equipment. For the first time since the darkness of grade school, I felt really in control.

It turns out that Dad was right all along about me. But the nuns and Mom, well, they were not simply wrong, they could not and would not give me the encouragement I wanted and needed. Now I told myself not to listen so faithfully to them. Instead, I took Dad's road, and continued to believe I could achieve anything if I wanted it bad enough.

CHAPTER 11

Life Was Good

B y the time I was a junior in high school, everything was changing. No longer was I just a slow kid that might someday make a good garage mechanic. Now I could fly. I was in charge of my own life. I was not out of the woods yet, but my classes were not as complicated as they once were, and I knew I had a chance to succeed at school. My skills blossomed, and at some point, in the year, I began to realize that I was not just a good photographer. Sometimes I could do really great work, and people started to comment on my photos.

Mr. Morrison encouraged me to apply for a photo camp at the Ernie Pyle School of Journalism at Indiana University. Of course, while it was modestly priced, it was still a lot more than I could afford. Amazingly, someone paid for my trip, with a small stipend and all the film I would need. Many years later I would discover that Jim and John Neal, the owners of the *Noblesville Daily Ledger* newspaper, had been the source of this gift. What a great gift it turned out to be.

After the camp, my photography really took off. Suddenly, the *Ledger* wanted me to do all the photo work concerning the schools, including sports, homecoming, and other school events. They also paid well, and the experience helped me get hired as a freelance photographer with Associated Press for the Indianapolis 500. Additionally, I was able to get hired out to film events like weddings that I had not ever planned to do. I was not interested in taking staged photos as regular wedding photographers did. So, I produced an unusual way to make these jobs more interesting. I would cover a wedding just as I would any newspaper event. The result was the couple got candid photos that the professional wedding photographers could not take with their large cumbersome equipment. My pictures were always natural and candid. Often the results were spectacular, even for this high school lightweight.

At the time, I had no idea just how good I was. But in fact, I was by then on par with just about any pro around the area, and often much better. Of course, none of that mattered to me. I just wanted to make the best pictures I could possibly make.

During my senior year, my grades continued to improve, and my photography took off like a rocket. Suddenly I was making a fair amount of money and could buy much better equipment. That summer Mr. Morrison and Mr. Wolfe both agreed that I needed better access to the darkroom. They gave me a set of keys to the entry doors and to the inside doors to the school. In addition, they allowed me to work any time I wanted, which was a tremendous help. You see, our family home on Clinton Street was just across the street from the front of the school. So, I was only seconds away from the lab at any time of the day or night. For some reason, I liked to work late at night when everyone else was asleep. I often was in the darkroom trying my best to create something new. Sometimes I failed, but I didn't care. I learned from each experiment, and on occasion when one worked, it really worked. There were times when Mr. Morrison was amazed at what I produced.

Mr. Morrison encouraged me to enter a contest for seniors sponsored by Wm. H. Block, the finest and largest department store in Indianapolis. The contest was for anybody interested in art, including photography. The grand prize was a scholarship to the school of choice. Mr. Morrison thought I had at least a chance, especially if we started early in the school year. His instructions to me were to just start taking pictures of everything, like frost on the window, bugs, and people. I decided to go along and give the photo portfolio idea a chance. It sounded like fun, so I began to take a lot more pictures than I had been already taken.

There was for me a particular joy in catching someone, something in the moment. Just as they were in that slice of time, happy, sad, crying, smiling. When you can see the moment and capture it just as it is, you capture life, you capture the essence of it all. When I captured the decisive moment, it became more than just a picture. It became magic. It was something that couldn't be taught, it had to be felt, it came from the soul and yes, it was magic.

There were times when I would shoot hundreds of photographs of a scene, a building, a person and in the end, I had hundreds and hundreds of pictures that captured nothing. Then among all the hundreds of negatives, I found it. The perfect moment, just as I wanted to see it, record it. Perfect.

CHAPTER 12

Changes

As I began my senior year, life was about as good as it could get, with just one little exception-- my dad. He was working night and day, seven days a week. I could see the weariness in his eyes. His business was not doing well, and suddenly he had people around him that nobody in the family really trusted. The worst was a guy named Howard Wess, a scumbag, a real jerk. He had made himself the president of the company, though he had no actual ownership. He was very much a bully, and he just put himself in charge.

Dad was really in bad shape physically, and we would find out later, financially as well. He had a serious heart condition, and Dr. Kraft had encouraged him to slow down and take some time off to get some much-needed rest. But as far as Wess was concerned, Dad needed to work more, not less. Wess created a situation where he would oversee the factory, and Dad would be the outside guy and keep sales coming in. One of the most despicable acts this thug did was confiscate my dad's office for his own, and then ban me from the premises. Unfortunately for him, Dad had given me a key to the place several months before, so on occasion, late at night, I would go over and snoop around.

Wess presented himself as this bright guy who was going to take care of business and show Dad how to run the place and make the big bucks. But what this fat, slick-talking bully was really doing was giving Dad just enough money to keep him on a tight leash. He even started a daily crooked poker game in the back room. Later I discovered that he had turned Dad's office into his little whorehouse, with his "private office secretary." If anyone dared complain, he was not above using a piece of pipe, covered at both ends with electrical tape, to give them his brand of attitude adjustment.

With so much conflict, Dad was working himself into a state of exhaustion, day in, day out. It was just a few hours before he died that I found him lying on the sofa, watching tv, eating his bowl of milk and crackers. It was all he could eat at that time, as his stomach and his heart were such a mess.

Once it was late when I finished the processing for the newspaper and hung the film up to dry. When I got home, everyone was in bed, all except Dad, who I found lying on the sofa. We talked for just a little. He asked how school was going, and was I ready to graduate. He loved to hear about my day and what new adventure I was into. The conversation was pretty short, as it was past midnight, and I was exhausted from the day's activities. I guess Dad went to bed right behind me. It was about two hours later when I was awakened and told to go downstairs. Father Gilman was there at the foot of the stairs. He put his arm around me and told me Dad had gone on the final journey to meet his maker.

In the next few hours, my brothers Joe and David and I would walk up Logan Street to the funeral home. We only had one thing to do, pick out a casket to put dad in. I remember they had a beautiful wooden casket that I thought he deserved, then they told us how much it was going to cost. They sold us the cheapest coffin they had that day, a battleship grey model. It would have to do.

In hindsight, I should have kicked Wess out when I realized how dangerous he was to Dad. But I was just a kid, and he was a prime bully. He even made himself part of the funeral service, prancing around, looking mournful and offering to help. My last memory of him is as one of the pallbearers, helping to carry Dad's coffin into the church. I guess there will always be a scoundrel or two in life, but that day I learned how hateful they really are. That day I also learned what a truly great man was all about. Dad fit the bill perfectly.

CHAPTER 13

Moving On

Sadly, after Dad died, Mom was in no condition to take control of the business. Soon the business was sold, and the building and trucks were taken by the bank to satisfy Dad's loans. Anything that could be sold for cash or moved, Wess took. Even Dad's tools, which I wanted for myself, disappeared. The warehouse was completely empty. But it could have been worse. At least with ten children to raise, Mom ended up with the house and a small insurance policy.

When I look back at that time, I can see the important lessons I was about to learn. Most important, I had to learn that when something bad happens, I had to just let it go. I couldn't fix the past.

At first, I had great resentment that Dad was no longer there to guide me. In those moments of grief, I didn't realize how much Dad had taught me, what a brilliant man he really was. This was a man that truly knew how to love life. His kindness, not just to his children, but to everyone, was impressive.

Years later I was standing on the courthouse square when an elderly couple suddenly pointed at me and asked if I was a Vincent boy. Yes, I said, rather startled. I could not imagine what was wrong. Then they began to tell me about the enormous kindness of my dad. They said once they found themselves in a difficult situation. They were out of money, and truly desperate. Dad didn't know them at the time, but he knew they needed help. He paused in his busy day and took them both to Kenly's Supermarket. He told them to fill up a cart with food of their choosing.

Then he took them home. They lived in a very poor area of town, on the south side just west of the train tracks. After he left them, he apparently told our parish priest about how he'd helped the family, and they were still going to need help. That was Dad, he never bragged or blamed. But he didn't know how to not be kind.

It seemed so unfair to me that he was gone. Then I thought of what Dad might say: "When you are handed a pile of shit, you have two options. One, it is a pile of shit, it stinks, get rid of it. Two, it is a pile of shit, which makes great fertilizer, so let's put it on the flower garden." Amazingly, it could be turned into fertilizer, and beautiful flowers were the end result. There is always a choice, make the right one,

CHAPTER 14

Doing My Duty

As my senior high school year was ending, so were a lot of other parts of my life. Dad died suddenly on January 8, 1966. He was only forty-eight when his heart failed. What a crushing blow this was for me and for us all. Until he died, I had not realized how much I depended on his opinion, and his always sound advice. He was a great guy, and I had no idea how I was to go forward.

As I stumbled and groped for my way through that year, everything was unfamiliar. I was lost. My last few months of high school were just a sad walk into tomorrow, without a plan or a direction.

Without Dad, there was no one else whose opinion mattered so much to me. For the first time, I started to make decisions alone without consulting anyone. But I did not care much about anything except photography. When Mr. Morrison announced to me that I had won the Wm. H. Block scholarship, I just felt wrong about it. I was not deserving. I was just plain lost and angry. Even though he tried his best to get me to accept, I turned the scholarship down. In my heart, I knew I would not do it justice, so that was that. After all, there were probably much smarter and more deserving kids than me. Without Dad's advice, this decision seemed perfectly logical.

At 17, I had no reason to get out of bed. Nothing held my interest for very long, friendships, everything I loved, were just slipping away. I was only seventeen, and a great cloud of sadness enveloped me.

Grief was like a deep black fog, and I couldn't seem to get out of it. With life turned on its head, I began to consider how I could escape without giving up the only constant I had left, photography.

This was the time of great build up to the military, and every able-bodied male was a prospect to be drafted. If you didn't have a draft deferral, going on to college for instance, you knew you were going to be drafted as soon as you graduated from high school. That was the biggest incentive to go to college: to stay out of the draft and the war. If you didn't go to college, the odds of being drafted were close to a hundred percent. The only other way to stay out of the draft was to volunteer to serve in the Navy or Coast Guard.

During that time, I occasionally did little jobs for an older friend, Garry Hiatt. We enjoyed each other's company, and we have remained friends right up to today. One day I asked Garry if he knew anybody in the Navy who could get me into Naval Photo School. I wanted to attend a basic photo school to start out. But I knew the Navy had a wonderful school for photojournalism, started right after WWII by John Ford, one of the great Hollywood producers. This was still considered one of the finest photo schools in the country.

As luck would have it, Garry's former Naval boss was now a captain and stationed in Washington, collaborating with naval photo interpreters. They had stayed close friends, even after Garry left the military. Garry said to me, "Let me call Washington and see if I can get something done for you."

Garry let me know that a naval captain was only one step below admiral in that branch of the service, and that his former boss would have a lot of clout. If he wanted to appoint a recruit right out of basic training to receive further training, he could not be denied.

Offered this opportunity, I decided to go for it—to enlist in the US Navy and aim to get into the photo school. I would turn eighteen in August, and hopefully serve as a photojournalist after attending the navy's photo school. After working as the school photographer and the local newspaper, photojournalism was a dream I'd had for a while.

I knew this was risky, because I could end up as just another seaman on a ship during a war. But I knew I had to take a chance to escape that fog of sadness. So, I enlisted. I was told to report to a second-floor office on New York Street in downtown Indianapolis, where I was sworn in and given initial medical tests and a test of my IQ. The IQ test took a little more than two hours and was supposed to be a broad measure of mental competence and intelligence. After completing it, I was led into a small office in front of two very nasty-looking Marines. Both accused me of somehow cheating on the test, and they tore up the results and made me take the test again. This time they stood on each side of me while I took the test. The second time, I scored even higher. In fact, I had the highest score of anyone who had taken the test in this office since the Korean war. So there, Sister Concepta, I was not as stupid as you thought.

Then I left for basic training, not sure what the future would hold for me. I was hoping that Garry was right when said he could get me assigned to photo school after boot camp. And with his friend in Washington's help, incredibly, he did. During my basic training at Great Lakes Naval Training Center, my company commander received a set of orders that I should be transferred to US Naval Photo School, Pensacola, Florida, upon graduation.

Usually, this school required a college degree in photography even to apply, and guys right out of boot camp were almost never accepted. Remember, this was the height of the Vietnam war, and if you were an 18-year-old male, you were probably going to be drafted, unless you were in college or voluntarily joined a branch of the military. They'd also started to draft recent college graduates, so there was always a ready supply of officer candidates and photojournalists graduating from college. These got most if not all the spots available for the US Navy Photo School.

There were very few ways to legally avoid the draft, the most prevalent being attending college. But the risk was just postponed, as the military would just wait until graduation before drafting you. Recent college graduates were considered fair game, and so a lot of the recent graduates would volunteer for naval service in order to keep themselves from getting killed in Vietnam.

Consequently, most of my photo school class members were college graduates with degrees in photography, and photojournalism. In fact, in my class, all but three—me, Bill Matela, and one other-- were recent college graduates. Nevertheless, I managed to finish with great scores. My class started with thirty-four members, but only fifteen graduated. At graduation, my class standing put me close to the top of the class.

Except for a bit of bad luck in my final project, I would have been at the top. During one of our last field exercises, we were told to take a photograph with a 4"X5" Speed Graphic, the photographic stalwart of the naval press core during the 1950s and early 1960s. The picture could be of anything we wanted, and I chose a mother and her small child sitting in the stands, watching a baseball game. My instructor, a Marine master sergeant, thought my last project was, in his words, "a stupid piece of shit." I wasn't one to take this comment lightly, so I let him know how I felt about his childish behavior. My grade was altered, and I finished fourth at graduation. That was still impressive, but had I kept my mouth shut, I probably would have finished first. In fact, a couple of the Navy instructors told me I was going to make first place, but my mouth was my own worst enemy.

What did I care. Dad was gone. I was a kid full of anger.

But it could have been worse. If you had scored a grade lower than seventy per cent, you were removed from photo school and sent to a new assignment, generally an aircraft carrier. During our weekly tests, one of the Marine instructors announced that two of our former classmates were on the flight deck of the aircraft carrier USS Forrestal when it suffered a fire and explosion. Both of our former classmates were killed. "Hope this helps with your test," he said with a grin, and then he turned around and left the room. I never forgot that comment. The sadness of it stayed with me for a long time.

With a little bit of luck, I might be assigned to Pacific Fleet Combat Camera, the unit with the best of the best photojournalists. With graduation from photo school and a willingness to serve in Vietnam, it just might happen. I have always believed that hope was always the best option, and I just needed to keep trying to move towards my goal.

But it was also during this time that drinking became a weekly, then a nightly sport for me. I discovered that I could out- drink just about anybody and often did. I also discovered that as time went on, rarely did I have much of a hangover the next day. Sometimes I woke up a little groggy, but I thought this was acceptable. In any case that is what I learned to tell myself. At first, it was fun to be able to out-drink everyone else.

After completing US Naval Photo School, I was given a week's leave and decided to go home. When I returned to Pensacola, my orders had been delayed. My classmate Bill Matella did not have orders as well and so, we waited, until one day, we were ordered to report to the commanding officer's office. We stood at attention in front of his desk, then he looked up and ordered us to stand at parade rest.

SECTION 2

Go West Young Man

*Three things cannot be long hidden...
the sun, the moon, and the truth.*

CHAPTER 1

Careful What You Ask For

"Well, men, I have here two sets of orders for each of you. The first set of orders will transfer you to San Diego, for training with a new, highly secret, and classified squadron, VO-67. That is all I can tell you. The second set of orders will send you to the fleet, aboard a yet-to-be-assigned aircraft carrier. Also, men, I need your decision, now."

I spoke up first. "Sir, I accept the first set of orders."

"Good. You will be given two weeks leave and travel time, and then report to NAS North Island, San Diego, California, no later than June 30, 1967. Are there any questions.?"

I shook my head. The commander continued, "Mister Matela, your answer is?"

Bill replied, "The same sir, I would like to be assigned to the secret squadron, sir."

"Very well, men, be ready for transfer by 0700 hours, tomorrow, at Photo School entry. Dismissed."

We both came to attention, smartly saluted, and left his office. After looking at me briefly, Bill said, "Well, what about it, Vince, did we just fuck ourselves or what?"

"Well, something very classified, dangerous, and with a high probability of death, sounds exactly right to me. I think this might be the adventure I was looking for."

This "adventure" could indeed be of great help to the family. My brothers and sisters all wanted to go on to college, and if I saved most of my money, I might be able to help the family with this. I knew if I ended up in Vietnam, I would also be given extra money for serving in combat, and I might also be able to get hazardous duty flight pay. If I got killed, well, with the life insurance policy being offered to all servicemen at that time, I could leave a trust fund for the kids. Now I had a plan. But this was also the beginning of not caring if I lived or died.

The next day Bill had his orders and shipped out for San Diego. But there was something wrong with my orders. They had not removed the offered vacation time, which I did not want, so the orders had to be rewritten. And naturally, the Commander was not in to sign them until the following day.

So, I flew to San Diego just a few days behind Matella and reported to special squadron, top secret, VO-67, Naval Air Station, North Island. It was just across the bay from downtown San Diego, but it might as well have been a million miles away from anything. After reporting to the duty officer, I found my friend from Photo School sitting on the stoop outside of the barracks.

Of course, I greeted him gaily. After all, I was all pumped up to start this new adventure. "Hey, man, what's going on."

Bill was not so happy. Honest to God, I thought he was going to cry, right there in front of me. "Vincent, you just won't believe what a shit storm we've invited ourselves into."

"Fuck, man, what are you talking about? I just got here, what's going on?"

Our barracks was right next to what was called the "flight line," the area where they parked most of the planes that were finished flying for the day. As I looked over at the line, I did notice a few planes in brown camouflage. These were P-2's, which I would soon learn was a plane that was not built for combat and very easy to shoot out of the sky. Usually, they had a crew of twelve and were designed to travel over the open ocean for many hours at a time. These had guards walking around them, with what looked to me like rifles.

"Vincent, those planes, that is what they want us to fly in, somewhere in Asia."

"Well, that's cool," I said.

"You fucking numb nuts," Matilla said. "These planes are supposed to be expendable, and so are we. This is bad, Vince, really, really bad. Shit, I have an awfully bad feeling about this. Tell you what, Vincent, just stroll over there and take a closer look. Then tell me what you really think."

"Sure, I think I will take a better look." As I got closer to the planes, a Marine quickly got in my face, shoved his gun at me and yelled, "Halt. This is a restricted area, and only authorized personnel are allowed to enter this area."

I growled, "Fine, dirt bag, these are my new squadron's planes, and I just want to get a better look."

The jarhead lowered his rifle and said, "I have orders to shoot any unauthorized person entering this area, and you ain't got a pass I can see, so you ain't authorized."

Shit, he was serious. Fuck me!

The next day I was able to get checked in with the squadron and meet my new boss, Chief Nagels, who turned out to be a real nice guy. He let me know that while here in San Diego I would be attending SERE (Survival Escape Resistance Evasion) School, and other necessary training.

Finally, after a few days of getting oriented, I learned from Chief Nagels a little more about what we were going to be doing. What he told me simply scared the living daylights right out of me. This assignment was the real deal. Our casualty rate was expected to be more than 60 percent. I thought, what the hell did I do, oh, my God.

It turns out I had volunteered for one of the most secret and specialized units of the Vietnam war. During the war, the Secretary of Defense Robert McNamara, one of the "whiz kids" left over from the President Kennedy White House, wanted a so-called electronics fence placed around the Laotian border. That was where men and supplies from North Vietnam were coming into South Vietnam. Also, he believed that everything should be done at once. He also didn't care at all about casualty rates or losses. His orders were, "Don't give me excuses, just get the job done."

It did not matter that this had never been done before and there were no delivery system or devices to see and hear the enemy yet in existence. The military told him that we had never developed the technology or had a plane that could deliver it, even if we did. His answer was "Bullshit, get this going pronto, no excuses, period, got it?"

But the Navy did in fact have devices that could be used and do the job if they could be implanted in the ground and trees up and down the Ho Chi Min trail. The Navy had been tracking Russian subs for years, principally with what they called sonar buoys and listening devices. These were incredibly exact, and both devices could not only hear the enemy but could also detect movement. With a good set of photographs showing where the devices were placed, we could in fact create that electronic fence.

All we had to do was place these devices both above and below water, record them as they were ejected out of one of our sub-chaser planes. With the use of the spy cameras, we had mounted on the rear of the plane, we could pinpoint within a matter of a few feet exactly where the sensors had been dropped. This way, we could know exactly where the enemy was when one was set off.

The difference was, when over the ocean, the P-2's had nobody shooting at them. But these missions would be over dry land, in enemy territory. So, every enemy soldier could take a pot shot at one of these planes, which used a lot of hydraulics to work and were known to be highly flammable, not to mention they had little armor protection. In addition, they would have to fly incredibly low and slow to track exactly where the listening and movement detectors had fallen in the jungle.

As expected, he green-lighted this idea right away, without any consideration of the aircraft's survivability, or that each mission would take a dozen men in this plane to accurately get the devices dropped. As far as McNamara was concerned, the planes and men were totally expendable, and throwing more soldiers into danger was a great strategy.

CHAPTER 2

SERE Survival Escape
Resistance Evasion

While in San Diego, I attended the SERE (Survival Escape Resistance Evasion) school, and I thought it was kind of fun. This was a course that was given to Navy SEALs and any force that would be going into an enemy territory. It was considered an extremely difficult ordeal, but without it, we wouldn't be allowed to fly into hostile territory. So, it was absolutely essential that we all take and pass this training.

Pain and suffering were perfectly acceptable to me, just the price paid to help the family out and honor Dad. Crazy, I know, but in the moment, I had accepted the fact that I might be killed. If it happened, so be it.

The school started out in a classroom overlooking the ocean. Each of us was assigned to a group and given two days of classroom instruction. The only unusual aspect was we couldn't eat or drink anything. Also, we couldn't leave the classroom, and we were ordered to remove everything from our pockets.

When that was done, all we had left was the flight suit we were wearing and a twelve-inch knife. We stayed in the classroom overnight. The next day each group was given lessons in starting a small fire, testing what was safe to drink, and making ourselves as invisible as possible. We also learned methods of hiding and escape, along with other survival skills that we might need.

After day two, each group was taken by truck into a deserted area, given a map, and told we had two days to get to a destination on a map given to each of us. If we were seen, we would be placed in a good replication of a North Vietnamese prison.

The idea was to evade being captured and tossed into their idea of a Viet Cong prison.

For the first day or so I managed to keep out of sight, and found a rattlesnake to eat, which turned out to be a very good idea. But after that, I didn't a have chance really. I made the mistake of trying to cross a dirt road at dusk. Of course, I got captured, and soon discovered these captors were real assholes. First, I was interrogated for several hours, slapped around, beaten, and put into a small wire cage (dog cage) for several hours. It started to feel very real.

Then they tossed me into a compound with everyone else that had been captured. By this time, just about everyone had been caught, interrogated, and generally kicked around. This was day five of SERE school, and I'd had almost nothing to drink and eat for the last two days. Quickly, I was running out steam to keep going. The guards, the compound, and the guard towers began to feel very real.

After several hours of this, some of the junior officers began to freak out a little. Some demanded to be released, and for their efforts got the shit kicked out of them. Many were flunked and sent home or removed from the squadron. We never saw them again. The majority of us, however, hung on and tried to help each other out.

As for me, I was not about to give up as long as I was not bleeding too much. The rest of the bullshit I really did not mind, and I just kept going. I began to really not care at that point, and nothing they could do to me was going to slow me down even a little.

After slowly walking around the perimeter, I soon realized that this was a tough place to escape from. The sun was just starting to come up, and a couple of the guards came into the compound. They ordered us to start a fire, and to put this large pot over it. Then they ordered us to fill it to the top with water. It held about twenty gallons or so, I think.

Shit, I thought somebody was going to get himself boiled in water. Instead, the guard opened a brown bag and dumped a lot of ground coffee and sugar into the water. The next thing I realized was they were ordering all of us to line up and stand at attention. A very mean-looking big dude stood there and asked for the officer in charge of our group to come forward.

Nobody responded, so he walked over and grabbed a Navy commander, and with both of his hands picked him up and threw him in front of us. Sweet Jesus, is this never going to end?

Then he got right in the commander's face and began yelling at him. "Do you want this exercise to end?" Then when nobody said a word, he yelled again. "I said, does anybody want this exercise to be over? If so, come forward and tell me."

Finally, somebody caught on and said, "Fuck yes, we want it over."

The guard then replied, "As of 0538 hours this exercise is officially complete. All those present have successfully completed SERE School. Line up and grab yourself a cup of coffee. We have a few instructions for you before you return to quarters."

He then warned us that we were all badly dehydrated, and our stomachs had shrunk and would accept little food. He told us all to eat just a small amount, a piece of toast or a roll, then take a shower and get some sleep. When we wake up, he then suggested we were to order the biggest meal we wanted, which by then should stay down.

That was it, done, the hardest school by far.

Somewhere during the exercise, I learned a most valuable lesson. Now I knew that if I really wanted to achieve, to endure, I had what it takes. Everything was suddenly possible if I just believed. Defeat had left my vocabulary.

CHAPTER 3

Last Task Before Leaving

Thank God. SERE was a school I would not soon forget. It was designed to teach our men how to survive, if they found themselves in enemy territory. While I did learn a lot about how to survive, which I'll never forget, I thanked God it was over. In any case, after a month of this and other training, I was sent to join the rest of the squadron in Alameda, California, just across the bay from San Francisco. By the time I arrived, it seemed like everybody on the base had heard about us and seemed to know a lot more than I did. Of course, all anybody really knew about the squadron was rumor and wild stories.

It became clear, however, that if you were part of the flight crews, those of us that got to fly around, you were automatically declared special. Of course, I was one of the first photographers to volunteer to fly, and so was quickly accepted.

The mission we were being prepared for required implanting these little electronic things that looked like a piece of foliage. We were going to drop them from our converted subchaser designed for dropping sensors into the water to detect and follow Russian submarines. These planes were never built to be shot at, because not many people were floating around on the surface of the ocean with a gun to point at the plane. But by the time we arrived in Vietnam, we had lots of people trying to shoot us down. In planes that were not designed to take enemy fire of any kind, we were sitting ducks.

For the devices to be of any use at all, we needed to know exactly where they had fallen. We needed not only to photograph the devices, but also know exactly where they were falling. To accomplish this, we needed to photograph a GPS device on board at the same time, so we could know within a few feet where each device was.

If all went well, bingo, we had sensors implanted and knew exactly where they were with the GPS location. (At that time, only the military had access to GPS, Global Positioning System, which was then a brand-new technology.)

We had very sophisticated cameras at the rear of the plane to photograph the terrain and the devices as they fell into the trees. The jungle canopy was often well over two hundred feet high, so the pictures had to be perfectly exact. As a consequence, the first thing Matela and I were going to learn, was how to load an enormous set of cameras under the plane and enclosed in a bullet-resistant plastic compartment.

It turned out that this was not a good plan at all. We would have to devote more than a day, per plane, per-mission to just load the cameras. And they had not left enough room in the glass enclosure for us to see what we were doing, so we would have to load these cameras blind. Bill and I spent hours on the flight line experimenting with different loading ideas. One afternoon we finally got onto a method to get the job done.

These cameras were very large and very heavy, I would guess about a foot square and fifty pounds each, and we had to mount two cameras on each plane. We built a wood rack to hang them on, about the same height as the plane's cameras were supposed to be. Then we took turns blindfolded, lying under the rack to load the cameras. This worked, as while one of us loaded, the other observed. That way we could easily see what would work and what did not. If we tried a method and it didn't work as planned, we simply took our blindfold off and figured out why. More importantly, we figured out from these mistakes how to do it right.

Our boss Chief Nagels never did figure out how to do it. At first, it took us several days to load them just once. But it got easier as we kept at it, until in the end, we could do both cameras in less than five minutes.

CHAPTER 4

Last Liberty

After this both Bill and I needed some deserved time off. Chief Nagels gave both of us a couple of days and I headed for San Francisco, which was just across the bay. I had to take a bus, but I was fine with that, as it gave me more time to gawk as we crossed the spectacular Golden Gate Bridge. The bus stopped near the area known as Fisherman's Wharf, close to the downtown area and lots of shops.

Back then, Fisherman's Wharf was not considered to be the must-see place it was soon to become, so it was not completely overrun with tourists. I took a trolley to the Wharf, and I found that to be a great deal of fun. Remember at the time, I was only nineteen, and on the trolley, just about everything was fascinating to me.

Of particular interest was the Nob Hill area, also very close by, where many of the most elite had built their estates and glorious homes. This was far and away my favorite area, with beautiful hotels and the famous restaurants. I only got the opportunity to go into the lobby of the hotels, but nevertheless, they were all spectacular. This was the first of several trips to beautiful San Francisco I would make when I was training there in the Bay Area.

Of course, I had not let what we would be doing really sink in. It all seemed so far off to me, hardly worth a thought. It still did not occur to me that in just a month I would be watching men being killed, and I would be helping in that death. My devil still had not got hold of me, but he was there, quietly waiting, in the background.

I could ignore the dangers of the future because our training was easy compared to the SERE training I'd just been through. The days were often long, and sometimes boring, but generally, life was good when I was part of a flight team. I spent a great deal of time in San Francisco, and it was right when Haight-Ashbury was the center of the hippie culture with music, drugs, and more drugs. One day I was able to find the band Grateful Dead's Victorian home in the Haight. Fortunately, I was smart enough to leave what I found there in the city and not take it across the bay and onto the base.

Seeing the city, going into stores, and just viewing the street life, was a blast to me. This was the first time in my incredibly young life that I had the opportunity to visit a town of this size and historic importance.

My last act in San Francisco was going into a very famous and very old tobacco shop started in the 1860s, so 100 years old at the time. Even after the Great San Francisco Fire, they managed to stay in business due to their exceptional service to customers. It was the beginning of a long love affair with a pipe. The staff there even helped me put together my own custom tobacco.

CHAPTER 5

Take A Trip

With the camera-loading problem out of the way, most of our other issues were minor-- except for one, the film sweating and gluing itself together, causing the cameras to fail. In the tropics, the humidity was remarkably high all the time, and we needed to somehow keep the film frozen until it was used. This would keep the film from sweating until we got into the air and had enough wind and cooler temperatures to keep the film dry.

Finally, somebody suggested we should keep the film in a giant cooler. Bingo, a meat locker would work simply fine, problem solved. We ordered a giant meat locker, and had it broken down and flown to Thailand ahead of us.

One of the last things the squadron did before leaving for Thailand was be treated to a large steak dinner and all the booze you could drink. It was all paid for by Martin-Marietta, the company that oversaw converting our planes. As it turned out, the purpose of the dinner was something that had nothing to do with Martin-Marietta.

The dinner was attended by a group of guys in dark suits and ties, which we came to call The Spooks, the CIA. They kept to themselves and sat in front of the group at special tables. When one rose to speak, what he had to say was brutal. He told us all to look at the guy sitting next to each of us, which we all obediently did. "Men, either you or the guy you are looking at will not come back. Because of the secrecy you will not receive any medals, nor will you get promotions for your service. Your wives and loved ones will be told that you just died for causes unknown. Further, you may never tell anybody what you are about to be doing, ever. If you do, you will spend the rest of your life in Fort Leavenworth, in an isolated cell. Are we all clear about this?"

We all stayed silent. He continued, "Men, either you or the guy you are looking at will not be coming home. So, if you want out, now's the time to get up and walk out of here." Nobody did.

Years later, I realized he was not far off in his prediction for the flight crews. Many of us never came home.

The next day, Air America planes landed at Alameda. You might know that Air America was a commercial airline owned by the CIA in the 1960s and 1970s. After we were airborne, we discovered that no alcohol would be served. That was no problem, as Wild Bill had a large attaché with the bottom left-hand corner featuring a small hole with a little handle of a faucet protruding. You can get right at four bottles of good booze in that attaché. We were golden, and all had a quiet, peaceful sleep to our destination, twenty-six hours away.

As we landed in Thailand, I was feeling fatalistic. At this point, as far as I was concerned, God had abandoned me. After all, he let my father die. Well, that's what I told myself anyway. There was the devil, right there with his hand extended to me.

Why not, I thought, maybe with the devil I will have better luck. Maybe he can make the pain go away. This attitude was a combination of anger and feeling sorry for myself. The disparity of this, feeling sorry for yourself, had not yet manifested itself to me.

Another World Thailand

Wars are not paid for in wartime, the bill comes later.

Benjamin Franklin

CHAPTER 1

A Whole New World

The Ho Chi Minh Trail became the most famous trail in the Vietnam war. It ran along the border of North Vietnam and South Vietnam, mostly under two hundred feet of jungle canopy cover. It ran right through the neutral country of Laos. This country was supposed to be off limits to US military including air flights. But to successfully attack the North Vietnamese on the trail, we had no choice but to fly into Laos from Thailand.

We flew in and out of a very secret and remote base right along the Mekong River which separated Thailand from Laos. The base was not really a military base in the normal sense, but instead was run by CIA groups and the US Air Force. We would be working primarily for the CIA and a handful of Air Force folks.

During this point in the war, the North Vietnamese were rapidly putting more and more men and materials into South Vietnam. They were doing this by traveling down the Ho Chi Minh trail through Laos of course, and then entering South

Vietnam. It was mostly a winding trail of foot paths, roads and trails through the foothills and mountains of Laos.

It was an exceedingly difficult area to bomb because of the hills and jungle. Also, the VC used a lot of bicycles and small carts to transport their equipment. The trail was largely covered with a two-hundred-foot canopy of very dense jungle. Remember, most of the time, bombs were dropped by a jet, which generally was going so fast it was almost impossible to see a small target. It was difficult to even see the trail under the jungle canopy. This was especially true for our highflyers and fast movers.

It was understood that we were not supposed to be there, and we were certainly not supposed to fly into Laos. We absolutely were not supposed to harm anything in Laos. All of this was absolutely bullshit, of course. That is exactly what we were going to do and did so every day.

If weather allowed, missions of all types were being flown day and night, seven days a week, from our base and several other bases. Most of the flights were flown by Air Force pilots who had volunteered for this work. If you went down, and were not rescued ASAP, your chances of survival went way, way down. And as far as the military was concerned, you no longer existed.

Of course, we were not even supposed to be in Laos, as Laos had declared itself off limits to the United States. For us, it was just a bad, bad place to die.

CHAPTER 2

Getting Ready

By the time we got to Thailand, I was beginning to feel much more like an adult than the nineteen-year-old kid I really was. Little did I know that becoming a man was going to happen suddenly, violently, and quite soon. It was going to be a shit storm of epic proportions. And it was going to be just what I wanted. A ride with the devil was what I had in mind, fuck me.

Actually, I do not think I really wanted to take the ride with the devil, but it was too late to back out. In a matter of hours, we would begin, and my first taste of what he had in store for me was not pretty.

When we arrived twenty-six hours after taking off from California, it took us a few days to get used to the heat and the on and off rain. It was the beginning of the monsoon season. I remember it rained most days at 10 AM and 3 PM, for about forty minutes. We could almost set our watch to it, and we quickly learned to work around the rain.

The tropics just did not compare to the cool climate of Alameda and San Francisco. As I got off the plane and walked across the runway, my breathing was already going nuts, and I was sweating like a living waterfall. This was the tropics in the rainy season.

Finally, we got the planes ready, prepped, and set up to fly missions. Our first couple of missions went well, but it did not last. My immediate boss was Wild Bill Coty. Bill was a Kentucky boy and a lifer. His goal was to stay in the Navy for life. He was the first of the photographers to do a complete mission.

So, my first question to Bill was, "OK man, what happened, did you see any Gooks?" The term Gook was often used to name the enemy. It was a derogatory term for a Vietnamese that was shooting at you.

Bill replied, "Naw, I did not see shit. We blasted away with our 50 calibers. The cameras all worked perfectly, and our Spooks (CIA) are incredibly happy with the film." (The .50 caliber machine guns were in the rear of the plane, one on each side, and each one operated by a crew member.)

CHAPTER 3

Low And Slow

I was enormously happy to hear about Wild Bill's success. Maybe this would not be quite as bad as they had told us. And maybe, unless a crew member was injured or absent, I might not fly much at all. We only needed one photographer on most missions.

The two rear gunners were stationed aft and also had to keep an eye on the cameras. A hatch in the floor at the rear of the plane was how we gained access to the rear cameras. There was a lot of electronics that worked these cameras, and without the electronics to run the cameras, the mission was a waste of time. So, we also needed access to the electronics that worked the cameras. Without the cameras electronics working perfectly with the equipment in the front of the plane, we were basically screwed.

When these devices were used over the ocean, we could see their exact locations, and photographs were not needed. But now the job was dropping these small devices into the tree canopy above the trail, and sometimes into the ground. They had to be photographed and recorded with GPS after they left the plane. That way we knew pretty much where each device was, most of the time within a couple of feet where they had landed.

Now remember these devices had been built for use in the ocean, and how they looked wasn't important. But on the trail, they might be noticed. So, we needed to convert them for use over land. What we did was convert one of them to look like a tree limb when hanging in a tree over the Ho Chi Minh Trail. The small parachute was camouflaged to look like tree leaves. If all went as planned, they would be dropped into the trees over the trail.

The other devices we dropped were designed to detect noise and vibrations. So, what we did with these was attach a piece of green plastic to the top of them that would also function as the antenna, while the main part would be buried in the ground along the trail. These were designed to send out a signal for months at a time, but all the enemy could see looked like a piece of foliage.

Of course, the problem was that for the cameras to accurately place their location with GPS, it was imperative to fly very low and slow. These were new systems at that time, and a lot could go wrong, so precision was essential.

Additionally, we were using planes that were designed to fly long missions over the ocean and were never intended to get shot at. Consequently, many of the planes had no protection at all or very little at best. We were sitting ducks.

In other words, you could shoot this plane down with not very much fire power at all. The VC and NVA had a ton of firepower, mostly provided by the Russians and the Chinese. We were the equivalent of a bunch of cows entering the slaughterhouse.

Quickly we all discovered that getting ourselves shot down was rather easy. Reality is really a bitch.

CHAPTER 4

Covering Air Force Ass

One morning I was standing in our photo lab which was right next to the flight line. Wild Bill came in the door with Chief Nagels following right behind. They looked at me and then at Matela. Both started to laugh, and Chief said, "OK, Vincent, you wanted to get more flying time, so I've been talking to the Air Force, and they have a really big problem that they want us to fix for them. Seems as though they lost several flight photographers recently, and they are short of photo reconnaissance men to work with the FAC planes."

FAC was Forward Air Control. They used the Cessna Sky Master which was very small, light, and agile plane that could stay in the air for hours. These guys flew low and much slower than the fighter and bomber planes were able to fly. Essentially the job was to fly around a suspected target, then if anyone started shooting, we could mark their position with white phosphorus rockets and pinpoint the target. That way the highflyers and other fighter bomber planes could destroy the target before they killed us.

In other words, we used these small planes as targets in order to find enemy convoys of men and materials hidden under the jungle canopy. Hopefully, the boys above us eliminated the target before the target eliminated the FAC. These FAC pilots were all former jet jockeys and had completed their tour of duty. It was also strictly voluntary, and they were the best of the best.

He said, "I'm told they only have two photo boys left, and they should have five men minimum ready to fly at any time. They have apparently lost several, and it is going to be awhile before they can be replaced."

Both Matela and I looked at each other with the same thought. "Lost several" really got our attention.

"I at once thought of you two boys bitching about never having enough flying time," Chief added. "So, I volunteered both of you to fly missions for them. Of course, you can both back out if you want. You know flying combat with FAC, in Laos especially, is always voluntary. But there you go. If you want it, it is yours. Make up your minds quick because they need someone flying tomorrow."

I didn't agree right away. Without talking it over with Matela and maybe Wild Bill, I just didn't want to commit just yet. "Hey Matela, let's go get coffee and doughnuts."

"Sounds good. How 'bout you, Wild Bill, Chief?"

Chief said no, but Wild Bill said yes and went with us.

I immediately demanded, "What the fuck's the deal, Wild Bill?"

He shook his head. "I'm telling you, Vince, we just found out about this a little while ago, and of course Chief wanted to just volunteer you both, without asking. I told him there was no fucking way we were going to volunteer you boys without your approval. So, you don't have to do these missions, and if you decide to fly one or two and then change your minds, it's cool. They've lost three photographers already, so it is a certainty that these flights are dangerous."

I asked, "Just how dangerous do you think these missions really are? I have heard quite a lot about these FAC guys, the craziest bunch on the base. A couple of days ago I was talking to one of the Jolly Greens." These guys in the rescue helicopters managed saving many enlisted men that had been shot down as well as trying to rescue downed pilots. "He said what these guys did was insane. I think he said, absolutely, certified out of their fucking minds crazy, the chances they took."

Bill broke in, "Aren't they now flying in front of our planes, to clear the target before we drop down?"

"Yeah, that's right, it's been decided that they will be doing that to help identify a hot zone before we go in there." Wild Bill stood up. "Well, you two think it over and let me know sooner rather than later. Damn, these doughnuts are fantastic, still warm. How did you folks find out about these?"

He left us with those questions. Bill and I looked at each other. We knew we were already risking our lives. But Wild Bill was offering another opportunity, and for some reason it seems cowardly to me not to fly these missions.

Danger is a funny thing; I always knew the danger was there, but then when I went out on a mission it changed. Suddenly I found myself in an adrenaline rush, and with that the fear fell into the background. Then it was all a rush, exciting and fun, something to look forward to. But after a while I realized what it really was, dangerous, very dangerous. Period.

Of course, I knew I didn't have to fly the FAC missions. The missions our squadron was flying were incredible dangerous as it was. But volunteering seemed like a grand idea to the Devil that was ruling me in the moment. By this time, I knew who was really in charge. My dance with the devil was ready to start, and I decided to give it a go. It was the beginning of a long drunken adventure, which wouldn't end for many years to come.

"Bill, I think I'm a go for this, should be fun, why not."

Bill said, "Well, Vince, I think I'm a go as well. It'll look good on my records if nothing else."

After just a moment, I guess it was decided. "I can't see a reason to say no, so let's do it. Navy boys are a lot fucking harder to hit in any case."

So, there you have it, Matela and I had both volunteered. Now I would have a new and important use for alcohol. After the adrenaline was gone, it kept me sane, with both feet firmly on the ground. At least I thought it did, alcohol and the devil.

CHAPTER 5

Getting Shot At

Bill got the first FAC flight, and I was damn sure interested to hear what he had experienced. As luck would have it, it was my turn to oversee film removal in the de-arming area, so talking to Bill would have to wait. When I finally caught up with Bill, he was taking a shower. His flight suit, lying on the floor, looked like it had been dumped into a lake. It must have been intense, this mission.

He said, "Christ, Vince, it damn sure was different once we got to the fence." (The "fence" was the Mekong River, the boundary between Thailand and Laos.) "Then things started to happen, and it did not stop for the next three hours. These guys are intense, to say the least. We started taking fire about one hundred miles into the mission, and it just turned this pilot right on."

Bill looked at me, looked at his flight suit lying in a pool of sweat, then looked at me again. "Down we went to about five hundred to a thousand feet, and what a roller coaster ride. The only time we went straight, and level was to get photos, and that was not long. We had three groups of planes, and we put smoke down for each of them so they could see the target. Man, I am telling you these pilots are just simply the best. They can fly the hell right out of these planes. Damn, they are the best I've ever seen."

He added, "The cool thing about it all was that I did not have to keep track of photo locations at all. Captain Johnson just grease-penciled it on the wind screen for me. When we got back to base, he copied all the photo positions onto a sheet of paper and took the camera with him. So, they made it easy for me. But I am telling you hanging out that window to get photos as needed was kind of spooky. I could easily see anti-aircraft fire and knew they were trying to bring us down, spooky."

Finally, he summed up, "By the way, I would recommend no drink or food before you go on mission. It ain't going to stay down, guaranteed. These fuckers do not fly in a straight line more than three to four seconds at a time. Man, they put that plane all over the sky. Could not tell where the hell I was unless I looked at instruments. Damn, these guys are good."

While what he had to say scared me on the one hand, on the other hand it got me really pumped up. Danger was what I was looking for, and that adrenaline rush was apparently what I could expect. It would be a few days before my turn came up. I was excited, but I knew the odds were not stacked in my favor. I kept telling myself that if things turned out for the worst, I would still be leaving a nice college fund for my brothers and sisters.

Of course, I knew the risks and I knew I wasn't invincible, but when you follow the devil's lead, you do really stupid things without thinking. These days, the on/off switch—alcohol-- was now essential for me to get through.

CHAPTER 6

Free Time in Villages And Town

In the meantime, it was back to free time for me. If you flew, you did not have to do much between flying. So, it was drinking, going into town, drinking, and carousing. After a while, it all became boring. To tell the truth, it became boring about thirty minutes into the trip to town, so I used my time to just walk around and explore the town. Soon I accepted my cameras again, and started to photograph everything I could visualize. When I had a camera with me, I easily got lost in another world. Photography was magic, just as it always had been for me.

At times I could spend the entire day with a camera just married to me, becoming a part of me. I photographed everything. Thai workers on base, villagers, women, kids, monks, water buffalo, I wanted to get it all on film. I was amazed by Thailand, the people, the way they lived, their homes, and the stores in town. I just could not get enough, as it all seemed to me to be so intriguing.

The bulk of the local people lived in small villages scattered within several miles of the base. Usually these were villages of fifty to two hundred people at most. The town of Nakhon

Phanom, about four miles from the base, however, had a population of around six hundred and fifty at that time. It was the only town of any size for many miles. Consequently, village people needed to travel to Nakhon Phanom for just about all their needs. On trading days, the town would swell to over a thousand for a few hours. Then when the sun was going down, the town would revert to its sleepy self.

By the 1960s, the town had been rebuilt, with most of the buildings being a combination of brick and concrete blocks. Almost all the buildings in the town center had electricity by that time, and most also had running water, and sort of modern sewage treatment. All sewage was carried through a pipe to the exterior of the structure, almost always in the front. It was just a ditch built about six feet deep and a couple of feet wide, which carried all the sewage away. Usually, the benjo-ditch was covered with boards to keep people from falling into the shit.

The homes in the countryside were built from mostly bamboo with thatch used for walls and the roof. Out there in the country, there was no electricity, and the villagers used one common well that served the entire village.

One interesting structure in Nakhon Phanom was a large clock tower built in front of government buildings just at the entry to the town. I learned from one of the town doctors that this was a gift from Ho Chi Minh, who in the early 1950's lived at an estate very close to our base and the town. The French had banished Ho Chi Minh and his political party senior members, and when they were forced out of Vietnam, they picked Nakhon Phanom and a villa close to town as a temporary refuge. Ho wanted to thank the town for its hospitality during his period of banishment until the French were finally defeated. Then it was agreed to make Vietnam into two separate countries, North and South Vietnam. Even though he vehemently opposed splitting his beloved country into two separate countries, Ho was forced into concession. After that period, he returned home a hero in both North and South Vietnam and became the first ruler of North Vietnam. And even after it was unified into one country about 25 years later, he was still revered as the founder of Vietnam.

Interestingly, his villa became the home of many of the spooks that worked on the US base nearby. First Ho Chi Minh, then the US CIA, stayed in the same house, go figure.

At the other end of the town was their town park, where festivals occurred several times each year. Close to the park was a walled complex for a Buddhist monastery, built for fifty to sixty monks. Mostly the town's population was either Buddhist or Catholic. Consequently, the monastery was very well supported by the town.

This was all so interesting to me, the monks, the clock tower, the whore houses, the bars. There was so much to see, so much to photograph. In my mind, it all needed to be on film, and so I began to document my experiences.

CHAPTER 7

Helping Hand

One morning I was sitting in the mess hall, eating dough-nuts, and drinking my tenth cup of coffee, when one of the paper pushers came through. I did not really know him well, but I should have. After all, he was the guy who cut my orders, made sure I got paid, and took care of all my other paperwork. He was picking up coffee and doughnuts for the CO Captain Sharp and others, and he had a little time to kill while the doughnuts finished cooking. I called to him, "How are you doing, Austin, how's the paper world?"

Austin responded, "Well, Vince, it's surprisingly good. My office is air conditioned, and I always have a nice clean uniform, beautifully starched and ironed, to put on every morning. Not like you nut jobs, flying around in itty bitty planes, asking to get shot at."

I laughed. "Yea, you do have a point, a damn good point. But I get flight pay, along with hazardous duty, don't forget."

"Yeah, yeah, I know." He added, "Hey, did you hear about the State Department job they got going?"

"No, what about it?"

"Well, they got our Doc Thomas and a bunch of engineers, going around to villages and trying to help folks out with their needs. I know that they are looking for a good photographer. You might check it out."

"Huh, thanks, I will."

A few days later I had occasion to go to sick bay to see about some photos that one of the corpsmen wanted. I said to him, "Morning, Mac, how's the sickly business, had any good cases?"

"Naw, just some scrapes and bruises, couple of guys cut themselves working on our planes. Just a few stitches and back to work they went."

Small talk over, I got to the point. "So do you happen to know anything about the State Department program that Doc's involved with?"

"Sure do," the corpsman said. "I am going out with him on occasion myself. It is really cool. How the hell did you hear about it anyway?"

"Well, I was sitting around at the cafeteria, and Austin came through and told me a little about it, said they needed a photographer. Is that right? He told me to ask Doc Thomas about it, but he was pretty sure they still needed a photographer."

"Yeah, I don't think they have one yet. It takes a lot of your time to go out on these missions, although they aren't all that frequent."

I said, "Well, I think I might be your guy. Why don't you ask him for me?"

Mac replied, "Happy too."

This might just be right up my alley, so I was anxious to hear back from Doc. This sort of mission might be a good way to accept the time between flying missions.

One thing I really hated about the military was the waiting around, the unused time. It seemed like I would be doing something meaningful for a few hours and then nothing. It was the downtime in the military that taught me how to drink coffee all day and tell lots of sea stories.

While a fairy tale always begins with, "Now once upon a time," a sea story began with, "Now I'm telling you; this is no shit...." A somewhat factual story might begin with, "Now I'm telling you, no shit, this really happened...." And of course, all the best stories must be told with a cup of java.

CHAPTER 8

Beer Hall

By the time I arrived at the beer hall, just to one side of the main gate, and across the road from the base chapel, I had forgotten all about taking pictures for the State Department. This was a wonderful place to drink beer, with lots usually going on. This was also the spot where we picked up the bus that took us into town.

As a spook base, we were highly classified, and not too many people got through the gate. The Thai workers were kept under a close watch, with US Air Force Guards keeping tabs on them at all times, and they were only allowed to go to certain areas, mess hall, bar, hooches (sleeping quarters), and common workers' duties areas. They were kept away from the flight line and the extremely sensitive areas. We had a lot of those. Some of the buildings were surrounded by several stacks of barbed wire. There were always many armed guards to keep the unwanted out.

This was the area where the CIA had a main frame computer installed and equipped with the machines that reviewed the film that we took on each mission. These CIA dudes were all dressed in casual clothes, and each carried a .38 caliber pistol, even when off base.

As I sat there in the beer hall watching people come and go, I noticed a bunch of Thais building a hooch for themselves right across the road from the main gate entrance. The Thai people were generally quite industrious, and these folks were getting right at it. They used bamboo to frame the structure, and right in front was a large fire pit with an assortment of pots next to it. After a few days, I realized it was going to be a two-story house of some kind. The walls were all covered with our boxes and plastic packing material from the base dump. We tried to burn most all waste, but these folks were industrious and clever. So we didn't much care they had found a new use for our trash. The guards left them alone, and so they continued like little busy bees.

Outside our gates, it was strictly any man's land, and there were a lot of Gooks (a very derogatory term often used for the Vietnamese, both NVA and Viet Cong, who would just love to cut your throat) around, right next to the base. I knew not to go fucking around on my own, especially after dark.

In fact, they tried to infiltrate the base on a regular basis, especially at night. Often, we could hear gun fire along the base perimeter wire. The guards were constantly firing at any movement, and outside the fence a lot of the area had been sprayed with Agent Orange to keep the foliage down. It was a damn good reason to be back on the base by sundown, if we were going into town.

We all knew our base was highly classified and because of that, of high interest to the enemy. We just could never let our guard down, even on base. The only times I felt really at ease was when we took trips to Bangkok, the capital of Thailand.

Even the house being built right outside the gate was suspect. We had no idea if the people building it were friendlies or North Vietnamese. We learned everything was suspect, so we lived our lives being suspicious of everyone, at all times. After a while, I got used to the constant tension. It really never left me until I was on a plane flying home.

CHAPTER 9

Deal With The Devil

Once when I was watching from the beer hall, Matella came sauntering up to me and said that the Chief was looking for me. So off I went. This was a very small base, and the photo lab was not far away.

"Hey, Chief, what is going on, did I forget duty times or something? Thought I did not have anything until my next flight time, which I thought was tomorrow."

"That's correct Vince, just wanted to make sure you were ready to go flying. We've adjusted your flight duties with the squadron, so we are making you guys available to the Air Force."

"Okay, got it."

"By the way, Vince, do not fuck up any of your FAC flights. The Air Force is now counting on us to save their bacon. These flights are important."

"Right, Chief, got it."

"Also, Vincent it's only eleven hundred hours and you smell like a brewery. Haven't you heard a sailor ain't supposed to drink until the sun is over the yardarm."

"Yea, yea, yea, but I was just sitting in the beer hall keeping an eye on the front gate for those Air Force pukes."

"Well, maybe you should have spent your time across the road at the base chapel instead?"

"Okay, Chief, it's under consideration. Is that all?"

"Yep, get out of here."

At the time, I had no idea what a profound change I was going through. I didn't think I was becoming a drunk. Drinking was just my on/off switch. When I was drinking, my mind and thoughts were a long way from flying and experiencing the killing and death of war. But when sober, I was always deadly serious, and paid attention to everything around me. So drinking was a terrific way to simply flip a switch, or so I thought. I could be part of a deathly serious killing machine one moment. But the next moment, I could be just a happy go lucky, nineteen-year-old kid. The deal with the devil had been made and signed by me.

CHAPTER 10

The Deal

Little did I know that my deal with the devil was just the start of an awfully prolonged period in my life. Nothing was the same after that. My life at home as I had known it was gone forever. My girlfriends and my friendships were all gone, by my choosing and the devil's. In my heart, I knew this was happening, but I would not be able to admit this profound change for years and years to come. My deal with the devil was now all I had.

That deal stayed buried deep inside me, where I thought my feelings could be controlled. It was all in a box, tightly locked and carefully kept deep inside me, where no light could shine. But no matter what, I knew the little black box was there, lurking in the shadows, wanting to get out, to escape.

I knew that if it did reappear, my life would turn upside down and I would have nothing to defend myself with. So it stayed buried, year after year, buried deep, inside a box that only I had the key to open. Or so I thought. But that would eventually all change. Even though it would take a decade or two, when it all came out, reared its head and came pouring out, I was completely defenseless.

CHAPTER 11

Sympathy For The Devil

Our squadron quickly got the reputation of a suicide squadron. Nobody in their right mind wanted to fly with us. For a while, everything was more or less copasetic. We had twelve planes in the squadron group, and we only flew one or two per day. So each crew got a four-to-six-day rest, sometimes more, before a mission.

But after the first few missions, everything changed. Things began to heat up a lot. First, we had crews coming back shot all to hell, but no one took a bad hit or was physically hurt. So, we thought we were a blessed squadron. That would turn out to be wrong, really, really wrong.

After all, the other squadrons were taking losses every day. You didn't have to look very far around the flight line to see a plane shot all to hell. Sometimes the cockpit hadn't yet been cleaned and it was full of blood. Sometimes the wind screen blown out, and I thought, "How in God's name did the pilot even get this thing back to base and, on the ground?" Sometimes they didn't. On occasion the pilot would manage to get back to base, and then crash the plane into the runway.

All the squadrons on base were taking horrible losses. We would see a lot of planes go out, and not come back. But so far, we were golden, no losses. Of course, we all knew, in the back of our minds, this would not last. It didn't.

To live with all this loss and destruction, some of us had to find a way to turn it off, in order to cope with the losses. My way was to join the devil because the devil's way was to enjoy the danger. In the moment, it was a good solution for me. But when the war was over for me and I returned home, I quickly learned the devil had heavy dues for me to pay. It would take years for me to finally realize I had already paid my dues, by just surviving.

CHAPTER 12

Devil's Payment Now Due

One day, it was my turn in the de-arming area to extract the film that was crucial to each flight. Because of the type of airbase, we were on, we had our runways and tarmac built with metal grids, kind of like a giant erector set toy built by the Seabees. The metal was coated with a gritty paint to keep the runways from getting too slick to land on. That didn't last. The runways quickly had the paint worn off with all the landings and take-offs. They became incredibly slippery when wet, impossible to land on safely.

Because the coating was dark green, it became as hot as hell in the sun. Like a piece of sausage in the frying pan, we sizzled. Consequently, we stayed off the grid if we thought we could get away with it. So, I did not want to be in the de-arming area any longer than necessary.

Naturally, on this particular day, our plane did not arrive as scheduled. So all we could do was stand around in the sweltering heat and wait. As we waited, we started to get anxious, then worried. After a few more minutes, we all started to look at one another, this was not good. Where the hell was it?

The ground crew chief finally arrived; you could just tell he was in shock. The plane was down, no survivors. We all were in disbelief. Crew Two, with Commander Olson, our Executive Officer, at the controls, was gone. I'd been talking with the photographer Widon earlier. His wife had just had a baby before we left the States.

They just could not all be gone, just like that gone. Now I did have to feel it, and I knew what getting bloodied up meant. One minute they were whole, then in a flash, gone. How can that be? Everything else was still here, clothes, toiletries, cameras, unprocessed film, and everything else seemed normal. Except they were gone. How was this possible, how could this be, where did they go? The vision of the empty bunks of the men who had been lost struck me hard. The bottom fell out of the world. None of them said goodbye, but they were gone. I did not understand. Why?

Hell has no sympathy for those working for the devil. At least that is what it felt like to me. We were all doing the devil's bidding, and I was perfectly willing. Now more than ever, I wanted to pay back, a way to get even, to kill those sons-of-bitches that killed my friends. How sorely mistaken I was. I was a badly hurt and terribly confused kid, who suddenly, violently, had been told to be a man. I was supposed to suck it up, do my job, let everything else sort itself out on its own time.

After Widon's death, I felt this heavy weight on my shoulders. It was as if I was carrying him around. I knew better, and I knew that no matter what, we had to keep going, keep flying. His wife would be told that he had been killed in Vietnam, but in fact he was a hero who had volunteered to fly into Laos on secret missions. The truth would stay buried for the next thirty-five years. Until then, no one would know how he had flown into harm's way voluntarily and given his life for his country.

It would take thirty-five years for the country to recognize the incredibly brave men of this secret squadron. Even after that, it would be a few more years until President Bush finally said, "Thank you." Finally, the president awarded our squadron the Presidential Unit Citation. It was a gracious thing to do, to finally recognize our sacrifice, thirty-five years later.

CHAPTER 13

Just Keep Trucking

Really, in those days in Thailand, we had no time to think about our feelings. After all, the war was getting hotter and more deadly every day. So, the FAC flights were more essential than ever, and about every three or four days, out we would go.

My next mission with a FAC was flat out horrific. Again, we were going to fly along the Ho Chi Minh trail on the Laotian side of the side of the border between Nam and Laos. The sky was overcast, but the ceiling was still high, so I thought of it as just another flight. But it wouldn't be that at all.

When we got to the Trail, we went a lot lower, under the cloud cover, lower than I liked to fly in any case. If you were badly hit at a low altitude, your opportunity to bailout was limited at best. This day, the FAC was low and scooting around all over the place. I quickly became disoriented.

We were flying through "karst," the foothills next to mountains, which were largely bare with a lot of rough sharp edges. Suddenly, the area between some karst that we were flying through turned into a cloud of shrapnel, and holy shit, we were in it up to our necks. But as usual, the FAC pilot had everything under control. I didn't realize a plane could do some of the things he was doing with it.

This guy could put the plane on its tail, then swing around and put it on its nose. Then he would skid in a tight circle on a wing tip, all of which meant that if you weren't flying the plane, you could easily become disoriented. It was almost impossible to stay oriented to horizon, wind speed, altitude, or direction in a plane that was dancing all over the sky. The bad part of this was sometimes, it was hard to keep my stomach settled. The good thing was that this made it really hard to be directly shot at.

We made it through and went around, then marked the area with smoke for the highflyers. They quickly turned the area into a piece of scorched earth, like a piece of burnt toast. Sometimes, napalm is a beautiful thing.

It was especially beautiful if it was either them or us. I would much rather it be them than me, and I was more than happy to make it them. However, this was the first time that I was really, truly scared, out of my mind. It was impossible to fly a plane through all that and still be in one piece. Here we were in one piece after all of that.

A bit later we finally got up to a little safer altitude and started to look around. At first it didn't appear we had been hit. Then my FAC pilot pointed to holes in the wing on his side. Holy moly, how lucky can you be? Well, apparently pretty damn lucky. We both knew that the plane might have taken a more serious hit.

I said, "Time to go home, Captain?"

He looked at me and just nodded his head yes. When we did get the bird on the ground and began to inspect the damage, all I could do was say, "Holy Shit" and shake my head.

Sometimes what happens in war can't be explained. You know it happened. You know you are still alive. You don't know why. You know today was just not the day to pay your dues. You know you're back, on the ground. You don't know why but feel it's grand. That's all there is to it: Today was a good day. Today you came home, one day done, and you get to fly again. Tomorrow, there is always tomorrow, and another dance with the devil.

CHAPTER 14

Time To Reflect

Finally, I was able to talk to Doc Thomas about the village program and became extremely interested. My first time out with them was kind of a return to my pre-Navy career. I knew how to be a photojournalist, and taking pictures of people and events was always my first love. To me, documenting life around me was the best use of my camera. It was a natural act for me, just wrap myself in the moment.

Doc told me to muster at the medical center at 0700 hours to go out with a group of Air Force guys. The village was quite a distance from the base. Well, it seemed like it was, because the roads were so bad, a few miles seemed like we'd been gone forever and might be on another planet.

When we arrived at the village, there were very few younger men. I was told they were all out working, tending rice paddies. In the center of the village was one large open-air hut, with women and kids scattered all around. The head mamasan was seated on the ground in the center. No doubt about it, she was definitely in charge.

In this neck of the world, the older folks, especially women, often chewed betel nut, the seed of the areca palm tree. It is a mild stimulant, giving the user a sense of well-being and euphoria. It also stains your mouth and teeth a dark brown. Mamasan had a large chum, or wad of betel nut mixed with limestone paste and wrapped in a leaf, stuck into her mouth by her cheek.

She and most of the old gals were using it, from what I could tell. Their mouth, lips, and teeth were permanently stained a dark brown. I guess, at their age they didn't care about the color of their mouths or lips. You had to be careful to not upset someone chewing the stuff, because if they spit on you, the spot on your skin would be dyed a permanent dark brown. And it did not wash off.

When we arrived, we all piled out of the jeeps and trucks and went to have a talk with her. She was serious but seemed to be kind and thoughtful. We took quite a long time explaining what we would be doing if she gave permission. The village had a very bad water problem and needed a new well desperately, and we were prepared to take care of this problem for them. We had brought several engineers and the equipment to drill a well. This she was happy to allow.

When Doc Thomas explained that he would provide free exams and medications as needed for the sick and elderly, she was a bit more skeptical but did agree. He asked if he could set up right here in the center of the village, and she agreed again. It was decided to take care of the children first and then older villagers.

We were off and running, trying our best to help this small village. My problem was that Mamasan did not want anybody, or anything photographed, and I had to respect her wishes. I stood around, trying to figure out how to get her to change her mind. She was adamant that there was surely something spooky about my cameras.

At this point, having nothing to lose, I carried my camera over to her and put it on the ground in front of her. We both stared at the camera, then I asked her, "Would you be willing to look down into the camera?" It was a Mamiya twin lens reflex, used by a lot of the pros shooting portrait and other types of photography, and my favorite. These cameras were much bigger than the popular Nikon 35mm cameras of the day. However, they had one advantage: You had to look down into the top of the camera to view the image, and the screen was much larger than a 35mm camera. So, she would not have to get her eye awfully close to the camera in order to see the image.

She was not sure at all. But I slowly picked up the camera and set it in her lap. Then I pointed down into the viewfinder, encouraging her to look through it. Slowly she did so, and I very carefully moved the lens and focused it, so that it was pointed at one of the children and in focus. At this point I could see in her eyes; she was fascinated with the image.

I asked our interpreter to explain to her how the camera worked, and that if she would allow me, I would take pictures of the village, and she would have them in a day or so. There would be no magic, just beautiful pictures for her to keep. She slowly agreed to trust me, and I got several magnificent pictures that day.

In any case, when we returned to base, I developed the film and made contact sheets right away. The contact sheets, just the negatives placed on a sheet of photo paper and exposed, were great for reviewing my images. Indeed, there were several great pictures of the villagers. As soon as time allowed, I made several large photos for the village as promised.

I gave them to one of the interpreters and asked that he get these photos back to the village as soon as could be arranged. A few weeks later, I was told that the magic camera guy was a big hit in the village, and I was absolutely thrilled.

While collaborating with the villagers was exciting and great fun, I knew my reality was going to return. We had a war, so dying was reality, killing was reality, and blood and gore and awful memories were the order of the day.

For a while I was like my old self, a photojournalist doing his job. But it was not going to last, and so, on and on it went. I was scheduled to fly the next day and had to prepare. The next day would be more of the same, another mission, another flight, another day, maybe we would return, maybe not.

So far, I had kept the devil and my little black box buried deep inside me, not knowing how long it could stay buried. Hopefully someday it could just go away on its own. After all, I hadn't heard of anybody coming back from Nam with bad memories. We now know that more veterans returned home from Vietnam with traumatic experiences than at any time since they started keeping track of these issues. But they were refused treatment for the most part by the Veterans Administration at the time. As a result, the suicide rate among Vietnam veterans skyrocketed.

It was unhealthy to ignore the trauma, but that was what we did—ignore it until it blew up in us. A feeling grew over me that we were all expendable, easy to replace. As the war went on, I tried to suck it up, to keep a manly face on it all. After all, real men didn't cry, had no time to think about losses. Real men knew how to shove it all into the background. That was the manly thing to do, and by God, I was bound and determined to be the manly type.

And this continued after we were discharged. It was generally accepted that it was gutless to seek help from the Veterans Administration. We decided we didn't need help, just as well, because it wasn't available. The psychiatrists at the VA took very few cases at the time. Our duty now was to forget or stow the feelings in a deep hole. That was, after all, the manly thing to do.

SECTION 4

Flying Dead Suicide Missions

It is foolish and wrong to mourn the men who died. Rather we should thank God that such men lived.

George Patton

CHAPTER 1

Like A Zombie

By this time, I had become like a zombie. Put my flight suit on, go to flight check, get my parachute, flack vest, survival gear, aerial reconnaissance camera, helmet, remove any identification I might have like a billfold, driver's license, and so on. Become just a number on a set of dog tags. Meet the pilot, FAC42, review again the mission, strap in, and off we went, across the fence again.

Although it was a rarity, sometimes missions were not so bad at all. This day would be one of those. The major was a great guy, actually fun to fly with. I think he was a little hung over or tired, so he let me fly a good bit, which I enjoyed immensely. He was also a damn good pilot and a surprisingly good instructor. It behooved us all that I had at least some skill in flying. If he got hurt, I could hopefully still get us home.

On this mission, things were quiet. The NVA (North Vietnamese Army) had a habit of putting some of their anti-aircraft weapons in caves, high up in the karst, rugged stony outcroppings between the mountain peaks. They were harder than hell to even see, and almost impossible to hit. These guys were certainly not stupid, and as time passed, I gained a strong admiration for their abilities and dedication.

We had been in the air for a couple of hours, with nothing much moving around below us. The pilot looked at me and said, "Let's go on a turkey-shoot."

What he had in mind was shooting at one of the guns up high in the karst. They had known for a good while where the gun was but could not do much about it. What the NVA would do is put these guns on rails or wheels and roll them out to the cave opening, take a few shots, and then roll them back into the cave. Naturally, they were awfully hard to spot, let alone hit. The major knew exactly where this one was.

So off we went on our turkey-shoot. Now all we had were white phosphorus rockets on our wings, which we used to mark targets for the planes assigned to us. In other words, we did not have much to work with. But it would improve our skills at putting our rocket markers where we wanted them. They were not always an easy target to mark, and this was not an easy task, but necessary.

We flew around one piece of karst after another, and into and out of one little valley, followed by another. I quickly became disoriented as to where we were, but the major knew exactly, and before I could even comment, he pointed out the cave we were looking for. You just could not help admiring these FAC pilots. They were so good at their flying ability. That little FAC plane was like a gnat, ridiculously small and in the hands of a real pro, almost impossible to hit.

He got us far enough away that they could not hit us very easily. I said, "Major, that is a pretty small target from where we are now. Can you hit it from here? Will our rockets even go that far?"

"Vince, ye of little faith, you just watch, maybe you'll learn something."

Around we went in a complete circle, and suddenly he pulled the nose of the plane up, so it was pointed well above the cave, and lit one off. The rocket flew in a giant arc as it approached the target. It just barely missed the opening of the cave. Boy, was I impressed with the shot. He was using dead reckoning from a long way out and damn near hit the target. Incredible!

He was mad at himself that he had missed. We flew around again, and he took another shot at the cave. This time he hit a dead ringer, right into the cave. My eyes must have been bulging out of my head, as he looked at me and chuckled. "See, told you I could hit it."

What an incredible shot. Wow. I suggested we come around and skid the plane past the cave so I could photograph it. When we finally managed to get close enough, the cave was really smoking, which led us both to believe that we had certainly hit something, and it was burning. Another one for the good guys.

As we moved on, and began again to scout for targets, he started laughing so hard that I thought for a second that I would have to take the controls. "Vince, confession time. I have been try-ing to hit that cave for a couple of weeks. Just could not get close enough to it, and when I shot from a safer distance the arc of the missile made it really hard to hit. But I figured out how to adjust the trajectory of the 'missile falling' as it traveled through space and thought I would give it the old college try today. The smoke from the rocket is made from white phosphorus and it burns very, very hot. So, if they were still in there, the heat should do some damage, and the smoke will at least piss them off mightily."

The rest of that mission was normal. Because of a falling ceiling, the clouds were getting low, and he decided to stop for the day after I got the pictures, I had been sent out to get. And I also got one good picture of the cave opening from up close.

On the way home he asked me if I wanted to fly the plane, and of course, yes, I did. He gave me a heading and told me to wake him as we got close to the fence, the Mekong River. I loved to fly and did not get too many opportunities to do so.

After we crossed the fence, the major decided to spend a few minutes just flying around. He said, "Let's practice a few low and slow passes." I didn't expect what he did next.

There were rice fields all around, and a rice field is generally surrounded by a hedge row, sometimes twenty to thirty feet high between fields. What he did was take us down so low we had to jump over the hedge row to the next field. I have no idea how we kept out of the water. After a few of these, he looked at me and said, "OK, let's put it down. Mission complete for today."

I was damn sure ready to be back on dear Mother Earth.

It was early afternoon by the time we got back to base, and the heat had picked up quite a bit. After checking back in, giving my camera to the major, turning all my flight gear over, and wiping all the sweat off, I went to the photo trailer to check with Chief Nagels. He was not in; Chief Tyndall was staffing the photo lab instead. I always really liked Chief Tyndall, as he was encouraging and wanted me to advance up the ranks. Hard guy not to like.

"Good morning, Chief, how's things?"

"Morning, Vince, how'd your mission go this morning?"

"Good, had a Major, really good pilot, came back with all the parts and pieces still attached. So, I got nothing to complain about. Am I scheduled to work with any of our planes?"

"Nope, you're free, just be sure and check in tomorrow AM."

CHAPTER 2

Going Across The Fence

One of my first missions began on a rainy day in monsoon season about 5 AM. I was told to report to Flight Preparation. I was given a flak jacket and a survival vest, then picked up a Smith & Wesson .38 handgun and a parachute. As I was putting these on, my pilot came in and introduced himself to me. "You Vincent? I am Captain Butler. Let's talk. First, let us get one thing straight. You do not have to fly this mission with me. Just give me your photo equipment, and you can stay on the ground if you want. I know that a lot of the photo guys do not like to fly with me. They say I take too many chances. It is your call."

"No, Captain, I am good to go. But right you are, your reputation does follow you. I was told you are a wild man in the air, but also that you were the best FAC pilot out here, and always got the job done. So, I am good to go." What I did not say was this was going to be only my second mission across the fence. My first was more like a training mission.

The "fence" was the Mekong River which separated Thailand from Laos. Our base was within a few miles of the

127

Mekong, but on the Thai side. Going across the fence meant flying into hostile territory, as everything in Laos was hostile. It was well known that if you went down and were not quickly rescued, your chances of survival were close to zero. So, no matter what, we could not get shot down.

The FAC pilots flew in Cessna Sky Masters, which were ridiculously small, with a push/pull engine set up. They were known for their durability and agility. I remember that right between the pilot and copilot seats was a sign riveted to the instrument panel that read something like, 'ACROBATICS IS STRICTLY FORBIDDEN.' What the hell? Did they think we would be flying straight and level, begging the enemy to shoot us down?

In the air, the FAC's oversaw about everything. They provided the eyes for the planes, mostly fast movers, or jets, to see their target. Targets were often exceedingly small and hidden by the jungle. So, we needed to mark the target with one of our rockets that were loaded with white phosphorus and produced a very dense white hot magnesium fire and enormous amounts of white smoke. This was so that the target could be hit by one of the highflyers attached to us, using smoke as the target.

I always flew in the right seat, which was usually used by the co-pilot, or just left empty. But today it was for me to use with the window open. I had an exceptionally good look at the ground, and generally got good photos of targets from the right seat. Most of the time it was kind of fun, hanging outside the plane taking pictures. I sure had a great view of the ground.

After we took off and cleared the fence and crossed the Mekong, it was not that far to the other side of Laos and the Ho Chi Minh Trail. I had not been told how incredibly beautiful Laos was. It was a sea of bright sparkling jungle green. This part of Laos was almost entirely mountains and foothills called "karst," made of large broken pieces of limestone. The sky was a deep blue with gorgeous fluffy clouds. It was breathtakingly beautiful, especially to someone like me, whose career centered on what I could see.

The area had very few villages, roads, or trails that could be seen from the air. But occasionally we would fly over a small valley between the mountains and karst. The little valleys often held a small village. The population of these villages was often Mnong tribespeople, who were fiercely independent and wanted mostly to just be left alone.

My pilot, FAC68, soon received a distress call from a badly shot up plane, still in the air, near to us. We found the pilot almost at once, and he was clearly in serious trouble. He was hit over a small valley, and it was clear he was not going to make it back to base. My pilot quickly got on the mike to me and told me to keep a close eye out for his parachute.

Within minutes, his chute opened, and quickly we had him on radio. He said that he was taking a lot of fire and was clearly scared out of his wits. We told him to just hang on while we went lower and tried our best to divert fire from him and make us the target instead. We tried everything we could think, but it was just not enough. They shot him as he was floating down in his parachute.

Why, why bother with the pilot? After all his plane had been destroyed, he was virtually defenseless in his parachute. Both my FAC pilot and I were ready for blood.

With nothing but smoke rockets to fire back with, we quickly backed off. The pilot called control and asked what could be made available to him for this target. It turned out that there was an Arc Light mission that had to be called off because of harsh weather. An Arc Light mission was a covey of B52 bombers, the biggest in our arsenal at the time. Arc Lights flew usually above thirty-five thousand feet, which made them almost impossible to see and shoot down with most antiwar guns. They were able to drop tens of thousands of pounds of explosives. We knew that there was enough firepower to turn the entire valley into the stone age. So, vengeance was ours if we wanted it.

We put several smoke rockets at both ends of the valley and identified everything in between as the target. When they finally dropped their load of bombs, the entire valley erupted into a gigantic ball of smoke and dirt. Nothing remained that I could see, not a soldier, not a villager, not a water buffalo, not anything. It was just a giant inferno, nothing left. Not a human, not an animal, all gone. I had never seen anything like it before that time. This was war about as ugly as it could get from the sky. Armageddon.

With most of our rockets used, we turned towards the fence. Home was just across the Mekong River. My second mission was behind me, and had changed me forever, in ways I did not realize in the moment but would affect me for the rest of my life. I had just witnessed hundreds of people killed in one giant inferno, a devil's cauldron—the cauldron of my devil, who now controlled me, at least some of the time.

CHAPTER 3

Death And Evil

Now I was spending day after day photographing the violence of war, watching people reduced to a target, to a spot in the jungle, naming them as anything else but human beings. They were targets, dinks, Gooks, but never humans, family, people, loved ones. Killing became something more, something I still don't exactly know how to explain. But everyone else made it sound perfectly normal. What did you do today? "Oh, killed a bunch of people, both young and old, men and females. It was scary, but what a rush."

But being able to photograph people, just people living their lives, was such a relief. Slowly, very slowly, I began to think about work that I could be doing for somebody besides the devil. I screamed at myself that there was still hope, that there was still a little beauty left in the world. My emotions felt like a giant soup, with a little bit of hope mixed with a dash of the devil in the broth. I was swimming in this broth and did not know what to make of it all. All I could do was keep swimming, and hope that my head would stay above it all.

It was a time of great loneliness. I did not think about tomorrow, or even the next moment. There was no guarantee that the future would come. I knew that the odds were that it might not, and sometimes the odds were heavily stacked in the devil's favor. This fatalism was the start of a long, long road that I would have to travel alone. It was a lonely road, something I just did not see coming, I guess. I was not the GI Joe of comic book adventures, just a sad and lonely kid trying to get the job done and hoping to get back to base in one piece.

Flying in combat for five or six hours at a time was stressful, to say the least. Usually as soon as we crossed the fence, my adrenaline would kick in. The funny thing about flying into hostile territory is it generally can all seem so peaceful, and then, like flipping a switch, all of hell's evil opens and you become the center of attention. Danger is a funny thing. It causes you to be high with adrenaline and everything around you become crystal clear. It was like Alice in Wonderland. Suddenly everything was different in my vision; everything I saw was crystal clear.

Then there was a disruption of time. Sometimes it just almost stood still. Something that took only a minute or two or three seemed to take forever, and everything and everyone was in slow motion. I could take it all in, soak it all up, in seconds. Then you needed to react in seconds. Sometimes guys didn't, and they paid a steep price.

The weirdest aspect was not only did events happen quickly, but the memory stayed with me forever. It was as if my soul had been marked, and that mark was going to be with me for the rest of my life, one way or another.

The war is now about fifty years in my rearview mirror. Sometimes I can still see it all, like it just happened.

Even as I remember most events that happened in combat, I can also remember the time right before. I remember the color of the sky, the sounds in the plane, the beauty of the land, like it just happened. Somehow my brain has been marked, and that mark is those memories, and they never go away.

Maybe it did not happen like that for others, and I hope it didn't. But for me, the memories left a mark that has never gone away. It has not gone away through all of life's ups and downs, my marriage, my children, all my successes and failures. It always takes front seat as most important. Nothing can be more important. It stays right there in front.

All of it is right there like it is just happening. In contrast, sometimes when I reflect on where I was or what I was doing two years ago, I don't have a clue. Of course, that's perfectly understandable. After all, our lives are full of tasks and details that fill our mind. But the one experience I have never forgotten is war. It is all still there, every second, every smell, every scene, all right there.

Sometimes the war comes back to me at odd moments, like when I'm in my car, driving, or on a hot beach, or sunning on the patio. Now it just comes to me for a minute or two. But there was a time when the memory of war would last for an hour or more and just go on and on. Then, like a light switched off, it would all be gone, all stored away, put into my own little black box. But I knew the lid would come off again. I knew I could never completely bury it. No matter what, it stayed right there with me, in the darkness, always there.

I wasn't always this broken. Before the war, when I was a kid, I tried to always be kind, to be the first to offer help if I could. For a few years we lived on the south side of Noblesville. The houses were much older, and there were a lot of the elderly that lived nearby. I quickly learned I could help a lot of these fine old women by running errands to the little neighborhood grocery, mowing their grass, putting in their gardens in the spring.

My favorite was Mrs. Mundy, a spry ninety-year-old. She heated her home with a coal-fired potbellied stove that sat in the middle of the living room. The stove pipe ran through that room, then through the bedroom, and then outside. One evening, I took out ashes from the stove and brought in enough fresh coal to get her through the night. We sat in front of her stove, and I intently listened to her stories and ate her oatmeal cookies. Man, her cookies were the best. Anyhow, as we sat there watching the fire, I told her again, how concerned I was with her living just two homes away from the Clarks, who were a rough family.

The father had been in prison, and his two sons had been in prison for theft. His daughter had been arrested on several occasions for prostitution. I kind of knew about that, after all, prostitution was in the bible, and it was supposed to be a terrible thing. I was genuinely concerned for her safety. "Mrs. Mundy, I'm always worried that the Clark boys might appear and cause trouble."

I remember she just said, "Rickey, you have nothing to worry about."

Then she told me to get up and get a piece of iron she had in a three-drawer chest in the bedroom. Of course, I imagined the piece of iron was just that, a piece of iron she could use as a club.

I was all wet. What she had in that drawer was a very long barreled .45 pistol. It was so heavy I could barely lift it out of the drawer. She very sternly told me to bring it to her but hold it by the barrel end only. So that's what I did, and very carefully handed it to her. I remember she took the pistol, flipped a little lever on the side, and the gun's cylinder flipped out. She smiled, spun the cylinder, and put it back together. Then she said, "Well, Rickey, don't worry about me. You see, if anyone comes in my house without an invitation from me, they will be counting bullet holes fast."

She meant it, and I was dutifully impressed, and also relieved. Now that I think about it, it was probably a gamble, that she could make it out of bed, get the pistol, point, and fire it. But I guess she just didn't want me to worry. She was always most thankful that I could take the time every evening to come over and help her out.

When she passed away not too long after that, I was told to not go to her house after school. But I couldn't help myself. I really cared for her and loved her. She only lived a half block away, so I walked over to her house. One of the relatives was there, and they seemed to be cleaning and preparing for the funeral. In any case, I was told that she died in her sleep quite peacefully and had gone on to better things. Even now, I sometimes think of her kindness, and the cookies and talks we shared together on a frosty winter day.

It was the only way Dad would have it: Be kind to everyone. Of course, I wanted more than anything to have Dad approve of me.

But once Dad was gone, somewhere inside me a switch flipped off. Perhaps when I went into the military, I realized that everyone has a dark side. Usually that dark side can be controlled by our goodness. It really cannot compete with the good we all have—unless something flips that switch! In my case, it was losing Dad. I thought that going to war would hide the pain. It did not, it just gave free rein to the devil.

I have always been an "all in or nothing" kind of guy. So, when it came time to go to war, I was all in, and I gave the devil a full ride. What a ride it turned out to be. Fortunately, I was eventually able to let my goodness back through the door, and it has stayed with me ever since that time. I guess you could say I had a rather long ride with the devil, and I know how he works, how he thinks, he is a trickster that is for sure.

I remember that during my time at war there was a Rolling Stones record produced with a song on it called "Sympathy for The Devil." It was my theme song, and often, when going into combat, I would repeat in my head the lyrics over and over again. In my way of thinking at the time, the only way anyone in their right mind could survive the killing, the blood and guts, the pain and agony, was to just join with the devil, for it was surely evil at work. What person in their right mind would get up and jump into a small aircraft, fly around until you found other men and women at war, and then try your best to kill them all?

What causes man to line up opposite other men and try to destroy them, to try to tear their arms and legs off? What causes man to kill in the name of some righteous cause? Can any cause be so great that we would feel good about ourselves for helping that cause along? Does man have no other way? Drenching ourselves in our fellow man's blood has been around for a long time, but why, why should it be? Can we not agree, agree to disagree? Must we always seek vengeance?

This is surely why, many, if not most of the world's greatest rulers have been drenched in blood. They know the outcome, the pain, the hurt, the damage to our souls, and try to avoid it. It cannot be worth the cost, can it?

Across the Fence Flying Into Death

Throughout this life, you can never be certain of living long enough to take another breath.

Hung Po

CHAPTER 1

Just Another Day in Paradise

When we arrived "in country" in Thailand, it was late in 1967, and things went well for a while. But as we got closer to a new year, the action heated up quite a lot. While we did not know it at the time, this was just prior to the Tet Offensive, when the North Vietnamese Army would attack every major city and all our major bases in South Vietnam. Tet is the holiday when everyone closes their business, goes home, and shares a great feast with their families, giving thanks to their gods. It is the most important holiday of the year for the Vietnamese. Traditionally, Tet was the one time when both the North and the South sides put down their arms to celebrate.

However, in late 1967, there was a big buildup on the Ho Chi Minh Trail which went right through Laos into South Vietnam. Laos was a country we were not supposed to be in, but of course we were, big time. Our secret little base on the Mekong River was there for one purpose, and that was to stop the supplies and the North Vietnamese Army from using that trail through Laos. Heavy traffic ran down the trail, day and night. What was going on? We were about to find out.

To detect activity up and down the trail, we put our sensors where they would work best. We were so effective that our FAC boys had targets galore. We had not lost our first plane at that point, and so everybody hoped for the best. We thought that somehow, we were blessed, invincible, and the luckiest group in the war, especially here on the border of Laos, working from a base right across the Mekong. Some of us thought as long as we prayed and tried to do the best, God was going to take care of the rest.

We were not facing reality. The Spooks and the Air Force were losing planes all the time. In hindsight I can't believe our naivety; we were not exempt from disaster. What we were doing was one of the most dangerous jobs in Vietnam. As it would turn out, it ended up being the most dangerous assignment given to any squadron in Vietnam. Our losses would indeed be staggering.

As for me, however, this young kid was just not going to believe that. No matter what, they couldn't hurt me-- so I thought.

CHAPTER 2

Reality

Then we lost our first plane, and everything changed. Reality was right there, hitting us right in the ass. With a tremendous amount of help from the FAC planes, we struggled on. But each day reminded us of this was an extremely dangerous game we were playing. At the end of a mission, sometimes we just sat there and shook, until we started to come down from the adrenaline high. Reality is a bitch, and we had reality in spades.

After our first loss, it was decided to have a church service for the crew. We had the service at the base chapel, just across the road from the main gate. The service was well attended and peaceful as far as I could tell. As for me, I didn't go. Instead, I just sat in the beer hall right across the road. I thought about going into town, but changed my mind, just sat there, and drank.

How could they be worshiping God? I just kept looking at the door to the chapel, wondering how they could trust God for anything now. This just did not seem right to me. It would not seem right for the next thirty years or so.

Sometimes we must walk a long, lonely road, and mine was just beginning.

CHAPTER 3

Popcorn, Ice Cold Beer, And Mary Poppins

After just completing a flight with one of the FAC's, I was ready to get my mind as far away from flying as I could get it. I needed to get my flight suit off and some fatigues on, with a nice long, long shower in between.

Bill was nowhere to be found, so I sauntered over to the mess hall for something to eat. I'd had nothing yet today and was getting mighty hungry after flying. By this time, it was close to noon, so I was able to get a couple of fairly edible sandwiches with some fries, chased down with a couple of beers, not too bad. About this time along came Bill, looking for some chow as well.

I gestured him over towards me. "Hey, Bill, how is it going. Had a good flight with the Major. He let me take us home, or almost home, pretty cool."

Bill wasn't as upbeat. "Well, Vince, so far, my day has sucked major. I just spent three hours in a darkroom trying to get some of my film processed and having nothing but problems with some Air Force puke. He thinks he knows just about all there is to know about photography. Of course, he doesn't know shit. Damn, I got so pissed at him, I just barely kept it cool."

I decided to help settle him down. "Let's go watch a movie at base theater. I am betting we will be the only ones there. It's Mary Poppins, and I want to hear the music. So, what do you say, let's go, get drunk later?"

Bill replied, "I would go if it were not for that obnoxious radio bleed from the Thai radios, right next door to the theater. It's bad enough we cannot hear shit over their jabbering."

"OK, tell you what, you give me a couple minutes and I'll cure that problem, at least during our movie," I said confidently.

"How the fuck are you going to do that? You got voodoo or something?"

"Nope, but I do have some help from Mr. Colt. You will see."

When we got to the theater, I asked Bill to get me some popcorn and some nice tall cold ones. I told him I would be right back. Then I stopped by the parachute riggers and checked out a Colt .45 for five minutes. It was a short walk to the Thai radio shack, and all I did was point at their radios and wave around the Colt. It was not loaded, of course, but they didn't know that.

When I walked into the movie theater, there sat Bill with plenty of popcorn and an equal supply of beer. We waved at the projectionist to begin and had the whole place to ourselves. It could not be better-- Mary Poppins, cold beer, and popcorn. It turned into a mighty fine early afternoon.

CHAPTER 4

Keep On Keeping On

Days off from flying were always easy, although occasionally we had a camera system that needed attention for one reason or another. That always took time to diagnose and fix. Generally, we just had regular flight line maintenance. Our cameras rarely needed much repair, and we just swapped them out for a good working camera most of the time. They were big cameras, about the size of a foot square box and full of electronics. They were very heavy, some weighing over fifty pounds, and so we generally didn't try to repair one on the flight line. We just removed it and put another in its place. Of course, then we had to lug this fifty-pound camera back to our photo trailer so Senior Chief Nagels could work on it.

On occasion we had to do electronic checks with the cameras and the other equipment needed to keep them running and exactly synchronized. It would be really bad news if those cameras did not work perfectly to photograph where our electronic sensors were being dropped. It would mean that the entire mission was for naught, and that twelve men had put their lives at risk for naught.

Sometimes what we did when we weren't actually in the air did not seem too important. But in fact, our post- and pre-flight checks were essential, because everything was dependent on those cameras working precisely as intended. When Bill and I were working on the flight line with the cameras, whether it was checking systems or loading cameras with film for the next mission, it was always deadly serious work. We never skipped a step or took any kind of chance at all. We ensured that the photo equipment was not just working but working perfectly.

The humidity at our base was always so bad that we never loaded the cameras with film until right before take-off, or as close to departure as possible. The film was kept stored in the large meat freezer we had sent over for just this purpose. It was the perfect solution for large rolls of film that we wanted to keep away from humidity.

Even still, the film would start sweating within an hour or so of being removed for use. So, we had to keep it sealed up and did not load it until just before take-off. That way it would stay as cool as possible and hopefully dry as well, for the short period of time we were on the ground.

Usually, we had to prep at least three planes every day and make sure all was ready, and then sign off on each one. There were times, however, that one of us would be flying as rear door gunners, and on those occasions, we checked our own planes out. If you know you are going to get shot at, you damn sure want the equipment in working order.

For our planes, each mission was a challenge. Usually, a crew would start preparing the day before the flight, to be as sure as possible everything was in its place and working. These missions were so dangerous, we did not want to have to do any of them twice because a piece of equipment failed. Our record for preparing the planes was darn near perfect, as we made damn sure nothing was going to fail. We did our best to check and re-check everything before each mission. We never had a camera system failure before a mission. Thank God.

Days could seem like years to us. We knew that what we were doing was incredibly dangerous, and there were no second chances. Ten percent of our squadron was already gone, and we had not been in country but a month or so. God, maybe that Spook had been right in his prediction about two-thirds of us becoming casualties. None of us wanted to talk about it, to even think about it, our number might be coming up. It had rapidly become just a roll of the dice.

It was impossible for me to wrap my head around everything that had happened. Just a few months ago, I was walking around the streets of San Francisco, enjoying the sights, the people, and now that life was all gone. It seemed like it was years and years ago. Suddenly, I was putting my flight suit on, getting into a plane, and flying into a hostile country to get shot at. And it was just a few months ago that we were flying on leisurely missions across the California desert and pretending to drop our little devices. Nobody shot at us, and it was kind of fun. It was now breathtakingly dangerous; we were getting shot at every mission. There was no denying I volunteered for these missions. But what was I thinking? I guess in that moment I thought I was invincible. Not anymore.

CHAPTER 5

Just Keep On Trucking

There was no denying, some of us were going to be dead to-morrow, or the next day, or the next. It went from "maybe it might happen" to "it's inevitable." Sadly, our losses began to increase. Suddenly, we realized that we could run out of planes for the mission, unless something changed, and our losses began to slow down.

That still seemed unlikely, so we just kept flying. Fortunately, for the next few weeks, the action settled back down. Each day that came and went was another day closer to the end of our mission, we hoped. But none of us could get over the losses we had already experienced, and none of us wanted to talk about it. The thoughts just rolled around in each of our heads like a whirlpool. Every day, two or three crews would awake, put their flight suits on, check equipment and weapons, climb aboard, and know that in the next hour or two they would be either alive for another day, or dead.

Most days I was flying with the Forward Air Control. Their losses weren't as bad as ours, but they still took at times very heavy losses. So, we still had to think about the risk we were facing. In my case, I had to contemplate watching one of our planes getting shot down, losing another crew, watching somebody die.

It was bad enough watching our bombs hit the ground, knowing all those poor bastards below us were going to be blown apart, or worse, incinerated. What really was worse, having yourself blown apart, losing your limbs, and writhing in unconscionable pain? Or burning to death slowly as the gasoline jelly covered your body and no amount of rubbing would put it out? You were going to melt and die an excruciating death. That's what we tried hard not to contemplate. Good guys or bad guys, it did not matter, we were all human and we were all close to death.

As for me, I just would not let myself think about it. I had a job to do. They needed good pictures taken, and I was there to do just that. What was under all the smoke and dirt and ugly black clouds rising into the sky was not my problem, at least in this moment. Not my problem. My job was to get back alive and hopefully still in one piece. I could be shot down during the two or three passes needed for my job, and if that were the case, so be it. The spooks needed the photos, and it was my job to supply them, and the risk was part of that job.

After each flight, I got myself completely shit-faced, as drunk as I could possibly get. It was so much better than thinking about the danger, remembering the losses. So, each evening I got myself totally stoned and did so for many years to come, every night. The drink kept the thoughts and the dreams at bay, and as my way of fighting back against the reality, it worked.

Or I thought it did, but I was just not being honest with myself. Someday the devil was going to take his due and destroy me. My only chance was to face the whole thing, and at the time

I just didn't think I could do that. So, every evening I took my medication, and for a while it did work. It kept the devil stuck in a box deep inside of me.

Then in late February, we lost another plane. When it happened, I was in town, just taking pictures for myself. On the bus back to the base, I noticed one of our guys looking disturbed and pissed.

"What's eating you, man?"

He answered, "Just heard from the Air Force that we have, well, we lost another, don't know who."

We got to the base about an hour later and went directly to our squadron workspaces. We could see it on the guys' faces. Crew five was down and declared missing in action. Still, we did not learn much else for the next several hours.

Finally, a FAC pilot let us know the real status. The plane had gone down on its second run. It was hit and badly shot up. It did not come back up above the clouds after the run. So, the two F-4's that were flying along went back down below the overcast and found the burning wreckage of our plane. There had been no parachutes deployed, and no emergency beepers were heard. While they were at first declared MIA, we knew that none of them got out.

As bad as this was, our losses were not over with. We knew that we had no choice but to keep on dropping the sensors where they were needed most. They worked just as advertised, but at a staggering cost. We had lost so many men. A third of our squadron was gone. It was hard to bear, all those men, all those friends, gone forever.

1968
Tet Offensive

*Excellent goodness speaks in
a whisper, evil shouts.*

Tibetan Proverb

CHAPTER 1

The Lying Never Stops

In January 1968, the Vietnamese celebrated their annual Tet Holiday. It is the most important holiday of the year for them, kind of like our Christmas and Easter all rolled into one big celebration each year. Sometimes the celebration lasts for over a week of family get-togethers, drinking, partying, and hoping the gods will present them with another year of prosperity.

But this holiday was going to be vastly different and became one of the most famous events of the Viet Nam war—The Tet Offensive.

As the new year began, we knew something was up, but could not figure out why traffic had picked up so much along the trail.

All we knew was everyone was glad that we were there to seed the trail with sensors. This made it so much easier for the FAC planes to find targets for the highflyers. But so many targets began showing up in December of 1967, and we had a tough time believing it was all just because of the effectiveness of our listening devices.

All we knew for certain was, our mission was successful, and our losses were not for nothing.

CHAPTER 2

No Time For Celebration

The US and its allies in the South Vietnamese army did not expect the strength of the Tet Offensive. When it began, the NVA quickly struck virtually every major military base and every major city in the country. The entire world was in shock. It appeared we were losing, but in fact, we quickly retook all lost areas and soundly defeated the North.

With the beginning of the Tet Offensive, the entire war was about to change. It would be the first stage of failure for US involvement in the war. Even though we were successful in defending all attacked areas, which wasn't the way the liberals back home wanted to see the war. Journalists, who for the first time in history had access to any battle or mission, began to change the story. They began to promote the liberal cause now in full swing in the US. Suddenly, US troops were bad, no matter how well they were doing.

The military brass wasn't used to such reporting and began to justify their actions. Unfortunately, they couldn't stop the reporting even though it was largely dishonest. This was to become the time of the Body Count, which was meant to prove that we were winning. Each day the military would report the body count of enemy killed, and the body count of US casualties. It didn't work.

The American public just didn't find the casualty numbers believable, even though the press inflated these numbers, and the military was also trying to manipulate the numbers to their advantage. It was a ridiculous way to report the war, as casualties only told a portion of the story. After the war, the military quickly realized the folly of using body counts, and in all future conflicts these numbers were always classified and restricted. In addition, the press corps was never again given the free access to the war zone that they had in Vietnam, and the military began to inspect their reports for accuracy.

The commander of the war, General William Westmoreland, advised all who would listen that we were winning, and we most definitely were. However, without exception, most journalists covering the war found this to be far-fetched at best, and most thought it was a flat-out lie.

Yes, we were not as prepared as we should have been and were taken completely by surprise. But then, after losing a good deal of ground the first two days, the US began to fight back and completely destroyed the North Vietnamese forces. Trouble is, because of our losses in the first few days of the offensive, most journalists covering the war presented this as a sign of complete defeat of US forces.

Actually, we were winning, especially towards the end of our part in the conflict. The US was inflicting stunning losses on the NVA and Viet Cong. The losses were so great, especially during the Tet Offensive, that the North Vietnamese would not recover for several years. The US media didn't want to report that, so instead they amplified our losses. After all, we were at war, people die, people get hurt. For God's sake, it was war. But the American public was told we were losing, and the losses would not end until we gave up the war. In truth, we never lost a major battle in the Viet Nam war. But when the politicians stuck their noses into the conflict, it quickly became a political liability, and the news media had little trouble selling the story of a defeat.

After Tet, we were winning the actual war, but losing the public battle, largely for political and journalistic reasons. The politicians wanted only what was popular, and the news wanted to broadcast only bad news, not necessarily the truth. Bad news always sells, and good news is bad for business.

In the end the press corps would never again be given full access to the US military battlefield.

But the damage was done. The story that got through at home was we were taking enormous losses and losing badly. Soon the public was firmly convinced that we had lost our military ability, and that our military could not be trusted to tell the truth. It was going to take more than twenty years for the military to erase the stain of the Vietnam War. Of course, the news media and politicians never offered a single apology.

CHAPTER 3

Marine Base Khe Sanh-
Help Is Coming

Before the Tet Offensive, the man in charge of the war, General Westmoreland, said this kind of attack was not possible, that it would be suicide for the NVA to attack en masse. He was wrong about whether it was possible, but he was right that it was suicide for the NVA. Their losses were so severe they would not fully recover for years.

At our own remote base on the border, we had become aware of the massive invasion of the South, and now knew why there had been so much traffic on the Ho Chi Minh Trail. For months, they'd been bringing in massive amounts of material, guns, men, and women. But Westmoreland stuck to his belief that it was just not possible for the NVA to attack the entire country. He was damn sure wrong on this score.

Then the general said it was all a ruse, that the NVA only wanted our Marine base at Khe Sanh, close to the Laotian border. This was only partially correct. They also wanted to take the city of Hue as well as many other towns and military facilities.

They did accomplish that, but only temporarily. Their success countered Westmoreland's supposition that the entire Tet Offensive was just a ruse to capture Khe Sanh. People in Hue or Saigon or any of several hundred other locations knew better.

The NVA had captured Hue for a few weeks, during which their soldiers and political cadre slaughtered tens of thousands of innocent South Vietnamese citizens. Both elderly and children were put to death and pushed into mass graves. Their crime was that they had not sworn allegiance to North Vietnam and were living in the South.

In a matter of days, the NVA was routed, leaving all the territory back in our hands. But the American press told the story differently, and the war-weary American public believed their lies.

And the NVA didn't get Khe Sanh. The Marines were hanging on, barely, though they were in deep trouble. They were surrounded by more than twenty thousand NVA soldiers with tanks and anti-aircraft weapons, along with artillery. The NVA had obviously put everything they had into conquering this base. The NVA were there to win and had a force they thought was big enough to get the job done. They wanted another Dien Bien Phu, the 1954 capture of a military base that ended the seventy-year French occupation.

Obviously, they had come to take this remote base that bordered Laos. But Westmoreland knew the base was vital and ordered the Marines to hold it at all costs.

In fact, the South Vietnamese wanted nothing to do with their Northern neighbors and just wanted to be left alone. The Tet Offensive did not bring a mass conversion of the South Vietnamese into North Vietnamese patriots. In that early 1968 conflict, the South Vietnamese and the Americans came back and defeated the North and defeated them badly. It would be several years before the North could rebuild their army and have any kind of major show of force in the South.

THE SECRETARY OF THE NAVY
WASHINGTON D C 20350 1000

The President of the United States takes pleasure in presenting the PRESIDENTIAL UNIT CITATION to

OBSERVATION SQUADRON SIXTY-SEVEN

for service as set forth in the following

CITATION:

For extraordinary heroism and outstanding performance of duty in action against enemy forces in the Republic of Vietnam from 15 November 1967 to 2 July 1968. Throughout this period, Observation Squadron SIXTY-SEVEN (VO-67), operating in the Republic of South Vietnam, successfully executed its primary mission of providing quick reaction, close air support, and combat logistics support for United States and Vietnamese military forces. In the face of extremely harsh climatic conditions at a remote operating base, while sustaining extensive operating damage and losses, the flight crews and ground support personnel of VO-67 carried out their highly important and extremely sensitive missions with outstanding skill and dedication. The Squadron flew countless missions implanting newly developed sensors to detect enemy movement. The support provided by VO-67 was instrumental in supplying real-time intelligence regarding the movement of North Vietnamese troops and supplies, which enabled U.S. Forces to prevent the total invasion of the U.S. Marine Combat Base at Khe Sanh during the Tet Offensive and contributed to saving countless lives. The squadron's operations were consistently characterized by prudent tactics while maintaining meticulous adherence to the rules of engagement, ensuring maximum deterrence of the enemy with minimum risk to friendly troops and civilians. VO-67's successful initiation of this new mission provided a significant and vital contribution to the art of warfare. By their outstanding courage, resourcefulness, and aggressive fighting spirit in combat against a frequently well-equipped, well-trained, and often numerically superior enemy, the officers and enlisted personnel of Observation Squadron SIXTY-SEVEN reflected great credit upon themselves and upheld the highest traditions of the United States Naval Service.

For the President,

Secretary of the Navy

CHAPTER 4

The Marines Needed Help

In our photo lab, everyone was talking at once, except for me and Bill.

"Man, this is unbelievable! I just heard that Westmoreland has his panties in a wad. He is saying it all is a ruse, that they only want Khe Sanh. Seems like bullshit to me. What have you heard, Chief?"

He replied, "Well, as far as I have heard, everyone is ordered to stay on Base, duh. All flight crews are to get yourself ready ASAP. Vince, you, and Bill will be flying FAC. But until we get a better picture of what's happening South, everybody just needs to stay cool."

I said, "Got it, Chief. Got any idea if we're working the trail, or what?"

"Not a clue, Vince. Just get ready, stay ready, stay sober. This is probably going to be a gut buster."

Later I was summoned back to hear more personal news. "Chief Tyndall, you wanted to see Bill and me about...?"

"Yep, sure did, remember when we made you boys take the Third-Class Petty Officer test back in Alameda? Well, you both made it, both of you shits are now Third-Class Petty Officers."

I laughed out loud. "Woo, Bill, did you hear what Chief Tyndall just said? We both passed and have been promoted, can you dig it?"

Bill just stared at me like a deer in the headlights. Then he said, "Where are we going to get our Third-Class insignias? I don't have any, do you?"

"Can't believe this myself, and no, I don't."

Soon Chief Nagels had the insignias problem under control. "Here you go, boys. Just do not lose these brass beauties. You will have to worry about your other uniforms when you get back to the World. We are all proud of you both."

Man, I tell you, Bill and I were both psyched by the promotion. But with the news about the South, we were also scared shitless. "Bill, how bad do you think it really is?"

"Vince, I am hearing it made every news channel in the world. I was able to pick up a little from the BBC, not good. They said what we just heard, but they keep talking about Tet Offensive. What is that all about? In any case, the VC must be putting up quite a shit show, at least along the border with Nam. So, I am betting we will be flying a lot of the trail close to this Khe Sanh base. If the Marines are asking for help, it must be a real son of a bitch of an attack. Guess we are going to find out, damn."

For the first time, I was truly scared, scared nearly out of my mind. I figured there would be a lot of ground troops shooting at us. They could easily hit a low-flying spotter plane with an AK47, not to mention whatever else they had.

My conversation was with the devil. "Shit, you scared little boy, they only shoot little bullets. Baby." That seemed to be all he had to say, but it was enough.

I didn't want to die; I didn't want to get shot at by any kind of gun. Why me, my God, why me? Bad omens were beginning to accumulate. The danger was very real, and this really could be the end. I wasn't ready, but there it was right in front of me.

As I imagined the worst, my mind worked frantically. I needed to write a new will, just to be sure all money went to the kids' education. What about all my equipment? Guess I can give that to the high school.

The next moment, I had weird thoughts. Am I already dead? Or am I going to be, and just when? Hopefully, it won't hurt much. What if I get sent home a vegetable, still alive and nothing else?

I told myself—You got to somehow stay cool. After all, all I have to do is climb in that plane, take good pictures, do my job. What could possibly be the problem with that?

Well, I was about to find out.

CHAPTER 5

Put It All In The Air

"Find out" is exactly what happened when we started flying in, around, and close to Khe Sanh. From the air, everything looked pretty much the same, just a lush green carpet running through the karst and around the mountains. Still beautiful, calm, and peaceful. But when we dropped down below a thousand feet or so, we began to see a lot was changing. There was movement everywhere, and sure enough, everything was headed towards the Marines. They were in deep shit.

Most of the planes in the air had been assigned to FAC pilots, especially in the area of the Khe Sanh base. So, we had lots of weaponry, whatever we thought we needed. We started using a lot of CPU, cluster bomb units, little brightly covered things that we hoped would attract the enemy. When picked up, the devices would sense body heat and explode, tearing a hand or arm off.

Several miles out from Khe Sanh, napalm was used, but never close to the base. Slowly the ground several miles out from the base began to look more like a treeless brown landscape. There was nothing but tree trunks, dirt, and debris everywhere.

It looked like there was nothing living left above ground. But the VC and NVA were there, we knew they were, and they kept shooting at us. These guys were not only brave, but damn good at their jobs. But then, so were we, and we fully intended to kill every last one of them.

Sometimes I'd find myself wondering, My dear lord, what was I doing here, in this tiny desolate piece of the world?

It did not take Westmoreland long to realize that we had a really serious problem, one that couldn't be solved by just bombing the jungle. The Khe Sanh base was completely cut off, and it was impossible to resupply the base overland. Trying to fly planes into the base was also damn near out of the question. The planes were shot all to hell before they could be unloaded, let alone take off again. So, the base began to be resupplied by helicopters and planes flying over the base and dropping their loads on skids, without the plane ever touching down or coming to a full stop. This was still dangerous; however, it began to work. But otherwise, the base was cut off with no relief in sight, and they kept coming at us.

I've never been exposed to a situation as desperate as this. It was sickening to fly over or even close to the base, where the Marines were outgunned twenty to one. They couldn't fight their way out; they would be slaughtered. Everyone began to think that this might just turn into another Dien Bien Phu, that we could lose the entire base, along with hundreds of men.

CHAPTER 6

VO67 THE GHOST SQUADRON

General Westmoreland was one of the very few that knew about our squadron and knew how effective we could be if we were allowed to do it right. We just needed to fly low and slow to drop each sensor and photograph its location clearly.

When we had the opportunity to drop, these sensors were superb at keeping track of the battlefield. If the enemy moved or made a single sound, we knew it and we knew exactly where they were. Well, not exactly, but we could tell within a couple of feet. If we then shelled them at the position given by our sensors, they were toast.

We would need to place sensors just a few feet from their outer perimeter and then in circles about every hundred yards or so. We decided to spread a field to about 1000 yards out all around the base. The Marines tried to place them by hand, but it was so hot outside the fence with rifle and machine gun fire, that idea was given up quickly.

Because Westmoreland knew about the secret US Navy Squadron VO67, he asked for us to place sensors around the entire base. He had been briefed on the accuracy of the sensors when placed where their position could be carefully photographed.

Of course, the Air Force, in its infinite stupidity, ordered us to release our sensors from five thousand feet or higher. We knew that this would not work, as the sensors would be scattered all over the place and ridiculously hard to photograph. From those altitudes, it would be impossible to do what the boys on the ground really needed. If we did not get down right above the ground, the sensors would be practically useless.

We were all willing to fly these missions to protect our Marines, even though there was no question that if we went down, we most definitely would not survive. We knew how many of our Marine brothers were in danger, and what needed to be done. Without question, we were ready to do the missions the right way, and to hell with the Air Force.

CHAPTER 7

Just Get It Done Right

We got the sensors placed where they would be able to do the best, and we all prayed they would work as advertised. Our brother Marines' lives depended on our accuracy, and accuracy was what they got. A story that got back to us was that one of our sensors picked up NVA movement over a hill close to the base. Of course, the Marines opened with artillery on the position. A Marine monitoring the sensor, and who spoke Vietnamese could hear the NVA cries, and one of them shouting to get men to the top of the hill and kill the spotter who was giving their position away. He didn't realize that the spotter was an electronic device dropped by an old, tired plane being flown by the US Navy, VO67.

On another occasion, a Marine transmission came across our planes radio as we are flying across: "Look out, here comes one of those green planes right on the deck again. Who the hell are those guys?" Even the Marines did not recognize us. We had very little identification on our planes, as all the lettering had been removed or painted over. Remember, we were a very secret operation at that time, very, very secret indeed. Nobody would know about us for the next 35 years.

Eventually we put enough sensors in the ground around Khe Sanh that the base could hear the VC and NVA coming long before the enemy had time to get there. While I doubt, we alone were the savior of the base, certainly we helped an awful lot.

Later, many years after it was

all over, the commanding officer of Khe Sanh prepared and sent a letter to the President of the United States. It was his opinion that because of our flights over the battlefield, the base was able to protect and defend itself. He said that without our efforts the base would have been lost and over-run.

It was nice to have this confirmation even if it was thirty-five years after the battle. His letter to President Bush resulted in our squadron receiving the Presidential Unit Citation, the highest honor a unit can receive, along with Naval Service Cross for those who did the flying, second highest after the Medal of Honor.

Finally, after thirty-five years, someone said, "Thank uou." It meant an awful lot to all of us. A copy of this letter and the awards were given to me at our first reunion, thirty-five years after it was all over.

CHAPTER 8

My Friend Baat The Monk

After our missions over Khe Sanh, it would have been nice if we could have all gone home and called it a day. That was not to be, as we had a long ugly road to travel still.

As February moved on, we continued to fly over the Trail daily. I was flying generally three or four times a week, sometimes more, which certainly did keep the adrenaline going strong.

Between flights, I started to spend more and more time in the village during the day. There was a religious monastery for Buddhist monks towards the end of the village, beside a small park. I found it to be quiet and peaceful. The monks at the monastery were from the age of about five to young men just about my age. They were a quiet bunch, and I watched them come and go, occasionally saying hello, but not much else.

One day, one of the older monks came into the park and sat next to me. His English was not the best, but it sure beat my Thai. It was the start of a wonderful friendship. Both of us were between nineteen and twenty. His family had sent him to the monastery at about the age of four or five, and he had been there ever since. As was often the case, he never saw his family again.

I learned from him that the monks would walk throughout the community with a bowl and ask for food. On most days, he had no trouble receiving something from one of the villagers. Apparently, it was good karma to give to a monk in need of sustenance.

As we got to know each other, I learned a lot from him and grew to have profound respect for him and his religion. After a while, I learned to address him as Baat, or something like that. I was never able to get the spelling correct.

He called me 'Bence,' although it should have been Vince. They just could not pronounce the letter 'V,' it always came out sounding like a 'B.' Our new friendship changed everything for me. Now I had a reason to go into town.

CHAPTER 9

Vince And Bence

M ost of the guys went into town to drink and carouse with the whores, who were plentiful. I just was not into either one of those things, although I did like to drink. My drinking was done mostly at base around the hooches, where a bunch of guys would gather to bullshit each other. Sometimes I just drank by myself. The most important thing was always getting enough booze in me to keep the devil and the memories all stuffed into the little black box, deep inside me, right next to my soul.

For me, it was like taking your medicine before turning in for the night. It let me relax and helped me forget, and I of course had no idea about the addicting aspect. All I knew was that it seemed like a great way to turn everything off, so I could sleep. It was just a way to flip the switch at bedtime.

One day, while I was in town, Baat came scurrying across the fairgrounds and sat next to me. He was out of breath and seemed as if he was in a hurry. "Hi, Bence, ask you this, you go help, help village with military men?"

I answered, "Yes, I go village, different village each time, help with medicine, food, water, yes! Take pictures with camera, give to big men, government, in Washington."

He was fascinated by this. So, I showed him one of my cameras, and helped him look through the viewfinder and take a picture. It was so funny; he could not understand where the picture was. He felt that he had offended my camera somehow.

As much as I tried to make him understand, he just kept looking at my camera with confusion. "Baat, I bring you pictures from camera, but you must wait till I come next time."

I think he agreed to this. In any case we continued to try to our best to talk and learn. Within a few minutes, he was all smiles, and all was well again.

Several days had passed before I was able to return to town. This time he was sitting in a lotus position, which I could never master, waiting patiently. I had a package of pictures ready to hand him. He was exactly like a small child sitting in front of a Christmas tree, looking with wonder at the pictures.

After a long time, we sorted through all of them. I had printed most of them into large 8-by-10-inch pictures, with a few smaller ones sprinkled in the package. When we were finished, I remember he very carefully placed each picture into a perfect stack, and very gently picked the entire stack up. Bowing, he tried to hand them back to me.

For the next hour, I tried my best to explain to him it was a gift from me to him. Monks have as possessions only the robes they are wearing, nothing else. They can have nothing for themselves, so we had a dilemma. But nevertheless, we talked and laughed, and kidded each other for a long time.

Finally, I agreed to take the pictures back, but asked to see his teacher. I asked Baat, "Do you have a boss, or a headmaster?"

This was totally confusing to him, so I tried again, "Do you have a 'papasan' or something like that?"

After a few more minutes of confusion, he answered, "Teacher, we have teacher. Yes."

"Yes." I said, "Yes" again for good emphasis. "May I speak to Teacher."

"Yes, maybe."

Off we went to the monastery, and I was in luck. The Teacher turned out to be more like the head dude, and he was more than willing to speak to me. Fortunately, he could understand a lot more English than I expected. He'd had a lot of meetings with a Catholic priest who was in the area from time to time. He spoke a combo of English, French, and Thai.

The first thing I asked him turned out to be about right. Dumb luck on my part. "Thank you for giving me some of your precious time. I have profound respect for all you do. Of course, I will not take much of your time. If you will allow me, I want to give you an exceedingly small gift, as a way of thanking you for the understanding one of your monks has given me."

As I said this, I handed him a silk-wrapped package, which held the pictures I had tried to give to Baat. He accepted the package, quite graciously, without looking inside at the contents. This was the absolute best for which I could hope. "I give you this small gift as appreciation of all that your monks have taught me."

He thanked me graciously, and that was that.

The next week I found out from Baat that the pictures had indeed been accepted by his Teacher, and that he was quite happy to have them. He had placed them on display in the monastery for all the monks to enjoy. Go figure!

Going into town was kind of like a valve to let out all the steam in my pipes before they exploded. When I was in town, I was away from the killing, the evil, the craziness of it all.

The town sat right along the bank of the Mekong River, and the main street of the town followed the riverbank, with buildings and businesses on one side and the river on the other. The town was built along a stretch of the river that had remarkably high banks on our side.

Across the river was Laos-- the other side of the Fence. The enemy. Very often I found myself standing or sitting along the river, just looking at the small boats coming and going from one side to the other.

"The fence" was almost so close I could touch. On one side of the river was peace, on the other was evil. It was like living a dream. At this time, it was no dream, it was a nightmare and would stay a nightmare for years and years to come.

Thank God, at least I had an on/off switch. I had the booze, and for now, it worked. What I couldn't understand was why it all continued to be so painful. Even when the flights were over, there was this pain, this deep inside me pain. I could shut it into the little black box that kept the devil and the evil away. But the pain couldn't be buried completely, and it was always there.

It was as if when I was sworn into the military, I had put my hand in the air and said I would follow all the rules and defend my country, and accept any pain given as part of this. It was my duty to carry this around with me forever.

CHAPTER 10

Bang-Bang, Not Coming Home

A s January slowly turned into February, our missions continued along the Trail. After Tet, though, life was a long
way from normal, and the intensity of what we were doing became crazy. "Normal" became just coming back alive, having
wheels touch down, safe again, for a while.

In this war, in our neck of the woods, nothing stayed safe for
long, and we were going to go through another loss very soon.

About the middle of February, Commander Hayden and
Crew Five were flying along the Trail and dropping Acu-buoys,
sensors that could detect movement. They had with them as
usual, a FAC plane to help spot and mark the target for us. All
was going well for a while. But then, after coming off the first
run, Commander Hayden radioed, "We've been hit by small
arms fire, but looks like everything is still good, and we are coming around for another run."

On this mission, we had a couple of F-4 fighter jets flying
as escort with our plane, and they followed our plane down
to keep an eye on things and see if they could see any activity
on the ground. It looked good to them on the second run. But

then they alerted Commander Haydon that his starboard engine was burning.

At this point Commander Hayden decided to abort the next run and try to return to base. So, the fighter planes came back up on top of the clouds, expecting to find the now wounded plane.

Both the fighters heard them saying, "We are beat up pretty bad." They both went back down to try and find our wounded bird. As they dropped down, they quickly found the burning remains. They found no parachutes and could hear no emergency beepers. The entire crew had apparently gone down with the plane-- no survivors.

What made this so tragic was that Commander Hayden was one of the most experienced pilots in the squadron. He had a lot of experience with multi-engine aircraft, and his co-pilot Lt. Thurman had experience with engines coming apart. Both these guys had been in planes with engine fires and were considered some of the best we had. It could only be assumed that they had suffered more catastrophic hits, but this was the one that brought them down.

Nine more men, gone. It was a lot to absorb, a lot to take in all at once. But nevertheless, they were gone, no survivors. All of us were numb, without words, just numb. We began to think, is my number up too, am I safe, or is tomorrow going to be the day? Christ, why did we deserve this? We all had to endure it, this empty space. It would stay with me forever, and there was so much more to come. I had to learn early on, to just stuff everything into a box and bury it deep inside me.

Oh God, please, turn this all off, I tried to pray. But the devil always seemed to appear, shaking his head, saying, "No, let's go kill, I'm not done with you just yet."

CHAPTER 11

What's The Point

During my first tour, I began to hear news reports and read articles that had been written about the war in Vietnam. They'd turned very negative. I did not believe much of what the news reports had to say, and I could not understand why they seemed so angry at me. Hell, what did I do that was so bad? After all, we were here to help another country, and we were not asking anything in return, as far as I knew.

Of course, we'd been told it was the communism that we were fighting, and the communism was leading the North Vietnamese to kill thousands of people. Just because the South Vietnamese didn't believe as the communists did, they could be shot on the spot. Sometimes a whole family, sometimes a village, would be slaughtered. To see these events was to believe that we were fighting for right. I believed that.

My naiveté was staggering, but not for long.

Within another month, our next plane went down, but this time things were different. This time most of the guys were able to jump out and made it safely to ground. Fortunately, our FAC brother was able to track all the parachutes and talk to everyone that had jumped. Quickly he alerted them that help was on the way.

He told them to keep their heads down and tell the FAC if enemy was sighted so they could lay down some suppressing fire to help till the Jollys got there. The Jollys were the Jolly Green Giants, our anacronym for rescue helicopters. If we had not been captured by NVA, these guys would risk everything to get us.

It took four Jollys to pick everyone off the ground. Now, I ask you, how do you thank someone that has just put his own life on the line to save you from a sure death? But these guys did just that, with only one glitch, and that was our fault.

One of the guys on that flight was Petty Officer Wang, whose parents were Asian. So, from the rescue chopper he looked a lot like the enemy. He needed to convince the rescue folks that he indeed was a US Navy boy.

By this time in the war, the enemy had recovered many of our pilots' survival radios, and would use those to lure the rescue chopper right into their position. It was an easy and always deadly way to lose one of the Jollys. As a consequence, on each flight, we were given a code name for the day. The Jollys of course wanted to hear the code before hoisting us up.

As a good and typical sailor, Wang let them have it with language that was quickly determined to be Sailor American, no t Vietnamese. We were sailors, and of course we knew how to cuss with the best of men. He was hauled up and out of harm's way without delay.

All but two of our men were successfully rescued that day. Sadly, both our pilot and our radioman had gone down with the plane. We knew the radioman was already dead and sitting at his controls. The pilot, however, was alive and unhurt, but he stayed behind and kept the plane flying in a straight line long enough for everyone to bail out.

His name was Commander Milius, and he was given some of the highest awards for bravery for his actions that day. What he did, not many men would have done. He freely gave his life for his fellow aviators. He kept the plane straight and level, allowing everyone to jump. Almost thirty-five years later, a new navy ship just coming into service would be named after him. Even today, the USS Milius, a destroyer, is serving the fleet. And those brave men that flew with him are now dwindling to the very few.

CHAPTER 12

Certifiably Crazy

By this time, most of us were incredibly stressed and beginning to doubt ourselves. Did we belong here, did we really need to fly right off the deck at three, four or five hundred feet? It was not that we were unwilling, it was just a suspicion that somehow, we might not be doing enough. And the tension was beginning to show up in extreme ways.

One evening, as was generally the case, some of our guys were playing poker at the Sergeant's Club when in walked Second-Class Petty Officer Litz. He was one of us, a photographer's mate, and also was on a flight crew. He was an all-right kind of guy, in the service for life. He mostly kept to himself. Now he was all dressed out in his flight suit and gear – and carrying a pistol and an M16 rifle.

Wild Bill Coty was playing poker at a round table with his back to an exhaust fan in the window. He was startled by this sudden appearance, then he realized it was one of our guys. "Litz, what the fuck! What are you doing?"

"I'm going to kill you, for a start." At that Litz looked right at Wild Bill and aimed his .38 at Bill's head. Fortunately, one of the guys coming up to the table realized what was happening and shoved Litz arm up and over Bill's head. Coty decided it would be a good idea to depart, and jumped through the window, taking the fan and window with him. He was not found for several hours.

We learned later that after jumping, Bill made a quick decision to hide and saw one of the bingo ditches. Now these ditches were used to carry restroom effluent to a central dump. They were about six feet deep and usually covered with boards to keep people from falling in. Bill decided that it would have to do as a hiding place, and it did work well. These ditches really stink, really, really stunk. Most everyone tried to just stay away from them. It was a perfect place to hide. He stayed there until the morning sun came up.

It turned out that Litz had become distraught when he realized he was supposed to be flying on the day we lost our last plane. He simply could not take it any longer. Fortunately for him, he was removed from the area and sent to a psychiatric hospital where he could be treated. We all felt bad for him, but we also were thankful that Wild Bill did not have to "take one" for the team. As for Litz, with care and time, he got well and was able to rejoin the squadron.

Time moved slowly, but eventually early spring came, and the weather began to change. One day, a small crew of naval photographers arrived at the base with a ton of photo equipment. This was the Pacific Fleet Combat Camera Group, one of the most famous groups of photojournalists in the military, and known for their work from WWII, Korea, and now Vietnam.

They checked in directly with Captain Sharp, our commanding officer, and told him Washington had sent them to document our squadron for the White House. It was quickly decided that would have complete access to the entire squadron with no restrictions at all. We were ordered to extend to them any help they might need. With access like that, we knew these guys were the real deal.

It did not take long for me to figure out they were all pros at their jobs. When they asked for permission to ride along on one of our missions, they were granted access at once, no questions asked. And when the next mission came up, they were all given the essential equipment, flack vests, parachutes, and weapons.

We carefully instructed these guys exactly how dangerous these flights could be. I clearly remember talking to them after that mission, when it was my turn in the de-arming area to remove film for processing. A couple of them got out of the plane and photographed me as I was removing film from the large photo reconnaissance cameras. Then we took them to the Sergeant's Club for a bit of liquid restoration.

They all said they would never go on another mission, that we must all be certifiably crazy, that no one in their right mind could fly those missions day after day and in Laos, for God's sake. Did we not realize what we were doing was against the Geneva Convention Rules, and that we were not supposed to even be in Laos? To top it off, we were working with the Spooks! I guess our secret mission just wasn't their cup of tea!

In any case, they were gone the next day back to Saigon, where they apparently had offices. After they left, I decided that there must be a way for me to get into that elite squadron.

After their visit, we knew that the rumors about us would begin again around and throughout all the services. We learned the film they took during that time became a documentary and was classified top secret. It remains so today. We too stayed top secret for years and years to come. Even in Saigon, where MACV (Military Assistance Command Vietnam) headquarters was located, only a couple of people, one being General Westmorland, Commander of MACV, knew anything about us.

Most paramount for us, however, was just trying to stay alive. There would be a lot of missions yet to do, a lot of killing and dying. We just wanted to live to tell the tale, and that got a lot more problematic as time dragged on, mission after mission. Then for me it was just fly, drink, fly, drink until I could at least sleep. Each in our own ways, we became somber, and there not much more smiling around the base. Our goal had changed. In each mission, we just wanted to get it over with, beyond that, nothing else. Just get through it and hopefully return to base.

CHAPTER 13

Thank God, Springtime

Finally, spring was here, and things began to change for us. After now having lost over thirty percent of our planes, the military began to consider whether the cost they were asking us to pay was just too much.

While Secretary of Defense McNamara did not much care how many of us were being killed, apparently some of those in government decided this question was worth bringing to the President or someone else with authority. Was this really worth the cost?

The answer must have been "no." By the end of March, most of our missions had been put on hold, and we were down to just a few missions a week. By the end of May, we were told to stand down. There would be no more missions, at least for a while.

Then, as suddenly as it had begun, it was over. Our mission was complete, and the squadron VO67 was ordered to pack and prepare to leave the theater and return to the US. Just like that, Observation Squadron 67 was disbanded, and all of us would be reassigned to other duty. It was a tremendous shock to be in active combat one day and told to go home the next day.

On the morning the Air America planes started to touch down, I entered the lab, and Chief Nagels asked me if I was ready. I thought he was asking if I was prepared for a mission. But he looked me right in the eyes and said it was over, get packed, and get on one of those planes. Air America would not wait just for me.

I thought maybe this was another bad joke. I just stood there and stared at him. This was the equivalent of being told that you were going to be beamed up to another world. As I looked around this Twilight Zone of reality, we all seemed to be reacting and feeling the same. Could this be real, just a couple of days ago, yesterday, we are flying around Laos, asking to be shot at!

It was real, it was really real. And it was over, just like that, over. My God, I made it, I was still alive.

Soon we were in the air, and a beautiful flight attendant was handing me a double scotch with a splash of soda. I looked at Matella, and he looked back at me. We both shook our heads. It was over.

On the long flight back to Alameda, nobody said much. We were on a flight to heaven, back to the world. I gave the devil his due, but he wasn't up to the task, thank God. In the moment, that was what I was feeling. But I was wrong. He wasn't done with me yet.

CHAPTER 14

Now What

By the time we landed in Alameda, it was about four or five A.M., and I had no idea what day it was. Still dressed in our combat fatigues, we got off the plane and were met by an admiral, who shook each of us of our hands. He told us to collect our bags, pick up our orders, and then go to a table set up for him so he could give us further instructions.

So first we went to retrieve our seabags, which had been left here when we departed ten months ago. Could it really be only ten months? Almost thirty percent of us were dead, and we all had changed forever.

Our plane was parked right in front of the same hanger we had used prior to leaving. Inside the hanger, all of our sea bags had been lined up in alphabetical order right down the middle of the hanger. We had forgotten that we were actually sailors in the navy. I just grabbed my sea bag and carried it with my other bag with all my stuff from the base at Nakhon Phenom. Then I joined the line to speak with the admiral.

It did not take long for my turn to come up with the admiral, who at once ordered me to stand at rest. Then he asked if I would like to sit, and quickly got right to the point.

First, I was to forget about everything I had done for the last year or so. It did not happen, and I certainly didn't know and had never met anyone from the CIA. If my memory needed to be worked on, I would be sent at once to a brig at Ft. Leavenworth, for a minimum of thirty years. At least he made it clear that this was the very last thing he wanted to do to any of us.

I replied, "Yes, sir, got it."

Then he asked me what my dream job would be for the rest of my time in the US Navy. It took me less than a second to declar it was my dream to be a member of Pacific Fleet Combat Camera Group. He asked if I was sure about that, and why?

"Well sir," I said confidently, "the unit was formed in WWII to document the war and became one of the most famous group of photographers during that war and then again in Korea. My lifelong dream was to be a photojournalist, and I would love to work with world-famous photographers like these."

The admiral nodded. "All right, son, Pacific Fleet Combat Camera Group it is for you, if that is what you want. But first let's send you to one of the advanced motion picture schools at Pensacola. That sound good to you?"

I was shocked and pleased. "Yes, sir, it sure does. Are you sure? I'm sure I'm deserving. But I am just a Third-Class Petty Officer, and I'm not sure I've even passed the Second-Class test just yet."

"Well, we better change that. As of now you are a Second-Class Petty Offir. If you will give us just a few minutes, your orders will be cut to PacFltCombatCamera and then to motion picture school. And I'm also authorizing thirty days leave time beginning now."

Then he extended his hand and said, "Son, what you have just been through, not one sailor in a thousand would have volunteered to do, but you did. Frankly I wish I could give you more. You are what makes our country genuinely great. All we can do is say it and mean it. Thank You."

As he shook my hand, my head was swimming with his praise. I was just doing what I thought was the right thing to do. Gosh! It was unbelievable. Only a few days earlier, I was getting ready to fly another mission. Now I was standing in front of an admiral and getting my dream job.

CHAPTER 15

Home And Change

Now I was on my way to the most famous military photojournalist group in the world, and I was not about to argue with these orders. I was put into a cab to San Francisco International Airport and told I could just stay in my fatigues. So off I went, but not without a surprise or two.

As I entered the airport, I realized just how tired I was. It had been a long three or four days, with little or no sleep. Luckily for me the ticket counters were all now open. I walked up to American Airlines and told them I was just returning from (almost forgot, do not mention Thailand) Vietnam and needed to travel to Noblesville, Indiana, well, Indianapolis.

The beautiful young woman at the counter was exceedingly kind and helpful. She told me I could fly stand-by for almost nothing, but unfortunately, I would have to wait about four hours for the next flight. I did not care; I just wanted to sit down and close my eyes for just a little while.

As I was walking towards the boarding area, a well-dressed elderly woman grabbed my arm and told me I was less than trash, a baby killer, and the scum of the earth. I was in shock.

I had no idea that while I'd been deployed, some people had grown to detest the war and veterans.

So, there I stood, shocked and embarrassed. I did not know what to do. There were restrooms for men just a short way from where she was laying into me. So, I made a hasty retreat to get out of the line of fire.

While I felt I was a man and deserved to be treated as such, this episode gave me pause. Frankly, I didn't know what to think. Would the public consider me a baby killer, and did I do anything to deserve this? After all, I was just doing my duty. Really, I didn't know what to think, but for some reason I was terribly ashamed.

It was almost more than I could accept. But what could I do but press on. I decided to keep going to the boarding area. There was, fortunately, no one there. So, I just sat and closed my eyes for just a little while. Well, that little while turned into a little bit more. I had to be awakened by one of the boarding attendants, who kindly asked me if I was flying stand-by to Indianapolis. I admitted as much, and she led me over to the plane's captain. Lord, please forgive me, I thought. I just want to get home; I just want to sleep.

Well, the first thing this captain did was pull me off the side of the people that were boarding the plane. He asked me if I had just returned from Nam, to which I politely replied, yes sir. I am trying to get to Indianapolis and promise, I would not make any trouble for him. After my last encounter with the elderly lady, I was not sure what to expect next.

He just smiled and took me onto the plane in front of everyone who had not already boarded and sat me in a first-class seat. He told me this flight was going to be compliments of American Airlines, and that as a first-class passenger I would be entitled to breakfast and anything I cared to drink. A flight attendant would be around shortly to take care of any needs I might have.

The whole thing just took my breath away, but this pilot was not quite done with me. As they prepared to close the plane door, the pilot came on the intercom and thanked everyone for flying with American. Then he did the most extraordinary thing. He told all the passengers that we had this morning a very special passenger and anyone that cared to do so should now stand and give him our thanks. "His name is Richard Vincent and just a few hours ago, he was flying in the deadly skies of Vietnam. I think we all owe our gratitude for his sacrifice."

The plane erupted, just erupted with applause. All I had left to give back was thank you, thank you so much, through a cascade of tears. I was finally able to feel that I had arrived home.

As soon as I reached Indianapolis, I found a payphone and called home to let them know I had made it through the ordeal. My mother's first comments were pretty much as expected. "My God, Rickey, what have you done now? I expect you have been thrown out of the service or something. Are you in jail, or what?"

I replied as politely as I could, "No, Mother, I am fine, and I just arrived in Indianapolis. Just wanted to let you and the rest of the family know that I am home, but just for a few days. I would really like to see the kids if possible. I guess I'll ask Vin Haggen if I can stay at his house for a day or so, but I promise I'll stop by as soon as possible. No, I'm not in trouble, but I'm very tired, very, very tired. Talk soon."

Then I called Vin and asked if perhaps he could put me up for a couple of days. "Hi, Vin, I'm home, well, at the airport and would like to ask for a big favor. Could you possibly pick me up and give me a ride to Noblesville, maybe let me stay at your house for just a couple of days?"

He was absolutely delighted to hear I had made it home alive. "Knucklehead, you are more than welcome at my home. Hang in there, I'll leave right now, be there in just a while. I'm so happy to hear your voice. We were all incredibly worried. Thank God, you made it back."

Within a half hour or so, I was in Vin's Cadillac on my way home. He had kindly had his guest bedroom prepared for my stay. This much kindness was all what I needed. Except for sleep. I was so tired. It was almost impossible to believe that my last good sleep had been in Nakhon Phenom, right on the border of Laos. My God, I was still alive. I didn't know if I deserved to be, but here I was, alive.

Within an hour, we were entering Vin's house. He said, "Okay. You are home, and your bed is made with fresh sheets. Why don't you just lie down and sleep? When you wake up, the fridge will be full, and of course, you know where we keep the booze. Help yourself. If I'm not here when you wake up, I'll be back soon."

I remember going into the bedroom and just stripping. My clothes were in a small pile, next to the bed with my jungle boots. For some reason, I couldn't help myself, I guess. I just stood there and looked at my jungle fatigues lying there on this beautiful, carpeted floor, in a wonderfully furnished room. The last time I saw them on the floor was in my hooch, with temperatures over ninety degrees. Now, almost overnight, here I was, home.

For some reason, I just couldn't wrap my head around it all. No more jungle, no more tropical climate. No more flying. Nobody was going to shoot at me today. How did I get here? It all seemed like a dream. Maybe after I got some sleep, it would change, go back to normal, flying, killing, because that was what normal was for me now.

CHAPTER 16

Sleep

I'm not sure how long I slept, but it must have been quite a long time. When I finally got out of bed, the sun was just coming up, and the river was quiet and peaceful. Vin's house was built right along the White River, a beautiful place I had helped build a lifetime ago. By the time I got out of the shower, the house was stirring, and I could smell bacon sizzling in the kitchen.

It took me a few minutes to dig out my street clothes from my duffel bag. By that time, just about everyone in the house was up and sitting in the kitchen. There were a few faces I had never seen before, but most I had known for a long while. Vin's house was always crowded. He was a confirmed bachelor, but he loved people, and he built his home so it would accommodate quite a few without being cramped at all.

Everyone was so kind to me, and so happy that I had made it home in one piece. Little did they know, little did I know, that "home in one piece" would turn out to be problematic. Every hour or so, I excused myself and went into my bedroom, just sat down, and cried. Really, I did not know what was going on, but even in the middle of these friends, I felt so lonely like I was on another planet. The friendship, the kindness being shown to me was almost more than I could bear. They were all so sweet and kind. Nobody called me names, and no "baby killer" accusation was heard from this crowd. It was really touching, but I didn't get why everyone was being so kind. After all, it was at least partly true I had killed or helped kill. But not kids, I prayed.

Well, what did I want then? I just wanted to sit on the patio, watch the river and the sun going down. That was all I really wanted to do, just be alone with my thoughts. In the moment, I had hardly a clue what was happening. I just knew it hurt to be home, and I could not seem to fix it. Maybe there was no way. Maybe I was going to stay lost.

I was feeling so weak. If I was going to function in this new reality, I needed to shove some of this pain down into the little box hidden deep inside of me. Everything must stay there for now; I just could not deal with the past. I did my best to suppress everything close to the surface, to put it all away and maybe deal with it all later, much later.

For some reason I had forgotten my best "deal with it" tool, but I soon remembered and put it right into use. During the day I would just keep the emotion at bay, then later I would take my booze medication and manage to make it through the night. It was a great working plan at the moment. When I got drunk enough at night, I wouldn't think of anything but having fun. But on the few occasions when I forgot to take my medicine, it was generally a nightmare, a vivid, horrible dream.

Those dreams were almost unbearable with the blood, the destruction, the killing, the bodies, the devil having a grand ole time. But the booze medication suppressed them most of the time. My conclusion was that it was a perfect way to keep it all under control. Take the medication, use the booze, and stay on an even keel. Alcohol gave me a switch that I could use to turn the pain off or on.

At this point, the drink was nothing more than, just an off-and-on switch, or so I told myself. During the day or with people around, I would always try and stay fairly sober. But then, when I was alone at night, I could turn it all off with a little booze.

Unfortunately, there were times when no matter what I did, the thoughts would just erupt, just come storming back. It didn't happen very often, but when it did, fortunately, I was able to quickly stuff it down into the little black box and inflict no harm on anyone except myself.

For some reason, I don't know why, this overwhelming episode happened a lot when I was driving. Obviously, that was dangerous, so over time I developed a method to keep it under control. When it started to really roar, I would just pull my car over to the side of the road and have at it. Usually a good cry, lots of screaming and occasionally beating on the dashboard, would do the trick. At first this happened at least once a week, but as time went on, it happened much less often. I was glad that nobody knew about it, and I really felt I was getting a handle on it.

Wrong.

The time spent with Vin and his friends, and my family as well, did wonders for me. After a couple of weeks, I was ready to carry on. I was even ready for another round of Nam, maybe more. We would just have to see how it went. Maybe I would live through it again, maybe not. I was fatalistic again. It didn't seem to matter to me if I had to go back.

During this leave, I was able to see most of the family. They had mostly adapted to having no father around and had moved on. I was worried about my brother though. He was sixteen, and he knew that if he didn't get into college pretty soon after graduation, he would be drafted into the service.

Fortunately, he did get a scholarship to a college, with a little extra special funding that was set up for him at least in the moment. As time went on, however, his situation would change as the rules changed about college deferments. Within a couple of years, he was facing the draft board. It did not seem at all fair to me. I knew he was still a devout Catholic and conscientious objector. If he was drafted, it would be a disaster for him. I feared for him, and knew I needed to try and prevent it from happening.

As luck would have it, I knew quite well the president of our local draft board, Ralph Waltz. Ralph had been the president of American National Bank for many years, the largest local bank at the time. It was also the bank that my dad had used for his personal and business needs, so I had known Ralph since childhood and generally held great respect for him. He always seemed to be a fair and reasonable man. He of course, knew all about the Vincent family's financial issues.

I figured the least I could do for Mike was let Ralph know my feelings regarding his being drafted. After a lot of thought, I figured that a personal letter would have to do. But I needed to make it strongly worded and give him a good enough reason to bring it up at the next draft board meeting that he would recommend that Mike be exempted from serving.

While I did not keep a copy of the letter, I remembered that I told Ralph about the Squadron I had flown with and the medals I had received so far to validate the deeds done. Then I told him it would be my intention to serve another term, in country, if needed to keep my brother out of this war.

As mentioned, I had not made a copy of the letter, but it went something like this:

> *Dear Mr. Waltz,*
> *As I am sure you must be aware, my brother Michael is facing the draft in the very near future. He has remained a Catholic and conscientious objector. I would beg you to consider what I have given to my country. For this service, I have been awarded several medals for service in the face of the enemy.*
>
> *Added to this, I have served well over a full tour in live combat. So, I would like to ask that you consider the time spent by me as at least partial payment for my brother, and of course, if you needed more time served in combat, I will give you whatever time is needed. But please, I beg of you, keep my younger brother out of this war. Let me serve the time if needed.*
>
> *I sincerely hope that you and the board will take this letter into consideration when considering my brother Michael. It is my most sincere opinion that his being drafted would not be in the best interest of our country and family, who need his steady hand at home.*

Of course, I meant every word, and just a week later, I received a letter from Ralph Waltz. He wrote that my wishes had been granted and that Mike would not be drafted. He thanked me for my service and willingness to give my life if needed in the service of our country. Thank God, that problem went away just like that.

SECTION 7

Disorientation and Withdrawal

*Only the dead have
seen the end of war.*

Plato

CHAPTER 1

Dreams Sometimes
Do Come True

After my brief visit back to Indiana, it was time to get back to serving my country. This meant criss-crossing the country, starting at US Naval Station, Miramar, which is where they decided to park us all until our orders could be arranged to our next duty station. For me, that would be US Navy Photographic Schools Motion Picture, all the way across America in Pensacola, Florida.

The Miramar base was largely unused. At one time during the 1930s through 1950s, this had been where we kept all the Navy blimps. But they had long ago been taken out of service. All that was left of the base was a lot of really nice petty officer sleeping facilities and the original blimp hanger. This used to be one of the largest buildings in the world, with doors at both ends that were so tall and heavy they had to be operated on train tracks to open.

It was home to the NASA Ames Research Center, which was pretty cool. Remember, we hadn't been to the moon yet.

And this base was right in the middle of what would become Silicon Valley, the birthplace of the computer industry. It also was right next to Napa, the valley of the most famous wine makers.

I was at Miramar only for a couple of weeks but enjoyed every minute of my time there. The only duty I had while there was one evening, I had to walk around the largest blimp building ever built. It was so large that the US Navy Blue Angels once flew in-formation through the hanger, with, I was told, a lot of room to spare.

A few weeks later, I was on my way to Pensacola. There I met another petty officer that was also reporting to Motion Picture school. He had a car and wanted to get an off-base apartment. We figured if we split rent, this would be well within striking distance of our base allotment.

So began my training in motion picture equipment, lighting, and editing. I'd been getting up every morning and climbing into a flight suit to fly over the jungles of Laos, so studying motion pictures as a photojournalist turned out to be a blast. From time to time, when we were just goofing around, I would think with amazement how fortunate it had turned out to be for this kid from Indiana. I was going to spend the rest of my military career with Pacific Fleet Combat Camera. Life was better than good in that moment.

For me, motion picture school came to an end far too quickly, and I headed to PFCCG (Pacific Fleet Combat Camera Group) to check in and begin my new tour of duty. It was more than a little exciting to be joining one of the most famous groups in the military. I hitched a ride to the airport to catch the next flight to San Diego, and then crossed the bay to Naval Air Station North Island at the north end of Coronado peninsula.

Of course, this was not my first time at North Island. The memories of the training that began here with my now disbanded squadron came flooding back. This is where it all started. All the guys I flew with, all the time in Laos, the dying. It was all still there, in that little box buried deep inside me.

But I had survived and now I had to keep moving forward. Here I was, now promoted to a new rank, and for the next eighteen months, I would be doing the one thing I did best, photojournalism.

CHAPTER 2

My Last Duty Station

I went straight to the Combat Camera Groups headquarters and checked in with the duty officer. He told me Commander Holmes wanted to see me when I arrived. I learned from the commander's secretary that he would see me tomorrow morning, first thing.

I asked him what time inspection was and he said 0700 hours sharp. Then I met with the station's barracks officer, who had already assigned me a room. I don't know why, but I thought I would be sent to a bunk in the barracks I stayed in the last time I was here. But now I was a Second-Class Petty Officer. I would no longer be in the general enlisted men's barracks. With my new rating, I would be staying in the Petty Officers' Barracks. He told me only about twenty five percent of the Combat Camera men were in the Petty Officers Barracks, but the majority lived off base. This was quite a surprise. I would have figured most of the unit would not be rated high enough to warrant the accommodation being offered to me, but this unit was different in a lot of ways.

I found my new quarters genuinely nice to say the least. Because of the coming inspection, I thought I had better look sharp. As luck had it, the base laundry was near to my new quarters, and I washed and ironed my dress whites. Then I went to the base chow hall and got a bite to eat. Navy food is always much better than any of the other services, I suspect because it was one of the few luxuries a sailor had when at sea.

This was all a huge transition for me. After all, just a month or so ago, I was getting shot at by someone that really wanted me dead. Now, here I was, living the dream. I got to spend the final months of my naval career as a photojournalist. Amazing, just amazing.

CHAPTER 3

Reporting

The next morning, I arrived at our headquarters at 0600 hours and had the good fortune to meet a few of my new colleagues. They were a very close-knit group. Almost all of them had already been working in the field, including in Vietnam. I learned that when they went out on a mission, it was usually as a five- or six-man crew. Most of them had already been formed into active crews of five to six men.

So, this was a very tight knit group, and there were not nearly as many men as I expected. It turned out that most of the film crews were on assignment, mostly to Southeast Asia. We had seventy-five to a hundred men in total, with about fifty stationed in our North Island office, and the rest in our Yokosuka, Japan office or in Saigon.

While I wasn't sure how many were standing for inspection, it must have been about a third of the squadron, probably a little less. The inspection was a quick affair, and the commanding officer was a genuinely nice man, with the rank of lieutenant commander.

After the inspection was completed, Commander Holmes stuck his hand out and introduced himself to me, then asked me to see him in his office as soon as coffee had been attended to.

When I entered his office, he said, "As you know, I know nothing about the squadron you were last in. I was just told you had served a year in Vietnam and were not required to do more time there for the rest of your time in service. Can you tell me if you were in the squadron that we sent a crew to document?"

I remembered that crew, whose documentary was immediately classified. "Yes, sir, I was."

"That is okay, son, I do not want to even ask what you were doing. Well, I will tell you that the documentary crew was absolutely scared shitless and would never ever want another assignment of that nature, and I assure you we left it at that."

I just nodded. We both knew the reason for that.

He added, "In the next week or so we will have another inspection, all hands required to be in attendance, in dress whites. You will be awarded the Air Medal. As I understand it, you have a handful of medals that cannot be granted just now because of the secrecy of your unit. Maybe someday, after this war is over, they will get around to awarding those medals. It doesn't sound like that's why you did what you did. But in any case, thank you for your willingness and courage."

"Thank you, sir."

He shifted to a more current issue. "Your standing from motion picture school has not been received but I assume you did well."

I replied, "Yes, sir, thank you, sir, and yes, sir, I finished close to the top. Sir, if I might, I would like to request the bulk of my duty to be spent in Saigon. It is where the story is, and I really want to be a part of it, sir."

"Damn, son, I was not about to send you to Saigon. It was my assumption and opinion that you had done enough for your country. And you deserve a rest, which is what you'll get here! You can take all the time you need. However, if rest is not what you want, I'll see to it that after a few weeks here to get your feet wet, we will send you to Yokosuka. From there, you can begin your first round back in Nam."

"Thank you, sir."

"If there is nothing else, you are excused."

Dad always told me, "If you want it bad enough, ask for it, demand it of yourself. You are worthy and you can achieve it. No matter what, if you want it bad enough, ask for it." Well, I did, I asked for it and to my amazement, I got it. For the rest of my Navy career, I was assigned to the group I had always dreamed of. I was an official member of Pacific Fleet Combat Camera Group.

By now, I thought I had the devil pretty much back under control. Now, I just drank at night, and just enough to keep him at bay. Smooth sailing from now on. No more nightmares for me.

CHAPTER 3

Getting Started

After leaving Lieutenant Commander Holmes's office, I began the tour of our facilities. The personnel were all great and made me feel right at home. From what they all told me, the commander wasn't kidding. They really didn't work all that much here at home port, and I would be able to take all the time off I wanted.

After hanging around for the morning, I was told that I had been assigned to First Class Petty Officer Penner for the next few days, to help with getting my feet wet. He was a great guy, had been in the Navy for a very long time, and had worked both in Hollywood and in San Diego for the Navy. So, he was just perfect for me. He had a ton of knowledge about the film industry both inside the military and outside.

One of First-Class Petty Officer Penner's interesting accomplishments was he had gone to the University of Southern California to take classes in motion picture work. During that time, he had the opportunity to work with one of the students doing graduate work, George Lucas. For his graduation senior project, Lucas chose to make a movie short about aliens. It would be his test run before making Star Wars. His little piece was only about one hour long, but included many identifiable parts of his latter movies that brought him great fame.

Penner got around in a little Nash Rambler, which he would keep on base when he was in Southeast Asia. It was a tiny little car, maybe the smallest car made in the US at the time. It was certainly an adventure driving it to Los Angeles.

John Penner, like all the others in the unit, was just a great guy and easy to get along with. He assigned me to my locker, where I could keep my personal camera equipment. Then he took me to the room where everyone hung out between assignments. It was a really nice place with had a full-sized pool table, and a coffee table with hooks for each person's personal coffee cup. Your cup was always kept at the ready, hanging there until you left the group for good. I noticed that most of them looked like they had never been cleaned and was told that to wash a man's coffee cup in this unit was the greatest of sacrileges.

The walls were covered with photographs from the Korean war right up to the Vietnam war. In addition, they also had trophies collected over the years, some of them were really interesting. These were items that had been confiscated over the years, well, mostly stolen. They came from all over, and some pretty damn interesting. There was an admiral's flag, which came from the whale boat that took the admiral from ship to shore. If memory serves, it was from WWII. Another one was a sign, very highly polished, which read ADMIRAL'S QUARTERS. Of course, the photographs were all just incredible.

I soon learned the most I would need to do was serve a shift at the Duty Officer's desk, for twelve hours, about every month. Also, I was told to stay out of the still photo labs, unless permission was granted. That was easy to understand with drying negatives hanging, and pictures being processed.

Those stationed at North Island didn't have that much work. However, I was assigned with Penner and a couple others to photograph some of the new Swift Boats under development at Mare Island Shipyard, which was close to Vallejo, California. This was mostly a test and evaluation facility for the Navy, located very close to San Francisco and right next to wine country. The base would eventually become part of Silicon Valley in the 1990s.

The Swift Boat was used in Vietnam to patrol the rivers and waterways. It was a shallow draft river boat, but heavy with its armament and weapons. So it couldn't traverse many of the canals, many of which were only a couple of feet deep in places. The weight was causing their props to dig into the beds of the canal. What they needed was a different kind of propulsion system.

These new and improved Swift Boats were fitted with water jets for propulsion. It was a good idea, and these boats could travel much faster and turn on a dime. At speed they could move and turn in less than six inches of water, which was just amazing.

A Swift is not very big, but when fully armed, it is heavy. That is no problem to a Swift Boat equipped with water jets instead of propellers. These things could fly and had plenty of power to spare.

One night a very drunk chief petty officer decided to see if they had enough power to jump from one canal to another, a jump of about thirty feet. Now one of the interesting things about some of the canals was that they were lined with trees. The trees were all fat, but not very high, maybe fifteen to twenty feet.

The chief's first try was successful, but he wasn't finished. He again came up the canal, this time at full speed. He was going so fast, and the water jets had so much force, that he launched the boat over the next canal, right into the top of one of the trees.

The boat wasn't badly damaged, but it took a large crane to lift it out of the tree. The chief also had to be extricated, as he had passed out when the boat launched itself into the tree. The next morning, only an hour or so after the launch, we were asked to photograph the boat in the tree. Our photos provided proof positive that the new improved Swift Boat was plenty powerful, even if it couldn't jump over trees just yet.

That was a good assignment. Otherwise, we at North Island had just a fair number of small jobs, and most took very little time, maybe a day or two. So, I had to find ways to fill my time. The pool table got a lot of use, and I found a nice chair to sit and read. But after more than a year of high action, this was pretty boring.

Consequently, I was more than ready to get back overseas to our Yokosuka office, where we would be rotated back and forth to Vietnam every sixty days. We would have more than our share of work in Vietnam, so much of the unit was in Saigon, and we were responsible for all Southeast Asia. From time to time, we had crews on ships off the coast of Vietnam, and also took stories in South Korea and elsewhere.

CHAPTER 5

The New Dream Japan

While I can't remember the exact transfer date to Japan, I do remember it was close to the end of the year, probably October or November. The Yokosuka office was a very interesting place, in one of the old Japanese Admiralty office. The Navy had taken this for our own right after the treaty was signed ending WWII. The Combat Camera group were there to not only witness the surrender, but to be one of the first to reach the shore afterwards.

The offices we confiscated for our very own use were in a brick building close to the docks. The Admiral's office was on the entire second floor of the large building. They now belonged to Pacific Fleet Combat Camera, and the walls were covered with trophies and pictures. The offices apparently oversaw a lot of very secret communications during the war and featured a big safe at one end of the Admiral's office.

During WWII, our planes were warned not to bomb this very large naval base. It had one of the largest deep water dry docks in the world at that time, and we wanted to use it after the war. During the Korean war, this base was essential to our aircraft carriers and other shipping, being very close to Korea.

But Japan had its own special hazards. I happened to be there for one of the many earthquakes and watched that enormous safe move from the wall in our Chief's office, which was formerly the Japanese admiral's office. It took a crew and several wenches to put it back into the wall where it belonged. This time the hold-down bolts were reinstalled and bolted extra tight.

The Japanese know how to build their navy facilities. The base was spectacular, with facilities for enlisted personnel that were way beyond the normal. The base also had one of the largest hospitals in Southeast Asia, left over from WWII. The city which straddled the base was largely dedicated to serving marines and sailors who were sent there from Vietnam. There were literally hundreds of bars and restaurants just outside the base. As one of the first units to come ashore after the war, the Combat Camera Group had its own dedicated bar, The New Dream Japan. I soon learned we had our very own corner in the bar, where comfortable seating had been installed for our use only. When we were not around, the area was kept roped off.

The entire area was patrolled by our US Navy and Marine Shore Patrol, all the time, twenty-four hours a day. It turned out that even the New Dream Japan had an occasional bar brawl. Remember, almost all the sailors were from the ships visiting port, generally for only a week or two. These guys had been at sea for months at a time, and many had not been in the States for a very long time. So, most of them would get drunk quickly and become rambunctious. When the Shore Patrol arrived, they never asked questions, just started clubbing guys with night-sticks and throwing them into a paddy wagon. When this happened, everybody in the bar was generally arrested and taken to the brig. We Combat Camera guys were, however, all ushered out the back door and into a narrow alley. We never had to worry about the Military Police, whether we started the fracas or not.

The bar was served by pretty girls, most of them single. Most would not consider selling themselves; however, they were risking scandal by working as bar girls. In Japan the social order is very rigid, and those outside are almost always shunned for life. I made friends with one of these New Dream girls, Kasica Nozawa. Although she was shunned by regular society, she was a wonderful human being. She was always the first choice among the girls that sat at our table, because she was both funny and smart. No one thought she should be working in the bar because of her age, the same as mine. Even the owners felt she should go back home. Inexplicably she refused to go and was one of the few girls at the bar who had her own apartment several blocks away.

We soon fell in love, and I moved into town with Kaz. It was crazy, I knew it, but I couldn't help myself. Not only was she beautiful, but she also had an amazing mind. This infatuation was going to turn into a painful mistake and take years to get over.

CHAPTER 6

Photographs My First Love

I was soon given my own set of press passes, which allowed me to come and go to and from about anywhere, including the brig. It turned out Shore Patrol could arrest us, but they could not hold us, because of our press pass credentials.

They had to release us to our duty officer, usually someone watching our phone in the office. Someone had to be next to the phone twenty-four hours a day. If anything of consequence happened anywhere in Southeast Asia, we had to have a crew ready to go and quickly. Even though we had offices in Saigon, on occasion they would call for extra men. So, when we got ourselves into trouble, all it took was a quick phone call to the guy on duty and we were released at once.

This happened on occasion, and I got used to it quickly. Here I was back in the thick of the action, and I still couldn't get enough. The devil seemed to have receded into the box, and because of my drinking trick, almost always, I was able to sleep even after a wild night.

That was the best solution I could hope for, and it seemed very workable at the time. It was sheer stupidity; I should have known. But I thought, "What else can I do? It works." At this point, I used this tactic, and didn't think about what the negative result in the future might be. After all, I was probably not going to make it very far into the future anyhow.

Living the Dream
November 1968
– May 1969

At the bottom of patience is heaven.

Tibetan Proverb

CHAPTER 1

USS *Pueblo*

November 1968

O ur press passes worked just about everywhere to get us into just about anywhere we wanted to see. They allowed us to see admirals and generals, and any active event going on. It turned out that military press passes were about as close to the golden keys as we could possibly have. While we might not be able to use our equipment, they still had to allow us to be there.

There was only one exception that I ever encountered, the USS Pueblo affair.

On 23 January 1968, the USS Pueblo, a Banner-class ship, was captured by the North Koreans just off their coast. The ship was far enough out that they should have been in international waters. But the North Koreans did not see it that way, and forcefully came aboard our ship and captured it and all aboard.

Yes, it was a spy ship we were using to keep track of the North, but we mistakenly thought we were doing it in such a way as we couldn't be contested or caught. We were wrong about that, and then our President faced a profoundly serious problem indeed.

The capture became international news immediately. The crew of the Pueblo became the news of the day all over the world. After negotiations went on for over eight months, we were told to send a full photo crew to Saigon to photograph the event. I was the only one that had my flight wings, so they quickly made me part of the crew.

Remember, I had just arrived in Yokosuka, Japan, our Southeast primary office, and they wanted us in Saigon asap. From there we would be transferred to the new ship Enterprise, at the time our only nuclear carrier. She was just off the coast of Vietnam, conducting air operations in support of our men in country.

CHAPTER 2

First Mission North Korea

November 1968

Upon arriving at Tan Son Nhat airport in Saigon, we were told to go to our offices and await further orders. We were transported to a Navy plane from US Aircraft Carrier Enterprise and all I knew was that I was supposed to strap in, tightly, very tightly. We were flown to an armada of ships, which I would learn later to be the largest naval armada since WWII. I had never seen anything like it, ships from horizon to horizon. It was the most impressive display of naval firepower I had ever seen, the most impressive display that almost any sailor alive had ever seen.

Within minutes, the plane captain got on the intercom and told us to prepare to land on the carrier. Landing on an aircraft carrier was an experience I shall never forget. It is just incredible to be flying flat out and suddenly come to a complete stop in the distance of a football field. After the gut-wrenching landing on the USS Enterprise, we were told to all go to the Air Operations, the staging area for pilots and crew.

Finally, we were joined by a marine colonel who asked us to all gather around for a briefing about our mission. First, he wanted to know if any of us was air qualified, and I immediately put my hand in the air. In the crew, I was the only one that had wings.

He announced that I would be in the lead helicopter when we went in. Then he explained that the President was ordering us into North Korea, to invade and take back the USS Pueblo. We would be given additional orders before going in. The rest of the crew was to go in with the rest of the advance marines after my chopper had gone in.

He ordered us all to stand by, and then left the room. After his departure, we just stared at each other silently. What could we say? The chances of us coming back from this were practically nil.

My God, I thought all this danger was behind me, but here I was again. It was exciting to be able to photograph this incredibly important event. But dying was no longer on my priority list. We all began to shake, a typical response when you knew you were going into great danger. Well, I didn't ask anybody else, but I was damn sure scared out of my head.

The one thought I had was that President Johnson must be really pissed off and was willing to risk a lot in order to get his sailors back. It was easy to surmise that the President would not be doing this unless they felt their backs were against the wall, and this guy was not afraid of a fight, when he thought he was being pushed around.

So, I got a flight suit and put it on, then strapped a Browning .45 on and thought I was ready. Apparently, my little devil had the door wide open.

CHAPTER 3

Waiting

November 1968

There we were, waiting, and waiting, and waiting some more. After several hours had passed, I knew by now we were into a new day as the sun had come, gone, and come again. This time a navy pilot finally told us to get ready to suit up. My first thought was, "This is it, the end." But he informed us that the President had told everyone to stand down. We were not going to invade after all and would all be going back to Saigon for now. The armada was to be dispersed.

In the meantime, they wanted us to put a couple of crews in the air and photograph this incredible armada. I must say it was unbelievably impressive. That sight, hundreds of ships all sailing together, from horizon to horizon, truly made an amazing and remarkable photo.

I guess I felt like I wouldn't have to worry quite as much about the devil that was inside me. Once again, I had lived to tell the tale. Still, at night before the booze kicked in, the devil was there waiting.

You can bet I never missed a night without my medicine. But somewhere in this period, I began to notice it was taking a bit more medicine to get that devil stuffed back into the box.

CHAPTER 4

Getting Off The Carrier

November 1968

After that, we were all ordered back to Saigon. It was sure okay with me and the rest of the crew. We piled back in the same transport plane that brought us to the ship, particularly careful to make sure everything was stored right. We all checked to be sure we had nothing un-stored, not a pencil in a pocket, nor anything else that could come loose and become a missile. With a plane being catapulted at takeoff, a loose piece of anything could be disastrous. We were going to be shot off the deck at several hundred miles per hour, and the deck is only a couple hundred yards long. It was truly like being shot from a cannon.

Along with us for the trip back to Saigon was a young Army lieutenant, attached to Military Army Command Vietnam, or MACV. Of course, this guy let us all know that he was next to a god, that his boss was the general that ran the entire show. Therefore, he was the most important person on the flight, and we should all pay homage to him. Asshole.

The pilot came back through and checked everything one last time, told us all to put our heads between our legs, just in case. Within a matter of minutes, the plane shot off the flight-deck. Because we all had our heads down as ordered, we could not see it, but we could sure feel it. Something went flying through the cabin just like a rocket. Whatever it was, it just missed the captain's head before striking the front windscreen.

He was a real pro, and brought the plane around, declaring an emergency to the carrier. They put the crash nets up, but he was able to put the plane down and made a perfect landing. Thank God, nobody was hurt, but we were damn sure badly shaken. The captain ordered everyone to remain in their seats, and as he came back through, he had the look of a very, very pissed off aviator. Luckily, it had nothing to do with me or any of the rest of our crew.

The Army lieutenant loudly declared himself to be in charge. The pilot was having none of it. "Lieutenant, did you store all your gear with all the rest of the gear, behind those safety nets?"

With a great deal of belligerence, the Army asshole replied, "Hell, yes, I did, do not look at me, you navy asshole. It was not my fault you can't fly this thing properly."

"Then Lieutenant, what did you do with that coffee thermos you had when you came aboard my plane? I told you to put it into your bags. Did you do that, or did you keep it with you?"

The lieutenant just stared at the captain, but not saying anything more. Finally, after making us all wait a minute or two, he acknowledged that he had not, but that he had put it on the shelf above his head, where he declared it to be safe. So of course, it was not his fault. Idiot.

"Lieutenant, I told you to store everything, including your thermos, behind the safety net. Yet you refused to obey the

228

captain of this ship and consequently you endangered every-one on board, and the plane itself. I am therefore placing you under arrest. We will see how you like the US Navy's version of the brig. I want everyone else to stay seated for a few minutes more."

He then exited the plane and ordered Marine MPs to take the lieutenant off his plane in handcuffs and put him in the brig. It was an absolutely beautiful sight to behold.

Then he asked the crew how quickly another plane could be prepared, and I guess was told that they already had one standing by. He went up to flight prep and asked permission to use the other plane, or whatever it was he had to do. In any case, we were again preparing for take-off within a matter of minutes.

After re-boarding a new plane, the captain explained to us that what the lieutenant had done was stupid beyond belief. He told us that the thermos, if it had hit one of us, would probably have killed us, and that we were very fortunate that it hit the windscreen. A little lower and it would have hit the instrument panel.

I guess we were all damn lucky. By this time, I pretty much knew that there was a reason you always followed procedure, be-cause your life often depended on it. Not following orders could get you killed in a war zone. But here I was, still untouched, still okay. I guess my luck was still with me. In the moment I didn't quite know the reason, I was just happy to be alive.

CHAPTER 5

Saigon -- A Beauty

December 1968

The rest of the flight went off without a hitch, and we were shortly back in Saigon looking for a ride back to our offices. Being launched off the deck of an aircraft carrier is certainly a moment to remember. That night, a fair amount of serious drinking went on. Thank God, all back, all alive, and I had my favorite scotch to keep me company. Life was good.

Because I was already in Saigon, they decided to let me stay around for a few more weeks, which was fine by me. This was my first trip to Saigon, so I had a lot to learn, and see.

It turned out that our hotel, The Lei Lie Hotel, was close to the central part of town, and right across the street from the very old, beautiful, and long out of order train station. It was built by the French during a more peaceful time, and still beautiful beyond anything I had ever seen.

Most of the glorious city was built by the French. There was an extraordinary racetrack with a few horses still there to run on occasion. There were villas and large estates, where many of the wealthy French landowners had lived when they visited the city.

The villas were now mostly being leased to the US military for smaller important groups. They were taken care of by a small cadre of employees that came with the house, servants, laundry maids, kitchen maids. The furnishings were, for the most part, original, and gorgeous as well.

One of the guys took me on a short walking tour the next morning. I was really surprised to find a French bakery remarkably close to the hotel. They had a charming little bistro attached. The French bread was to die for, as were the pastries, and the coffee was from heaven. I remember a fresh hot loaf of bread, and pastries just out of the oven, with coffee, cost thirty to fifty cents. It was naturally all the coffee you could drink, no extra charge for anything.

After a long, leisurely break with coffee and pastries, I decided to just walk around the city on my own. The city central district was very beautiful, a bit run down, but nevertheless beautiful. I guess after experiencing over thirty years of on-and-off war, you had to expect things to be a bit frumpy. It was a gorgeous city, with charms galore.

I was given directions to some of the finer shops and hotels, which I found after locating the Rue Catinat. This was the main street of the old city and just full of beautiful shops, small and large eateries, lovely bars, and cabarets, with beautiful homes scattered in among it all. It appeared I had awakened in Paris, with a Southeast Asian twist.

CHAPTER 6

The Job At Hand

December 1968

The next day I rode in our Econoline Ford van back to Tan Son Nhut, where our offices were located, and called Yokosuka to let them know more precisely what had happened on the ship deployed to Korea. They told me again that I had been nominated to stay in Saigon for a while, and that they had several jobs that I would be needed for coming up soon. I was to stand by in Saigon, and orders would be coming in the next few days.

On the way back to the hotel, the drivers were nice enough to give me a bit of a driving lesson, along with instructions how to get to the hotel. The driving lesson was one for the books. You see, in Saigon the streets were always packed with cars, mopeds, bikers, trucks, with any remaining space filled with pedestrians.

Along with all that, they had roundabouts all over the place. Streetlights or stop signs were just meant to assess one's skills at drag racing, along with turning a doughnut if needed. The roundabouts were always packed with every kind of moving vehicle, pedestrians, even an occasional live pig hitching a ride on a moped or motorcycle.

My first drive through town was a cross between a nightmare and a demolition derby. To drive in Saigon, it was required to be certified as insane, or legally blind and insane. The first rule to learn was that you can get right up to, but you can't touch anything or anybody.

The last piece of info I was given was to always back into the parking spot at the hotel. Even with the van securely backed into the wall next to the hotel, it was necessary to check the vehicle before climbing in it or driving off.

It seems the Vietnamese Communist or VC had infiltrated the city, and you never knew when or where they would appear. They were very clever when in the city and always dressed like one of the civilians, so it was impossible to know if you were looking at the enemy or just a civilian living their life. A favorite activity was to wire a hand grenade or some other explosive device to a US military vehicle parked next to a hotel.

The VC were just everywhere, and you never knew. One of our guys, Murphy, was sitting in a little bar one evening when a shoeshine boy asked him if he wanted a shine. He declined. Later he noticed that the boy had left his shoeshine box and was nowhere to be seen. Well, Murph knew enough to immediately fall onto the floor and cover his head. The explosion happened right after he dove for the floor, and several US servicemen were either killed or blown apart.

This was nothing new. It happened almost every day. You always needed to be aware who was around, what they were carrying and doing. I learned quickly to always be on guard, and this behavior was something I took home with me. Guys like me would find themselves back home, but still with the caution of Saigon.

It was a lot like flying the missions in Laos-- you just never knew. At least I will say this work was a lot easier. We almost always were in the company of others, and usually carried a weapon. But still, you never did know.

It could be a boy, or a young girl, or a mamason, or old man. It was impossible to tell. They used all sizes, shapes, and genders. As with Murph in the bar, they would often walk right up to you and pretend to be friendly or servile. Murph sure had learned this the hard way. The guys told me that he had previously been shot and wounded photographing the racetrack during the Tet Offensive.

CHAPTER 7

Finally, A Real Job

February 1969

After a few days of sleeping in, roaming around the city, eating fantastic meals, I was itching to get started doing something. So, I volunteered for the next job that came up, and they were delighted to give it to me. It was always much safer in Saigon, so the guys always preferred to stay in the city if they could. On this job, Eugene McCawley and I were assigned. He was a nice guy and good photographer.

The MACV (Military Assistance Command Vietnam) folks wanted film to show somebody, the media I guess, just how effective their new use of Agent Orange could be. They had sprayed huge areas along some of the streams and tributaries, not too far from Saigon. This included villages that were often built along these waterways.

It was a sight I hope I can someday forget. Miles upon miles of foliage along the banks of the stream were just dead. Every living thing was dead. In its starkness, it didn't look like another living thing had ever been there. The scenery we were to photograph was terribly sad.

As we traveled down the stream, everything was dead along the stream and about a mile inland. But this was not the worst by a long shot.

After a while, we came alongside a now-vacant village. There was still a dock that went out into the water, so the PBR (Patrol Boat River) dropped me off. Then it traveled further down the tributary so that McCawley could photograph the river from the boat. It was just so sad, the village was quiet-- no birds, no animals, no villagers, just deafening silence.

Many years after the war, the US military admitted that the use of Agent Orange was unsafe. But the damage was by then irreversible. It was perhaps one of the saddest things I ever photographed. I certainly hope there is a special place in hell for the civilians that developed this horrible agent without properly evaluating it before it entered service. Thousands of Vietnamese villagers were badly harmed by Agent Orange, many suffering for years after the war was over. Especially injured were the children who suffered from many cancers as a result of Agent Orange.

After this trip McCawley and I were certainly ready for a few days off. For me, it took an extra heavy dose of forget-it-all to lock it up in the little box where it couldn't get out. I stayed drunk for a couple of days, slept, walked around the city, and the blasted villages finally became a memory stuffed deep down, where it could not hurt anybody, ever again.

CHAPTER 8

The Coroner

February 1969

For me at least, the only way to stay afloat was to stay busy.
So, I got in the habit of asking for another assignment as
soon as I had completed my current assignment and the film
had been shuttled on to wherever it was supposed to go. That is
exactly what I did after completing our mission photographing
the Agent Orange results.

Maybe for comic relief, who knows, when we got back to
Saigon, they immediately assigned me to a small shoot in Da Nang.
But you never knew with Combat Camera whether you would be
in the shit or doing just a little puff piece. This little assignment
was sort of in between. What I had been asked to do was film our
Marine undertakers as they prepared bodies for return to the US.

This was not a job I was looking forward to at all. But that
was what the bosses wanted, and so that would be what they
got. They had their set up in an area right next to the airfield,
where the caskets could be put right on a plane and shipped
home. This was not a job I was looking forward to shooting,
and I just wanted to get it done and get the hell out of Da Nang.

The first thing I needed to do upon arrival was find the mortuary and make arrangements with the two guys operating it. I needed to check their schedule so we could get the footage needed with the least amount of turmoil as was possible.

I was glad to find out that the guys I was going to photograph were decent guys. Their workspace was in a tented area with refrigeration, there was no air conditioning. The work was being done behind a canvas curtain that surrounded the field tent where the work was done. The canvas wall at least provided a little privacy. Of course, the bodies had already been prepared and just needed to be placed into metal containers for shipment home.

My goal was to get this footage shot and done in one day and get the hell out of Da Nang and back to Saigon. The undertakers were decent enough, but their mission was to me just so distasteful it was hard for me to stay on it.

About mid-morning both stopped work and wandered outside the canvas covering their workspace from anyone walking by. Nearby was a gedunk truck, a food truck that served coffee doughnuts, hamburgers, and other food. It always stopped close to their workspace a few times a day. It had just arrived, and they were ready for a break and a bite to eat.

They went over to the truck to buy a burger, chips, and a coffee. But these guys didn't stand around and eat their food right there. They took their sandwiches and coffee back to their working spaces and set up a table on top of a stack of metal coffins.

They also were wearing aprons, which I thought were covered in blood, but probably not. The aprons were tied with a long string, and their rubber gloves were stuck there as well. Now to these guys, it was just another day, another day closer to going home. They were not doing anything disrespectful. It was just another day working on the corpses of our dead.

So here we were, eating hamburgers with the dead and mutilated bodies of our men. To these guys, it was just another day on the job. But to me, watching them eat their hamburgers and drink their coffee, with coffins as a place to sit and eat, it was just too much. Quickly I walked over to a corner where a large barrel was being used as a trash can and began to get sick. I just couldn't help it. The scene was just more than I could endure.

After I was done being sick, I returned to my job, and photographed them eating their burgers and sitting on the caskets. Just another day to them, and I guess it was. But for me, it was an ordeal. Saigon never looked as good as it did later that afternoon. It was at that time I realized our work ran the gamut of happy times to scenes of brutal hell. Each day was different, and each photo shoot had to reveal itself. What would it be tomorrow? There was just no telling, maybe blood, maybe not.

It was a lonely, sad feeling, and I wasn't sure of where I was going. How do you work with death right there in front of you? There is no happiness in killing. The glory, the bravery, was all bullshit, and I knew it. Sometimes it was needed I suppose. If they are shooting at you, there are only two choices, run or fight. Most of the time we had only one choice, and that was to fight. None of us enjoyed it, I guess.

The braggarts and the self-important seemed as though they did enjoy it, but I don't think they really did. It was just their way of covering it up, of hiding behind their self-indulgence. But that's just a guess on my part. What I did know was that I was always scared in the face of the enemy. I would shake before and after the fighting. It was only during the moment of combat that I would flip that magical switch and become centered. Everything would slow and move steadily, slowly towards a final. You lived or you died, with not much in between, you just did.

What would it be tomorrow? There was just no telling, maybe blood, maybe not.

CHAPTER 9

Give Love A Chance

March 1969

As luck would have it, my next assignment was a lot more fun, with hardly any danger at all. Chief Jones was putting together a crew for a story he was producing in the Philippines. It was based around a new US program to help the Philippines rebuild their horrible school system. Most of the education outside the major cities was done in one-room schoolhouses, with barely enough of anything to go around. In this respect, they had not yet recovered from the brutal years they suffered under Japanese rule during WWII.

In the Philippines, there was a very active Communist group trying to convert as many villagers as possible. They had on their side the fact that the villagers were largely uneducated and had little chance of obtaining any kind of education for their children. The villagers all wanted to provide an education for their children, or at least some education.

After WWII the country was completely devastated, and the small villages in the countryside had almost nothing to help them get back on their feet. It remained like this for the next fifteen years before US aid finally started to trickle into these small villages. Unfortunately, the only way these folks could survive and stay out of starvation was with the help of everyone in the family, including children.

So, the idea was to use a new program called Helping Hand, to try and right the ship, and the first steps were to provide medical aid assistance. Then it was felt that the only way to really provide these families with concrete help was to get their children educated, to build each village a schoolhouse and provide funding for educators to run them. They knew it would have to be Philippine educators, so education schools had been established in colleges in Manila to start producing the teachers to get this done.

We were supposed to help them build the schoolhouses so they could operate efficiently. But it was also known that just providing money to the Philippine government would not work. The money would never make it to the villages as it was always stolen by the politicians first.

It was going to be our job to teach them how to build and electrify these simple buildings. We needed to have a film that could be used in the US to demonstrate their needs. In addition, the film was needed to demonstrate to the village that we would provide the help and the materials needed. But they needed to provide a location and enough men to do the work. We would provide everything else, including a funding program to produce teachers to run these new schoolhouses.

Pacific Fleet Combat Camera was sent to get enough raw footage with sound to produce these documentaries. This is how I got nominated to be first camera, with Chief Jones running the show. First camera was just a term for the principal camera being used in a five man or more crew. As was usually the case in this type of job, the first camera operated a camera connected to sound equipment, so the film would have live footage and audio.

We flew into Naval Air Station Subic Bay, Philippines from Saigon and were really loaded down with equipment. For this job, we had thirty-five large aluminum suitcases, loaded with equipment and film. I was the only one in the crew that had a firearm, a Colt .45, which I almost always wore while in Vietnam. Before leaving Saigon, I had simply forgotten to leave it there, but that turned out to be fortunate for us. When we arrived, it quickly became a needed tool.

When our plane came to a stop, we all piled out. Chief said to just hang around while he went to flight operations to pick up a couple jeeps that were supposed to be ready for our use. So, there we stood, when a small group of Philippine men showed up to unload all of our equipment from the plane. We realized we had better keep a close eye on these guys and keep our equipment surrounded.

I was standing there watching all the hectic activity, when I noticed one of the unloading crew, a little Philippine kid picked up one of the camera cases and starts to walk away. This caused me to yell out one of the nicest, "Stop Motherfucker" screams I could muster. But he kept walking towards the fence separating the airfield from the village we were parked close to.

He not only did not stop, but he also began to run towards the fence where his companions in crime were waiting. I felt the only thing I could do was introduce him to Mr. Colt .45. As soon as I fired one round into the air, he came to a complete stop, fell on the ground, spread his arms and legs, and began to beg for forgiveness.

I yelled, "I just want my camera equipment back, asshole. Make yourself scarce before I change my mind." It is amazing how fast a kid can run when he puts his mind to it.

Everybody just looked at me, chuckling, and a moment later the Chief arrived with two fully fueled jeeps. Within minutes we were loaded and ready to depart, and I was a little lighter after giving Chief Jones my firearm.

Our first stop wasn't far from the airfield at all. It had been decided to spend the night close by at one of the resorts set up for officers on their rest and recreation trips from Vietnam. It was really very nice, with great rooms to sleep in. It took an entire room to store our equipment. The rooms were right next to a gorgeous club, overlooking the harbor. The food was incredible as well, and the drinks were plentiful and large.

The place had been built with all the amenities, very nice indeed. I wasn't sure how Chief got us into this facility, but with our press passes, I guess we could get into and stay just about anywhere we wanted at the government's expense.

Naturally, our illustrious Chief Jones had already been in contact with the authorities needed to photograph the documentary. The next morning, we took off for San Miguel. This was the local district's main town, but to us it looked more like a tiny village in the middle of nowhere.

The villagers were very nice to us and excited to have their village in a movie. We were going to need a lot of help, moving equipment around, getting things set up, and then just shooting film for one scene, before going to the next. It was time-consuming, laborious work.

Of course, the best part for me was they weren't shooting at us. There were no guns to worry about, no bombs, no death. We didn't have to look over our shoulders every other minute. It was weirdly peaceful, in fact. Everything was quiet, no loud talking, no one was bragging about having killed, or just staying alive. It was just beautifully quiet. I could feel it, the peace.

CHAPTER 10

Helpful Kids

March 1969

The chief wanted to meet the gal that was in charge of the school program and our coordinator with Helping Hand and the schools. Well, it turned out that Chief Jones really knew what he was doing. After these meetings, we had a ready supply of kids to help us move equipment, hold lights steady, and do other tasks. They were wonderful kids and always willing to help where needed.

These kids and the village were fortunate to have us there. Because of our presence, they would indeed receive special attention, at least while we were there. Of course, these folks were very poor. They mostly lived in small homes, and sometimes not much more than a single room with walls of thatch.

In the center of the village, there was a bar restaurant, that we quickly made into our office and home. Of course, they were happy to have us. The beer in the Philippines was a brand called San Miguel, really delicious, and it only cost a nickel a bottle.

Suddenly, we had all the beers we would ever be able to drink, and the food being provided, while simple, was also very good. The two essential ingredients a good sailor needs, food and booze, were now taken care of.

The food was mostly local, which was fine by us because local meant fresh seafood, not more than an hour or two old, with rice and vegetables grown in the village or close by.

Most of the men worked in the rice fields or growing fruit for export, primarily pineapple and mangos. While most of the village was very poor, they were all very kind to us, and seemed to enjoy their lives much more than we enjoyed ours.

The village did have some electricity, but not a lot. So, we had to have a generator brought in to do the kind of lighting we needed, especially when we got into the schoolhouse itself which had just a couple of outlets and a single light bulb. We needed thousands of watts to run our lighting alone.

At first, I didn't realize how the village was governed but quickly found out. It seems at that time all government in the Philippines was corrupt in one way or another. We noticed that among the huts, there were a couple of very nice homes, with electricity, kitchens, and bathrooms, along with beautiful furnishings. We would soon learn these belonged to the head dudes that pretty much ruled everything in the province.

Naturally they were considered government officials, so their rule was absolute. Corrupt doesn't really describe their position. They literally controlled just about everything. Their control extended to how much the villagers could keep when they got paid. The rest had to be surrendered as local taxes, sup-posedly for their healthcare and education. If a child was given a scholarship to attend school in Manila, it would mostly be confiscated by them as reparations. When they did allow a bit more to be kept, there was always a catch.

So, we needed to deal with these folks carefully.

Of course, this was all well-known, and it was assumed that a payoff must be made. So, prior to our arriving arrangements were made. But nevertheless, we still had to acknowledge their importance, and let them know that we knew all about the pay off, and that they had agreed to a payoff for us to be there. Hopefully, we would not need more. All in all, it was a good enough reason to get our work done and get out, before they stuck their hands out again.

Fortunately, everything went well for all of us. I was able to snatch a little kid about seven or eight years old, and he was just thrilled to death to help me each day. We made sure all the kids got a little something in pay every evening.

He was just amazed at what could be seen in the viewfinder. I was a bit surprised at how observant the little guy was. He caught on fast and became a big help, especially in the rice paddies. After shooting a scene in the paddy, the camera would have to be moved for the next shot, and this required us to carefully move all the equipment, keeping it all out of the water and dry, of course.

This required me to have my shoes and socks off with pants legs rolled up, so I could stand in the wet fields for sometimes hours at a time. My little guy became my fetch and get it, so he needed to learn what some of the equipment was called, as most of it was sitting in cases on dry land.

He caught on quickly, and when he did not, we generally had a member of the crew to help him pick out what was needed. He was a wonderful little guy. I tried my best to make sure his parents were rewarded for his help, without the village gangsters knowing of course.

This was an enormous change from going into a rice paddy where you knew you were going to get shot at or worse. We all had the time of our lives, and it quickly became for us a job that we didn't want to complete.

No matter what, we all knew we were soon going back to Saigon. So, when it came time to shove off from the village, we were all really bummed. The villagers all got together and provided us with a wonderful celebration the evening before we departed. How kind, how wonderful they all were. While they were all very poor, especially by our standards, they were all the kindest and happiest people I had met in a very long time. No matter what, I could feel it. Peace and love were in the air.

CHAPTER 11

A Good Piece Of Bullshit

March 1969

When I got back to Saigon, it was decided that we should all have a little time to rest, and consequently, were all sent to Japan for a month. During this stay in Yokosuka, we crafted a little job that we actually talked the Navy into letting us shoot.

It started one afternoon as we were all hanging around our ready room, drinking coffee and lying to each other. One of us, I don't remember who, came up with the idea that we should send a full crew with interpreters to Mount Fuji and photograph the crew as it climbed the mountain to the top. This would require at least two days to get up the mountain and one to get back to the mountain base. It would also require a few days at the base to prepare.

Now we all knew that this had already been done several times before and getting the Navy to approve this trip was probably not going to happen. But we had a secret weapon to use, Master Chief Denning. The rank of master chief is rare in the Navy, and there are only a handful in the service at any one time. We were fortunate to have Master Chief Denning in charge of our Yokosuka headquarters at the time.

He was an old salt, and knew the Navy inside and out, having been in it for almost forty years at the time. In addition, the master chief took an especial liking to me, partly because of my service with VO67 in Thailand, which he had heard the rumors about. He knew that those guys were lucky to be alive.

After all of us had spent the better part of a day sitting around our large recreation room, or more officially our ready room. We had put together what we thought was just a perfect official request, which now would have to be submitted and approved.

We all knew that our chances were slim, at best, to get this approved. This was one of those things that we rarely had a chance of getting beyond first base. But you never know what piece of shit will stick to the wall until you give it a try. So, we all laughed a little about our chances and submitted the request.

For a while, absolutely nothing happened at all. But suddenly, one day Master Chief Denning called me into his office. Now Master Chief Denning was always perfectly dressed, and I do mean perfectly. Never did know how he managed to keep the creases of his shirt and pants like they had never been worn, absolutely perfectly straight. He was the only enlisted man I always felt deserved coming to attention and saluting to when entering his office. It was not required, of course, but to my way of thinking he earned it. His career went back to the Korean War, and he had the medals to prove it.

So, I came to attention, and gave him my best salute, which he returned, and then pointed to a chair in front of his desk.

"Good morning, Master Chief Denning. How may I be of service?"

"Well, Vincent, you definitely have good manners. I have here a request that I believe you are a part of, is that correct?" He handed me his copy of the request we had submitted to him.

"Yes, sir. That's correct, sir, I am a part of the submission, Master Chief."

"What, pray tell, gives you the idea that we need such a film made?"

"Well Master Chief, it is my understanding that Mt. Fuji has already been photographed; however, I feel that with a new set of fresh eyes on the subject it can be better done. Also, Master Chief, it is my understanding that it was not done with a good script. We can create a better one prior to shooting the story."

"Well, Mr. Vincent, that's a very good piece of bullshit. How many interpreters do you suppose you will need?"

"Oh, yes, I do believe that our request would need to come with at least one interpreter, if that would meet with your approval, that is."

With a chuckle, he said, "Okay, I'm going to approve this request. However, I will expect continuing extraordinary work from both you and the rest of the team."

"Yes sir, you can count on us for the very best at all times. Thank you, Master Chief Denning."

"You're welcome. Now get out of here before I change my mind."

With that I made the hastiest retreat I could manage without stumbling all over myself. Everyone sitting around drinking coffee was mighty interested in the outcome of my little talk with Master Chief Denning.

"Well, guys, it's on. We just need to put together our five-man team, and one interpreter. One was all we can have, but how about Kazuie Nozawa, my girlfriend, at the time. She would love to go with us, and she speaks English well enough."

There were no disagreements with her as part of the team, so all that was needed was the approval of the papasan at the New Dream Japan. Everyone in Combat Camera Group knew the papasan well, and over the years had found him to be a reasonable guy. So later that day I walked over to the New Dream to have a talk with him about borrowing Kazuie for a four-day trip to Mt. Fuji. We were prepared to pay him for her help, of course.

When I walked into the bar, papasan was in back, doing I don't know what. So, I sat at the bar, waiting patiently for the elderly gentleman to come out and talk to me. After a short while, papasan reappeared and sat down at the bar next to me. He was always jovial with all of us and today was no exception. He listened to me intently for just a bit before he said he would prefer that we take the senior girl at the New Dream, Junco. I realized that Kaz was not going to be permitted, so I let it go, and agreed that Junco would be simply great.

CHAPTER 12

Red Light Kaz

April 1969

The bar owners, the papasans, controlled the red-light girls who entertained the men, and their rules were extremely strict. They would not let a girl go out with anybody that was too drunk, and then it was always understood that they had truly little time, and papasan would take all money transacted, no exceptions, period. It was a good system; in that it kept the girls out of trouble and protected. The bars all had bouncers, and they were good at their jobs, really good. If one of the girls was gone for a bit longer than expected, the bouncer was sent to find out why. Messing with one of these guys would get you a quick trip to the base hospital.

The main job for the girls was just to hang out with these very lonely sailors, get them buy the girls drinks (really just iced tea in drink glasses), and be nice to them. On most occasions, which was all a lonely sailor really wanted, to spend some time with a girl that would listen to them kindly. Of course, if one of them got even a little aggressive, they would soon find themselves in the alley behind the bar with their faces rearranged.

But this rarely happened. Consequently, the Shore Patrol rarely had any trouble at the New Dream.

I was fairly sure that Junco was indeed the oldest and most senior of all the girls. You could tell at one time she had been very attractive, but now was cursed with a little extra weight, and not as pretty as she once was. She was however one of our very favorite girls to sit at our table, as she was funny and just plain nice to be with.

Shortly after my conversation with papasan, she came strolling through the door. She walked right over to the bar stool I was sitting at and greeted me gaily. "Hi, Bence, you back to stay for a while, I hope. We miss you very much."

"Yep, I think I'm going to be in town for about a month, after all I need to catch up with my favorite girl," I replied as I gave her a gentle hug.

"No, Bence, you are so silly, you have eyes for much younger girl. Ney!"

CHAPTER 13

Junco Can Go

April 1969

"Well, Junco I have a very special request to ask you. Before you say anything, I have already talked to papasan, and he thinks you would be perfect. Would you like to go to the base of Mt. Fuji with a five-man crew to photograph the mountain and the people hiking the mountain?"

"Oh...Bence, you are sure, you mean it, when?"

"Well, we haven't set up the time and the date yet, but probably very soon. We just need to get some orders, and money to pay for the trip. Of course, we will pay you, as well as papasan. Hopefully, we can leave by no later than Monday, will that work with you?"

"Oh, yes, yes, you sure you want me?"

"Absolutely." With that, everything was apparently in place, except obtaining transportation and lodging when we got there. Also, we all felt we should send Junco on a shopping trip so she could refresh her wardrobe. This would take a little collection from all the members of the team to fund her, and everyone was more than happy to contribute, including me.

CHAPTER 14

Kazue & Sister

April 1969

Now the way all the bars in the red-light area worked for sailors was about the same, apart from Combat Camera Group. Because we had been using this haunt for over twenty-five years at the time and were the first to claim this as our bar right after WWII, we were special to the red-light district. Also, we all carried press passes, which prevented the Shore Patrol from doing much more than giving us a warning. So, we were in effect sacrosanct, and it was relied on for us to stay out of serious trouble, which we did do, usually.

The way the red-light area worked was that the girls that worked there were more or less all prostitutes, but of a very special variety. They almost all lived above the bar in kind of a large dorm, although some of the older ones, and some of the more famous ones did live away from the bar, in their own homes.

In the case of Kazuie, exceptions had been made. She wasn't a prostitute, but she did work in the bar and would sit with the sailors. If they were after something more, they would be passed off to one of the other girls.

She came from a home far from Yokosuka and wasn't recognized as a bar employee when outside of Yokosuka. She had lived alone in a small apartment for a long time, but then I came along. The papasan of the New Dream had made a rare exception with her so that she did not have to work as a prostitute and could live alone. It was a mystery to me as to how she found herself in Yokosuka in the first place, and I was never told by either papasan or by her.

After she and I became involved, I began to stay most nights with her. As a consequence, I felt it necessary to pay for her apartment. Nobody on the base seemed to mind, at least I was never told I couldn't do that. That was the beginning of our relationship. Never in all the time we shared would she explain how she had gotten into working at the bar, why she was in Yokosuka.

I just could not understand how she had gotten herself into this type of work. She knew, and I knew, that she didn't belong here. She was far too smart, and quite beautiful as well.

I never did figure out whether Kaz and I were in love, or just very good pals. But when I was in town, she and I spent all our time together. Papasan had no objections at all, which was rare. I think he was of the same opinion as I was. She really didn't belong here at all.

So, on one occasion Kaz asked me if I would like to meet her sister and her brother-in-law. At the time I had no idea that Kaz even had a sister. They lived in a large town about an hour or so by train from Tokyo. It sounded to me like a fun trip, so I agreed and asked Master Chief Denning if I could be gone for a couple of days, and he had no objection.

As it turned out, her brother-in-law was a rather famous chef who had recently been working in Tokyo. Because of his recent marriage and the arrival of their first child, they had decided to move out of the city and into a better area to raise their new family. So, they lived about thirty-five miles from Tokyo, and he had taken over a small but very nice little restaurant. They lived above the restaurant, as most store owners did. In Japan, space is more valuable than gold.

The time spent with Kaz, her sister, husband, and their little girl was one of the best times I remember from that period of my life. Her brother-in-law was a wonderful cook, just as advertised, and we quickly bonded and enjoyed each other's company. I would sit at the counter right next to his cooking space. He made a lot of lunches for businessmen and for their meetings. So, when he was preparing for a delivery, he would make a small dish for me to try. I thought I had died and gone to food heaven; he was so good at his work. It was amazing.

This was also a great time for me to try and learn a little more Japanese. His daughter was between three and four years old and the perfect teacher. She would giggle and clap her hands when I figured out what she was trying to tell me. When I conquered something kind of hard, she would run around the tables, giggling, and clapping her hands, as if I had just won a major prize.

It was so much fun that I could have easily stayed for a much longer time, but I needed to get back. Our Mt. Fuji trip was going to be starting in just a couple of days. I still needed to firm up with papasan how long Junco would be with us.

So, back to Yokosuka I made final arrangements for our trip, which was supposed to begin in just a day or so.

CHAPTER 15

Booze & Baths

April 1969

It looked like we had just about everything in place, except transportation, lodging, and how to get our funding from Master Chief Denning. The master chief had already taken care of most of it for us, good man that he was. He suggested we use a private limo service because of all the equipment we would be taking with us. Of course, we agreed whole heartedly with the master chief's suggestions.

He also asked if we had found our interpreter and if she was ready to go. We told him yes, we did, and that it was Junco from New Dream. Of course, he knew her and thought she was indeed an excellent choice, and that because of her age she would probably keep us out of trouble.

We left within a few days for what we thought would be a four-day trip. It turned into a bit more than that. The master chief's suggestion of a limo turned out to be right on the money. If we had taken the train, it would have quickly turned into a nightmare. Even with private transportation, it took us the better part of a day to get there, and we were all just blown away by what we found.

At the base of Mt. Fuji was a beautiful small town, with everything laid out just so. It was almost like a fairy tale. The village was very small, and quite obviously not at all a cheap place to be staying. Of course, the Chief knew this, but we of course didn't. He had made reservations for us to stay at a small hotel with a spa and unbelievable food service.

We were all like ducks out of water, but with Junco carefully guiding us around, it quickly became a lot of fun. In that we were staying in a strictly Japanese establishment, we needed to follow, as best we could, their customs. Junco was absolutely a godsend in this department.

After we had checked in and found our rooms, Junco said that we must be tired from the drive and that we should all take a long relaxing bath. None of us really understood what she meant. But being young sailors, we all nodded our heads yes and asked her how to accomplish this. She said with a big grin, "You boys put on your kimonos," and she would be right back. As promised, she was only gone for a minute, which was good as we all felt a little like small kids.

We put on our kimonos, and she ushered us into a steamy room with a bunch of round tubs. Each tub was about five feet in diameter and four to five feet deep, with a bench to sit on. The tubs were all recessed into the floor which was a kind of a straw mat. Her orders to each of us was to take a tub, get in, and soak. Next to each tub was a cup on a long handle which we found was used to pour water onto yourself.

We all had a slight problem stripping and getting into our round tubs. The water was incredibly hot. Once you had forced yourself into it, however, it was divine.

We thought this was going to be a bathtub, but that was not exactly right. These were all round tubs and were used for only soaking. There was a separate room where you could clean your body and rinse the soap and residue off into a drain.

The very wealthy could always afford to bathe in a smaller area or private space and have refreshments served. But for most, it was common for men, women, and children to all share a bath together. Nobody cared what you looked like, and if you followed customs, nobody seemed to care that you might be sitting in a round tub, not too far away from somebody else. Man, this was wonderful, really wonderful.

Next, we all retired back to our rooms, and Junco ordered for us the equivalent of hor d'oeuvres, and of course the assorted beer, scotch, and sake. I had never tasted the difference between cheap sake and fine sake. Junco helped teach me the difference.

The establishment we were staying at was indeed one of the finest. After a short period of time the food and booze arrived. It was all laid out on trays, and it was all quite beautiful. After bowing, I assumed I should give a tip to the waiters after having set everything up. But Junco quietly grabbed my arm and whispered to me that no, don't.

When the servants had left Junco explained that while she understood it was American custom to tip, in Japan it was not. In fact, it was considered one of the barbaric customs that the round eyes displayed. Instead, the Japanese habit would be to have the person responsible for the rooms and payment, to decide with the management to pay the final bill and leave extra only if the stay had been exceptional. Then it was always split among all that served, in various proportions, which was decided by the management.

From Junco I learned a lot about the culture. I didn't realize that most Japanese lived in only one room, which served also as their dining room and general living space, including a bedroom at night. The one living space was quickly turned into whatever was needed in the moment. To have more required enormous amounts of money. In other words, to have anything like an average American home required millions of dollars to own and maintain.

It was during this time that I finally began to understand that Americans didn't have a corner on the market when it came to exaltation and love of family and home. I began to understand that in many ways, these people had more, much more contentment than we could ever hope to obtain with all our stuff.

They did not worship money or things, and they put little stock in ownership. But they did have a great admiration and love of peace, thought, and wisdom. It occurred to me that they were right. Really, money and material things didn't matter nearly as much as I once thought. When compared to our values, their priorities seemed much more in line with the universe.

CHAPTER 16

Quiet

April 1969

The next day we split up into two groups and started photographing the village, train station, and people arriving. During the photo session, I noticed that some of the Japanese were leaving the mountain with walking sticks, and emblems that had been inked or stamped with a hot iron into each side of these square sticks. The walking sticks apparently indicated they had climbed the entire mountain, and had been stamped by the monks to certify their deed. Interesting, but everything was interesting to me.

The village had only one purpose, and that was to serve those that had come to visit the mountain. This was not at all a rowdy town, like we would have in our vacation stops in the US. Instead, it was very quiet, and a feeling of peacefulness surrounded everything. It seemed as if everybody was moving in slow motion, and when someone spoke, it was very quietly, and with the utmost of respect for one another.

Before long, I had caught on, and was myself also caught up in the quiet, peaceful mood that surrounded us. Everything became relaxing. Even just walking became a wonderful, bliss-ful experience. I was discovering the Japanese idea of a peaceful vacation to revive their souls, and it was a lesson I would never forget.

It was impossible to describe, and yet I'll never forget that time. Quiet, if done correctly, can be a bigger joy than laughing.

CHAPTER 17

Summit Stamps

April 1969

O nce it came time to climb the mountain, we made the decision to go all the way to the top. With all our camera equipment, getting up the trail would be quite a task. Fortunately, we were all young and in excellent condition.

The trail itself was managed by Zen Buddhist monks, and at the base, each climber was given one of those walking sticks. They told us that the walk up to a midway point and back could be done in one day. However, if we desired to go all the way to the top, it would take two days to do so and return. The midway point had a large hut which could be used for rest before finishing the next day.

After talking it through, we decided that all five of us would try to get to the top. But Junco agreed to stay behind, given her age and condition. We agreed to also leave for Yokosuka immediately after completing the climb.

Right before we started to go up, our walking sticks were stamped with a red stamp. The trip to the top was uneventful; however, only three of us went all the way to the summit. A couple of the guys stopped at the halfway station, so we left a lot of the equipment with them and took only the bare minimum of camera gear to the top.

Those of us that went to the top found that the going was a bit more difficult. We could tell the air was a bit thinner, so we had to move with a bit more thought. When we did reach the top, we stayed for only a short period of time. It was cold, windy, and we were exhausted, so we decided to go down quickly, but not before getting the film needed taken. After we reached the camp at the midway point, the other guys were ready, so we could leave without delay.

When we three returned to the midway point, we repacked all equipment and headed down to the base. The trip down was easy and uneventful, so we managed to make exceptionally good time. At the bottom of the trail, a Zen monk stamped our sticks with a hot iron, which indicated we had indeed traveled all the way to the top of their most revered mountain and volcano.

By the time we got to the bottom, got our walking sticks stamped for the last time, and retrieved the car and Junco, we were all set to return home. We just had to make sure all payments had been made to the hotel, which we did with Junco's help.

We were all exhausted, and the trip home was quiet. But the result was wonderful, and for me especially so. Having climbed Mt. Fuji was a special event that I had wanted to accomplish for a long time and one that has stayed with me.

Of course, it was also one of those times when I took note of the pleasure I could still experience in life. Good things can happen to anyone, if you just try hard enough.

CHAPTER 18

Photographing The Secretary

May 1969

Right after we returned to Yokosuka, Master Chief Denning grabbed me and said, "Don't get too comfortable." Things were happening in Saigon, and they were going to need another crew right away. More would be coming soon, so stand by.

Within the next twenty-four hours, I found out from Master Chief Denning that the Secretary of the Navy was going to be making a trip throughout the Far East, and he wanted me to get the story.

This of course was a surprise, because I knew I was by far not the senior person available. Of course, this was bound to cause resentment, especially in Saigon. The other photographers would be really pissed at me.

Naturally, about everyone thought that I had been playing Master Chief Denning to give me this important assignment. That couldn't have been farther from the truth, but I had no way to convince anybody. So, when I got back to Saigon, I knew it was going to be a bit ugly for me, and it was.

As a Second-Class Petty Officer, while I outranked a lot of enlisted men in Combat Camera Group, I was far from senior to most. There were a lot of First-Class Petty Officers and Chiefs that should have been assigned this story. With the Secretary of the Navy coming to Nam, I was a bit uncomfortable being put into a senior position.

But Master Chief Denning wanted me to be the crew chief on this job, and that was the way it was going to be, period. I wasn't going to argue with him.

The first thing I needed was to quickly put a crew together. Next, I needed to get equipped to do this job, and there I hit a bit of a snag. According to the guys in charge of our equipment, they had no Arriflex cameras. The Arriflex was a 16mm camera that could be used with a Niagra Recorder to shoot in sound, and it was our main stalwart for shooting film that included audio.

I knew that this was all bullshit, because the Arriflex/Niagra was our main camera and sound system. But I had no choice but to take them at their word. So, I had to settle for an incredibly old Mitchell. With the Mitchell, you could record sound with a special magnetic strip that ran down the side of the film. The camera was ancient and rarely used at all. It was not built to operate in the high humidity that we would be shooting in. My gut told me it was going to be a problem, even on a good day.

I knew that the only reliable way to shoot this assignment would be with our Arriflex and Niagra equipment. But the situation was not going to change, and there was little I could do about it. I picked out the best guys available to shoot this job and explained we had no choice but to use the cameras assigned to us.

When the secretary arrived, we discovered that most of the visit was not going to be photographed. We were told to meet up with Secretary Chafee in Da Nang for a one-day visit, and then go on back to Yokosuka. There we were supposed to photograph his tour of the hospital where a lot of the Marines were transported from Vietnam.

At the time Da Nang was the largest Marine and Navy base in Vietnam. We had all been to Da Nang many times before this and knew the lay of the land well. There were only two events that we needed to photograph. The first was a visit to a small village where a small pig farm had been built by our stateside folks. Its purpose was to show the Vietnamese people how to raise pigs properly. Without exception, nobody bothered to ask the locals if they needed help with pig farming work, they had been doing this for at least the last four or five centuries. In other words, the locals had been raising pigs much longer than the United States had existed.

So here we were at a small little farm, with all the buildings freshly painted, and everyone was smartly dressed to impress the entourage with the brilliance of US pig farming. What a joke this was rapidly becoming.

The chopper set down, right on time, and the generals and dignitaries all piled out for the pig exhibition. The pigs were ready, all nicely cleaned and combed for the occasion.

Now the barn they were all marched into was not just any pig barn, no sirree. This barn was freshly painted, the floor of the barn was tiled in a black and white check porcelain, and of course there was not a piece of bare wood anywhere.

Very impressive, but nevertheless it was just a glorified pigsty. Now Secretary Chaffee, being dutifully impressed, told us to be sure and get a lot of good photos of this impressive display of American generosity to the South Vietnamese

I guess we were supposed to show that pigs everywhere here in Vietnam lived in the comfort of porcelain tiled floors and antiseptically painted walls. They even had fans to help cool and disperse a lovely smelling deodorant throughout this marvelous pig barn.

It was so ludicrous that my guys were hardly able to shoot anything without laughing, which of course I warned them to absolutely not do, at least in front of the dignitaries. Oink.

The next stop on the secretary's agenda was just before he was to depart for Japan. He was going to give a speech to a large group of smartly dressed marines and sailors. Starched uniforms in the tropics were something to be amazed at, especially in the broiling humid sun in Da Nang. And this sweat-box was where the Mitchell Sound camera was supposed to be used.

We worked for several hours in the heat and humidity to get the camera set up at the back of the gathering space. Somehow, I just knew this was not going to work, and it did not. In fact, it was much worse than I could even imagine. The film we had to use did have a magnetic strip down one side, but this film was very old, and probably hadn't been properly stored or refrigerated to begin with. In this tropical environment, it was doomed to be glued together and not usable. But it was all we had, so we had to at least try. Maybe the film gods would bless us on this hot tropical day.

They didn't.

Even worse, when the camera jammed, a warning buzzer would be set off in the camera to alert the operator. It was loud enough to be heard by the speaker, Secretary Chaffee. We tried in vain to get the camera running. All we could do was shut the camera down so we could stop receiving ugly, very nasty looks from the secretary.

When the secretary realized we hadn't photographed his speech, he was very angry with us. We learned later that the photos were going to be for his own use and to be used only by him. I tried to take the entire blame for this screw up, and Senior Chief Denning did seem to understand what had happened, thank God.

Two days later we were back in Japan, preparing to record the secretary at the Naval Hospital in Yokosuka.

He was to award US Navy sailors and marines medals for the bravery they had displayed in battle. In the past, these award events were solemn affairs and always done with great respect and dignity for these battle-tested men.

By this time, I had access to our Arriflex camera and a good Niagra recording system to work with. Everything worked as it was supposed to, but the crew still had a really challenging time doing this part of the secretary's trip.

Right before entering the ward where all the men that were to receive medals were located, Secretary Chaffee approached me and made it clear that he expected excellent work from us. He insisted that I should be sure and photograph his right side only.

He wanted close-ups of all medals he was going to distribute. It was quite clear he was the center of attention, not the wounded men he was going to use as props. I really wanted to tell this arrogant person that what he was asking of me would be considered disgraceful and inappropriate, to besmirch these brave men. But all I could say was, "Yes sir."

As we entered the Marine ward, everyone got a lot quieter. It was clear to most that this was a special place of reverence. These were the men that really paid the price. The first bed we stood before had a marine with no arms, no legs, and was clearly not psychologically present. Usually when we approached a patient like this, the medal would be carefully pinned to their pillow, and the presenter would whisper into the person's ear a short solemn message.

The secretary looked at the man in the bed, turned, and walked to the other side, completely ignoring this valiant marine. The medal wasn't given to this brave man at that moment. Later, after the event was complete, we asked a Marine colonel if he would give this man the award he so valiantly earned. The colonel was outraged by the behavior of the secretary, and quickly agreed.

The secretary was making such a despicable demonstration of self-indulgent behavior that it was all I could do to stand there beside this horrible excuse for a human being. As he walked among each wounded marine, he of course made sure we were doing our best to have him photographed as if it were his finest moment. Quietly, I told the sound man to lower the input to the recorder, which he did. Then I motioned to our camera to not work so hard, which he understood.

I wanted under no circumstances to have this unbelievable, self-pious jerk get any usable film at all. These men deserved so much better than what was taking place.

Fortunately, we didn't have much else to do as the secretary stopped at only a small handful of beds. He then told the person with the medals to be awarded, to just pin something, on each pillow, didn't matter to him if they were the right medal or not. He ordered, "Be quick about it. I have a plane to catch." He did indeed, and I would have to say, it was wonderful to see him leave. A man like that didn't deserve to be in the same room as these brave men.

SECTION 9

Goodbye Vietnam
June 1969 – June 1970

*Moral courage is the most
valuable and usually the most
absent characteristic in men.*

George Patton

CHAPTER 1

Final Answer

July 1969

Returning to our offices shortly after the hospital debacle, I thanked everybody for doing their jobs as well as could be expected. Of course, I knew the Secretary would probably be complaining. So, I found Master Chief Denning and told him about everything that had transpired and that I would under no circumstances lay blame on anyone but myself. Furthermore, I would do this job about the same if asked to do it all over again.

The next day Master Chief Denning asked to speak to me outside. He told me that he had checked into matters, and that I had done the best that could be done. Nothing would ever be said about the matter.

After all was said and done, with all footage sent back to Washington, there was never any mention of the inadequately filmed Secretary of the Navy. To this day, I still remember every detail of this self-serving Washington dignitary. It was my first excursion with the selfish, arrogant Washington crowd, and I could only hope it to be my last.

The arrogance displayed by the Secretary of the Navy was not particularly unusual when you were in Saigon or working with senior officers not involved with the actual war. I had found that most of these arrogant assholes loved to pontificate about how well they were doing, and that they had just done a stellar job. It was the "look at me" crowd. They did everything with only one purpose in mind-- to further their own careers and nothing else. These arrogant guys had a profound love for themselves, and not much else.

But it was a good learning experience. It taught me that no matter where I was in life, this crowd would be in attendance somewhere along the line. But in the end, the guys that made sure the job was not only done, but done well, would almost certainly end up on top. The only place this didn't seem to be the case was in political circles. In political circles, the best liar tended to end up on top.

Because of these experiences, I always tried to just do my best. Doing something in a half-assed way stopped being acceptable during my military life. I learned to always try, just try my best, and let everything else take care of itself.

CHAPTER 2

One Last Time

November 1969

By this time, it was late into 1969, and I wanted to have one last trip to Vietnam. Of course, going back to Nam was still easy: Just put my hand up and they would cut my orders right away. And once again it worked for me.

Upon arriving in Saigon, I quickly noticed that the work had slowed down quite a lot for our group. But they did have a job coming up that really interested me and so I asked for it.

In the delta areas around or close to Saigon, there was always a lot of action. The area was overwhelmingly marsh with very little dry land, perfect for cultivating rice, which grew best in this type of landscape. Naturally the Viet Cong and NVA liked to stay in the area because it was all very swampy and was hard for us to move around in.

For a long time, we had heavily targeted the delta, but always the VC or NVA came back. Even finding them in these swamps was difficult, and as soon as we moved to the next area, they came right back.

We kept a lot of Patrol Boat River squadrons and SEALS in the area, and they did their best to keep them at bay. Both of our groups collaborated closely with each other, and often took a lot of casualties.

My assignment at first seemed simple enough. I was to pick up a detachment of SEALS at My Tho, and travel with them by barge upriver to a PBR (Patrol Boat River) base. From there we were going, the next day up a much narrower stream that constricted into marshy passages too shallow to travel by our boats or barges.

At this point the SEALS were going to enlarge this little tributary into a channel large enough to take a PBR or barge through and into a larger stream or channel. This way they would have access to an entire region that had been in Viet Cong hands for a long time.

The first task was to travel up to the PBR base camp. With our fully loaded barge, this was going to take some time. Otherwise, I figured that we wouldn't have much trouble getting upstream. But as time to shove off approached, a chopper showed up with a young, clearly wet-behind-the-ears Army first lieutenant, with a uniform that was crisp, clean, and sharply ironed with nary a wrinkle. We all looked at each other and thought, "What is this shit-head doing here?"

I soon found out. At the last minute, MACV (Military Assistance Command Vietnam) decided to send its very own photographer to make sure the event was properly documented. He made it clear that he was there to do just that, and that he was here at General Westmoreland's request. When he saw me, he just had to jump all over the fact that there were now two of us doing the same job. He let it be known he was now the senior officer on this job, and that what he said was to be always followed. This did not sound quite right, but I chose to say nothing in the moment.

However, the SEALS weren't so reticent. One thing you did not due to a SEAL was tell him how to behave. When we did shove off, one of the SEAL Team members came over to me and said with a big grin, "Do not pay much attention to Mr. Spic and Span. We've bumped across these reprobates in the past and there'll be a show to watch in little while."

I dismissed the lieutenant's assumption of command and took the SEAL's instructions to heart. The trip upriver went as planned. The barge was loaded with what looked like a black firehouse hose with brass fittings on each end. I didn't think anything about it as these barges were used to transport all kinds of odd stuff upriver.

But as I sat on top of one of the large rolls of fire hose, enjoying a Marlboro cigarette, one of the SEAL's sauntered up to me and begins to laugh. Finally, the guy asked me a question, "Must we all die today?"

"Well, I wasn't planning on it. Why are you asking?"

He said calmly, "Well, you know that we have our ordinance on board, and the big coil of firehouse hose you are sitting on is a new kind of explosive designed for underwater use. Amazing stuff. It is one of the most powerful explosives ever developed, and we're really excited to try it out on this assignment. It was just put into the field for us to use. But one of the cautions was to keep it away from intense heat." He grinned. "Now you are sitting on top of the entire load."

I looked at my cigarette, and then at him, and put the entire cigarette in my mouth and swallowed it whole. Naturally, this caused the entire to begin a loud, uproarious laughter at my expense. Holy shit, I had no idea.

In this war, you just never knew when your string was going to run out. It wasn't going to be today, and for that I only had a very brave SEAL to thank. These guys were just the best.

CHAPTER 3

Always Love a SEAL

November 1969

Despite my stupidity, the two-hour trip went as planned. Because of our sensitive load, they chose to go slow down the river, keeping an awfully close eye on the riverbanks. The little PBR (Patrol Boat River) base was heavily protected, with two lines of barbed wire and claymore mines strung into the wire. In addition, they had heavily fortified bunkers. Obviously, this place had been under fire in the past.

After we arrived, everyone shook hands, and someone put a PBR (Pabst Blue Ribbon beer) in my hand. For obvious reasons, this beer quickly became the PBR boat crew's drink of choice. When the lieutenant asserted himself, he was insulted right off. The base commander, a Chief Petty Officer, told him that if he really was put off, he was certainly welcome to swim home.

If not, he had better learn to keep his little mouth shut on this base, where he had no authority at all. Chief Dale Swinford took the arrogant Army clown to one side and told him that when he was needed to speak, Chief would let him know. Chief also explained how he was going to behave in this forward base.

Thank God, our lives depended on everyone working together, so out here rank meant nothing, or very little.

It was the end of the lieutenant's unruly behavior. At least, he behaved much better for the moment.

The next morning, we departed early to the area that needed work. Along the way on the starboard side, we passed two very dead Viet Cong. They had obviously just been killed; their bodies left to rot. Upriver a bit further, we crossed paths with a squadron of our guys that had been on ambush all night. The word from them was stay alert, the area was hot with VC.

Shortly after, we came to the little stream that needed to be enlarged. We were supposed to connect these channels with another channel about three hundred yards to our port side. The SEALS got right to work. Our tag-along lieutenant ordered me to stay on the barge. One of the SEALs heard the conversation and came up to me with a suggestion. "OK, I just heard what that asshole ordered you to do. If you want, I'll talk it over with the rest of the team and get you in the perfect spot when we get ready to light it off, and we'll take care of that dickhead, trust me."

I replied, "Sounds good to me. Just tell me what you need me to do, and I'd be happy for your help. Thanks."

"No problem. Get your stuff ready, and one of us will come get you in a few."

"Roger that."

About that time, one of the SEALs was placing the plunger to set off the explosives about seventy-five to a hundred yards away in a little revetment. This would give them some shelter from the explosion. I would have thought this was the best place to get the perfect pictures needed, but I was wrong.

A few minutes later, one of the SEALs appeared out of the water next to the barge. "OK, if you are ready, get in the water.

It shouldn't be higher than your hips. I will help you with your equipment. Let's go."

He then led me very slowly to a little spot about two hundred yards from the blast area. This was a little area that was above water and dry. It was not much but nevertheless had plenty of space for me to set up and be able to hold the camera steady. It was a perfect spot.

Then he told me he was going to disappear but would be within a few yards of my position. Right before disappearing, he told me to turn my camera on when I saw white smoke and to turn my camera right on the smoke. By the time I had the camera set up, he was nowhere in sight.

Well, it could not have been better. My position was perfect, and he indeed did have my back the entire time. He was hidden in the water with some reeds around his head and his gun which was sealed in plastic was also mostly underwater. These guys deserve all the accolades given to them. Even in 1969, they were just simply the absolute best.

When the explosives were touched off, an enormous line of water and mud erupted in the new channel. The mud went several hundred feet in the air and then came down right over the firing station, which included the lieutenant. When the men stood up after the explosion was complete, they were covered in at least an inch of mud from the eruption. All I could see were eyeballs.

The lieutenant was also covered in mud. His film and camera were ruined, a complete ball of mud. There would be no pictures for the lieutenant today.

After the shoot and a couple of beers with the PBR folks, we headed back to our original launch point where I would get a chopper back to Saigon. The lieutenant, arrogant little prick that he was, tried to confiscate my footage by saying he was part of MACV and had to be obeyed. I told him he was totally fucked; I didn't work for him or MACV.

At that point I pulled out one of my press passes. "Sorry, Lieutenant, I do not work for you and the footage I have will move through Naval channels as was ordered. But please, feel free to whine all you want to MACV. You will find this press pass gives me the authority to conduct my work any way I feel is best. Furthermore, my work cannot be infringed upon, especially by a lieutenant who fucked up his own work. Sorry, sir, I will not comply. You outrank me, but you don't outrank my mission."

Later, a copy of the film went to Washington and MACV with US Navy stamped all over it, along with my name and rank: Photographed by Petty Officer Second Class Richard Vincent. We never heard another word about the lieutenant and his temper tantrum.

I always felt if I did my best, that was all I needed. Well, that and a little help from the Navy SEALS.

CHAPTER 4

Goodbye Saigon

December 1969

By now, I was beginning to get run down, and started to feel like I had been mighty lucky. My charmed luck was running out, I just knew it. Also, there was an announcement that enlistees who had done at least one tour in Vietnam could be considered for early release in order to attend a school of higher education.

By my calculations, I had completed about three tours in South Vietnam or adjoining countries. I asked Master Chief Denning if I could leave Vietnam and return to Yokosuka and/ or the States. Within a few days, I had orders sending me back to Japan. But of course, there one last little problem.

Remember, our hotel was several miles away from Tan Son Nhut Airport. Traffic to the airport was always an issue, so I wanted to leave the hotel a little earlier than usual. My driver to the airport was Tom McCaulley, who was not as anxious as I was to get there.

As I suspected, the roundabouts were packed with people, mopeds, bikes, hand carts, and everything else, including small motorbikes with a live pig strapped to the back and bound for the market or a restaurant.

We suffered through one roundabout after another, and the time melted away. We finally made it through all but one last roundabout, and we still had a bit of a hike to get to the security gates and then to the airport itself.

By this time, I had lost all patience. I was being unreasonable and knew it. McCaulley was doing the best he could to keep moving, but these roundabouts always became overloaded with people trying to come and go.

Finally, I exploded and jumped out of the van, I yelled at McCaulley to keep moving, I'd clear the way. In my frustration I pulled out my .45 pistol and began waving it around. At first it was the winning formula. But then things slowed down again.

I fired a round into the air, and it was like Moses parting of the sea. Suddenly we had no trouble at all completing the distance to the road we needed to the airport. We made it in plenty of time, and as I got out of the van, I handed McCaulley my sidearm. I said, "Dear Lord, I hope I never have to see one of these again. Sorry for all the yelling and screaming. I know you were doing the best you could to get me to the airport."

Tom grinned. "No problem, Vince, hope you have no more problems getting back to the land of the living."

What could I say? I just turned around and walked into the airport lounge. My plane was not ready to board, but I breathed a sigh of relief. It was over, finally over.

The rest of the trip to Yokosuka was uneventful, but it seemed to take forever. Still, it was over. Vietnam was hopefully behind me. My God, I was still in one piece. How did this happen and why/ I just didn't have a good answer at the moment. I just knew if I took my evening medicine I would survive.

That's what I thought, but still I had no idea where the devil was going to drag me. He was going to hold onto me for years and years to come.

CHAPTER 5

Keep Moving

Early December 1969

It was good to get back to Yokosuka, where not only were they not shooting at me, but nobody was carrying a gun. It was November, and I knew I would have to wait my turn to get back to North Island in San Diego.

In the meantime, Master Chief Denning asked me to go on one last simple job. He needed someone to cover some military exercises in South Korea, and that seemed safe enough.

As it turned out, South Korea was fun. I had only two days of work to do and a week to putz around a nice city. Seoul was completely rebuilt after the war, with many very tall office buildings, most of which were quite beautiful. It was like Saigon in that everything was inexpensive, so I did some shopping. I found I could ship about anything I wanted through the US Embassy with the use of my press pass. They had a US Post Office which avoided all customs inspections.

At the time I could not think of much to send home, except booze. If memory serves, I sent several bottles of good scotch to myself in Noblesville, Indiana.

Of course, every night in Korea, I got myself shit-face drunk, mostly drinking scotch. The formula was still working perfectly. I could sleep and the next morning be as good as gold, no nightmares, no dreams. It was, I still thought, the perfect solution.

The master chief was true to his word, I was back in Japan in about two weeks.

CHAPTER 6

The Folks Hanging Around

Late December 1969

Christmas was rapidly approaching, and consequently everything slowed way down, except for Nam of course. We still had three or four guys rotating in and out every month, allowing the guys to stay fresh. Short of that, we had much of each day to lounge around. Some of us played pool, some read, some slept, and some of us were able from time to time to go to see the old and famous Zen Buddhist temples.

There was one in Kamakura, the Taiizan Kotokuin Shojosenji, which was always open. I loved sitting on a park bench for hours admiring its beauty. It was a huge structure built with enormous timbers. I marveled at the precise way each piece of wood fit with the next piece of wood. The entire structure was built by using joinery, with no fasteners of any kind, and still standing after almost 850 years.

Always I considered it my good fortune that I was able to encounter Buddhist monks and begin to understand this simple religion. Well, it just looks simple. In fact, Zen Buddhism is very complicated to understand. Or maybe it is very simple but cloaked in mystery. Of all the various Buddhist sects, I found Zen to be the most difficult. Even the type practiced in Thailand was very hard for me to fully understand.

But no matter what, I always felt I was learning from the various monks I met. For some reason I wanted to just dive in and hang out with as many different people as I could find. This became very useful as I went through life, having met all these amazing and different people.

But I finally realized they all had many of the same life struggles, happiness, and desires that this Christian boy had. It was just amazing to realize our commonality.

CHAPTER 7

Last Gig

February 1970

Hanging around doing nothing was never my strong suit. So, I asked Master Chief Denning if I could have a word with him. It was a rainy day, as I recall, and with little going on at the time. I said, "Master Chief, as you know, my enlistment is going to be up in just a few months. I recently heard of a new program which allows Vietnam veterans to leave the service a little early if they wanted to attend a school of higher education. I have taken a couple of courses by mail with Indiana University and thought I would try to enroll with them for next fall term. Of course, I realize that I will need to apply to leave the Navy a couple of months early. What do you think my chances of getting my tour shortened by just a couple months would be?

The chief nodded. "Well, Vince, let me look into this program you are speaking of, and I'll get back to you as soon as I've got something."

"Thanks, Master Chief, I would really appreciate your help."

A couple of days later, Master Chief called me into his office. "OK, Vince, here is what the Navy has to offer. You can leave early if your senior duty officer recommends it. But first, you will need to apply to Indiana University and be accepted. Then you will need to take the paperwork from the university verifying you have been accepted and give this to Commander Holmes." Commander Holmes was the unit's commanding officer in North Island.

That was it. I knew that with Master Chief Denning helping, it would happen if I did my part. A couple of days later, Master Chief Denning called me into his office and dumped a wonderful surprise into my lap. "Well, Vince, I have one last job for you, if you want it."

"Well, Master Chief, does it require me to get shot at, and if so, not interested."

"No, it doesn't. They were going to send a crew out from North Island just to do this story. However, I think it is entirely right for you before you head back to the States. It will give you a reason to stay in this man's Navy. We need a crew to report to the commanding officer of SEATO."

SEATO was Southeast Asian Treaty Organization, the Pacific version of NATO. But it only existed for a few years, whereas NATO is still in existence even today. The chief continued, "The big dogs at SEATO have decided to run a naval exercise, leaving Manila, and transitioning to Bangkok for the end of the route. You started your first tour in Thailand, didn't you? Thought you might like to see it one last time."

I replied immediately, "When would I need to shove off, Master Chief?"

"Don't know, but probably quickly. I'll have to check and get back to you on the timing. See me later today."

"Master Chief, thank you."

"Get out of my office," he said with a little smile.

Suddenly, I found myself getting ready to head to Manila to the United Nations offices and headquarters for SEATO. From there I went to check into my accommodation, the Miramar Hotel, a famous old hotel close by and overlooking the bay. The Miramar Hotel was built in the 1930s and at one time was "the" hotel to stay at. It was General MacArthur's home while he governed the Islands, as I understood it. He had the entire top floor for himself, his wife, and family.

The US Navy would not be putting us in such incredible nice quarters, for sure. I guessed SEATO on the other hand could always afford the very best.

In any case, the accommodations were spectacular and right next to the harbor. From there, I would be taking a whale boat to my ship, the HMAN Melbourne of Her Majesty's Australian Navy. That was where I was to report to the Admiral of the Australian Navy. The navy was also accommodating, provided me with working space for my equipment, and assigned me two Aussie sailors to help me around the ship. My instructions were simple. The Admiral wanted to have the ship and all dignitaries filmed. In addition, he suggested that I go to one of the British ships for a photo shoot. Of course, I thought that was a grand idea.

I understood I was going to be at sea for only four days and would be dropped off or sent ashore in Bangkok for return to my home port in Japan. Of course, that was fine with me, but first I was to be treated to the Australian Navy's idea of hospitality, and boy, was that the best.

My two guides met me at the dock in Manila, where a whale boat was moored. They suggested I go ahead and get aboard, and not to worry about my camera equipment. They promised to take care of it and me, which was very nice, I thought in the moment.

Well, the boat quickly filled up with mighty drunken sailors. Nice to see that these Aussies knew how to play. One of the guys that boarded was really plowed, and his uniform looked like it had been run over by a garbage truck. Under his blouse he had tucked a duck, a live duck. Holy shit, how did he expect to get that on board?

A few minutes later we pulled alongside the carrier, and the men began to disembark. Now it is naval custom, when approaching the duty officer at the top of the ladder, to first salute the flag and then salute the officer of the deck and ask permission to come aboard. But guys who had spent the evening on shore were going to be very drunk. In that case, the duty officer usually waved them on board quickly, so they could stumble to their rack.

All was going well for a few minutes, then it came time for the sailor with the duck. He drunkenly saluted as expected, but the duty officer stopped him.

"What the fuck do you have under your blouse, sailor?"

"Oh, my friend, Mr. Duckie," he drunkenly replied.

"Well, Mr. Duckie isn't going to be given permission to board. Get rid of it."

So, he drunkenly pulled his little duck out from under his blouse and placed its neck on the railing and begins his farewell. "Sorry, little duckie, guess your sweet time on earth is over. I have been ordered to remove you from this ship and so you must go to duckie heaven."

As he began, the sailors down below us, still in the whale boat, began to all become very, very sick. You see, while a carrier is so heavy, it will not rock or roll much, even in heavy seas. But a little whale boat in a harbor with choppy water is going to rock and roll all over the place. It's mighty easy to get seasick if you are drunk and in a moving boat, and these guys were all really drunk.

At this point the duty officer looked at the whale boat full of vomiting sailors, and then at the sailor giving his duck a last elegy. There was really no choice, and the officer waved the drunken sailor, with duck, to come aboard, and get out of his sight. Even at that, the duty officer had one hell of a puking problem. It did not stop for several minutes, and the trail could be followed all the way up the stairs and past the duty officer, before disappearing below deck.

The next morning, when I jumped out of my rack and headed right for the shower, I saw it-- Mr. Duckie, happily swimming around in the flooded shower stall. These Aussie guys knew how to have a good time, and I knew I was going to really have fun with these clowns.

My two tour guides arrived then to give me a thorough tour of the ship's spaces. This was an aircraft carrier, immense and complex, and without their help, I would have been lost in a matter of minutes.

However, after the tour, we had an awful breakfast. It turned out the Australians were not as good as the Americans when it came to feeding their sailors. The Americans always had tremendous food; the Aussies had horrible food, but they did have a redeeming feature. The Australians issued on every other day one large liter of Foster's Beer, made just for the Australian Navy, and man, was it delicious. All this alcohol was perfectly normal to me at the time. I still had not figured out that drinking every evening was not the on/off switch I thought it was.

After that, it was right to work. The admiral asked me to his quarters and gave me the itinerary, all typed out for my use. Then he wanted to know if I was planning to board some of the other ships, and if so when would I feel that was best. By that time, I had already thought it best to board a British frigate, if possible. He said that arrangements would be made at once to get me transferred in the next day or so.

That's exactly what I did the next day after leaving the harbor. I was taken by chopper to one of the frigates sailing with us. Getting on the chopper was easy, because I was on an aircraft carrier, which hardly moved around at all in rough seas. But getting off the chopper onto the frigate in rough seas turned out to be a whole lot of a problem.

The seas were much too heavy for the chopper to land on the frigate, so the only solution was to lower me down. I just had to stay calm and let the chopper and the frigate do their job of coordinating the drop. By this time in my navy career, it was not the first time I had been asked to stay calm in a dicey situation. On the third try they got me on deck.

As it turned out, the British were even more hospitable and generous with their time. First thing, I found myself being taken to the conning tower, which is exactly where I wanted to be. The CO (Commanding Officer) of the ship asked me how I could be assisted. I let him know I had wanted to photograph the conning tower, and one of the guns in action if that could be arranged. Indubitably it could, was all he said, and left me to do as I wished, first telling the officer of the deck to make sure I was taken to the guns when ready.

Later that day, the British blokes took me to a room where they hung out when off duty. They quickly told me that the horse piss the Aussies were given to drink was not at all acceptable. Only a good mug of British grog (a very toxic rum) would do the ticket. The grog, I must say, was mighty, mighty good. I wish I could have stayed on the frigate a bit longer.

However, I knew I needed to return to the carrier to photograph festivities on board the next day. So now they had to get me off this tossing and turning ship. The seas at the time were so heavy that the helicopter could not land. So, both my equipment and I were going to have to be picked up by hoist from the helicopter. As advertised, these guys were just as good as I expected, and they got me onboard the chopper with ease, but only after they practiced missing the hook on the hoist from the helicopter a few times. The misses were, I assumed, just to let the American know how tricky it could be to be lifted off a pitching and twisting British ship. Yes, I got it, in fact, I got the bejesus scared right out of me.

That night the Aussies treated me to the officer's mess, where the food was indeed much better. Then, after an awfully long day, I decided to head down below and find my bunk. But I wasn't quite done yet. When I got below, over the ship's intercom came the following: "Ship's smoking lamp is now lit, beer ration is now available." This meant you could now smoke in designated areas, and you could get your ration of beer. Hell yes, I wanted to try Australian Navy Beer. Foster's Brewing made this superb beverage for navy use only, and to remarkably exacting standards. Boy oh boy, was it good and strong. I believe it was stronger than their exports to the US but never knew for sure. At that time, 1969, Fosters was only distributed to the Australian Navy, and I don't think was available to the public even in Australia.

Not too long ago, in the 2000s, because of draughts and fire storms, the Aussies were not able to brew the amounts of beer normally brewed for the public. To help, the Navy volunteered to lend the public their stash, to great applause, as I understood from the news articles. It was indeed declared that Fosters was a special beer, and to be treasured.

When the ship finally pulled into Bangkok, I felt I needed to reciprocate for all of their kindnesses. I left the ship and checked into my lodging for the night. Then I went to a US Navy ship's store and bought four gallon bottles of the best rum that they had. Next, I had to get the booze onboard. As I was leaving the liquor store, I noticed a telephone truck. Now, at the time I remember, phones were a lot bigger than today, and of course always had to be plugged into a receptacle or land line. They each came in a nice large box, bingo. They were perfect, just the right size for one bottle.

All I needed to do was steal four boxes of phones, remove the phones, and, of course, return the phones themselves to the truck. Next, with a little carving, I was able to place each bottle in a box. Now I had to figure how to get them onboard the ship.

Luck was with me. The Officer of the Deck that day was one of the officers I had met before. He took one look at my cargo and asked me what the fuck were the boxes of phones for. My response was, "These phones are for a final meeting with UN folks and the admiral. They will need communications with the embassies."

He bought it and said, "Carry on." Off I went below deck, where absolutely nobody was present. They were all on shore, doing what all good Australian sailors do best, getting really shit-faced. I needed a place where the booze would survive. So, I went to the head (the shower and toilet) and removed several towels.

It took a few minutes to make the exchange look right but I finally got it done. All I did was remove each pillow from the pillowcase, put that under the bed, and then refill the pillowcase with a towel wrapped around one phone box. They looked good, I must say. Of course, I also composed a short letter thanking them again.

CHAPTER 8

Last Stay Yokosuka

March 1970

The trip back to Japan was uneventful, and I arrived at Yokota US Air Base around 3 PM. Then it was a short trip to Yokosuka by our company van which had been sent to pick me up. The next day I reported to Master Chief Denning and handed him my film along with a report of the mission. He was pleased with the job and told me to pack and prepare for transit to the States in the next few days. It was now April, and I was more than happy to comply.

It seemed like the war always had an uptick in early spring, so I was mighty happy to be left behind. No more war for me. After three years, I was done, and so very tired. Home-- what a thought, no more death, no more blood, it was finally done.

By the time I had said goodbye to everyone at the New Dream and on the base, they were finalizing my orders. But I still had to leave Kaz in a kind way, and the more I thought about it all, the more confused I became.

My heart was twisted, and I couldn't decide what was best for her and for me. Finally, I told Kaz we were going to a really nice restaurant, not as good as her brother-in-law's, but the best I could find here in Yokosuka. She was her always perky self that evening. As much as I knew I needed to have the conversation, I just couldn't do it. So, we went home that night with my reluctance in tow. As was so often the case with me, I waited till the last moment. Then with time about up, I just jumped into it and began to discuss our future.

It was awful, just awful. She completely understood what I had decided to do. But nevertheless, her heart was broken, and I could sense it in her behavior. This was the first time I had to leave a girl like this, and I prayed it would be the last. It was so painful for her, and me. We agreed I would try to get back to Japan within a year, and she wanted to wait for me, but no promises were made. That was the last time I saw Kazue Nozawa.

CHAPTER 9

Pack Up, Time To Return

April 1970

Around the middle of April, I was officially transferred back to the US. My days in Vietnam were over finally. Thank God. Along with the remaining days left in the Navy, I would soon be finished with it all. I was foolishly looking forward to no longer having to deal with the memories and the little black box buried deep inside me. Somehow, I thought when I left the Navy, everything would be left behind, and it would be over.

No, there were thirty more years of dealing with it all before I could really say it was finally over.

It was actually a bit melancholy leaving Vietnam, and now Japan. With the final moment coming into view, it wasn't at all what I expected. For the first time in over three years, I allowed myself to think about it, all the guys, the blood, the body parts, the gore, the flying, getting shot at, killing, crying. It all came back. It wasn't so much I blamed myself for anything. I'd committed no war crimes, although I had seen a few, but I was still sad, just sad. Why, I asked myself, why be so sad? I should be happy. Incredible as it was, I had finished the journey. I was alive.

CHAPTER 10

Home, North Island

May 1970

But I was ahead of myself. I still had a couple of months left, and that depended on my being able to start school for the fall term. So, the first thing I did upon returning to North Island was talk to Lieutenant Commander Holmes. He understood exactly and gave me wonderfully good news. My acceptance at Indiana University was all that was needed to have me retired from active-duty on August 8, 1970. I had already received my acceptance from IU, so I was good to go. As I handed my acceptance letter from IU to Lt. Commander Holmes, we both just looked at each other. No words were spoken. The end was near.

I was still alive, just tired, very tired.

Because I was now a Petty Officer Second Class, I was permitted to stay in new genuinely nice quarters that had just been built. Finally, I had my own room, and a separate dining facility just for petty officers. What a treat that was. Barracks for me were a thing of the past, now that I only had a few months left in service. It was great to have my own sleeping quarters, where I could be left alone with my thoughts.

For the next couple of months, I had noticeably light duty, although I did have to endure a lengthy conversation with Lt. Commander Holmes about staying in the military. With my already fast advancement, he told me, I was practically guaranteed a shot as a Chief Petty Officer in the next few years. But I was done, tired of the killing, worn out from all the stress of being in combat.

I just wanted the whole thing to be put into the past, to be buried somewhere in my little black box, where hopefully it would never rear its ugly head. Well, I couldn't have been farther off. I wanted to leave it all behind, but it didn't want me to go anywhere, not just yet. First, I had to endure the nightmares and the silence about it all from everyone around me.

It might have seemed that silence was preferable to the loud protests from some people back home who believed we had turned into killers of women and children. But that was why we had to stay silent, not talk about what we'd been through. We wanted to seem normal, unaffected by what we'd been through—not crazy.

But the silence imposed on all of us was beyond destructive. We couldn't talk even among ourselves about the traumas.

Why, I asked, why. I really wanted to know why it all happened, and the more I asked myself, the more confusing it all became. There was only why, and why. But soon I was like so many others, telling myself just to stuff it all away, pretend the last years didn't happen. It was easier to stay silent, to be like everybody else, to grow my hair long, smoke dope, go to school, get a degree, move on. It did not happen, did it? Even if it did, I decided to keep it to myself.

CHAPTER 11

Man Animals At The Zoo

June 1970

Besides working out my position with the Navy, I had to fulfill a promise I had made if I returned alive. I was going to have a truly magnificent meal at a restaurant next to the harbor. So, very shortly after returning to the San Diego area, I made reservation for myself for a table overlooking the water.

It was the first opportunity in an awfully long time to put my dress whites uniform on. But they were needed at the restaurant. I didn't have a civilian suit, and I had no problem at all with formal naval attire. When I arrived, my table was ready for me, and I was so excited to be there alive.

I remembered I ordered a wonderful bottle of red wine. My great waiter asked if anyone else would be joining me tonight, and I told him no, it was just me, celebrating.

During the dinner, I was preoccupied by the same old questions. How in the hell did I pull this off, back, alive? What would I do with myself now, and just how was I going to accomplish my life's goals? Now I didn't have to answer to anybody but myself. Nobody was ordering me around, no one was watching me. No one gave a damn if I was doing what I should be, nobody but me. It wasn't scary, just disorienting.

But I reminded myself of the little black box, the memories. I knew I had to put everything in the little black box, to never talk about it, to never tell anyone. Unfortunately, I had a very hard time shutting it all away. But I knew that to survive in present-day society, somehow, I needed to do just that. There would be no welcome homes, and very quickly I learned to just keep my mouth shut, pretend my service just didn't happen, never show, or tell anybody about my medals or my experiences. In order to survive in a school setting, I had to change my looks and my demeanor. I needed to look more like a "hippy." That I thought at the time would be fun. I had been around Haight-Ashbury in San Francisco quite a lot, and I could get into the pot generation easily. At least I knew I liked marijuana.

Changing my looks, letting my hair grow a foot or two, that was all easy. But quickly I realized it took more than that. Conversation would require either strict silence or the ability to badmouth the military, the war, and everyone connected in any way with it. It would be hard to do, to pretend, to act like the last two years didn't happen, to keep quiet about the killing, the hurts, the sadness of war. My soul would not do well lying about it. Each time I tried to conceal what I'd been through, it was painful.

At the time I didn't think the advice was necessary. I could certainly figure out how to put one step in front of the other, couldn't I? Well, the answer was no, not always, not exactly. I subconsciously thought the war was somewhere in the distant past and need never to be thought about again. Wrong, oh, how wrong I was, how much more I was going to endure before it would finally be in the past.

After that wonderful harbor self-celebration, I returned to base to find there wasn't much of a place for me. Because I would be discharged soon, my unit had little for me to do. The kind of projects I was used to would sometimes take months to be prepped and completed. As luck would have it though, my idleness did not bother anybody all that much. In fact, most of the lower-ranked guys were I think a bit jealous of my status.

The time drug on, but mostly I had enough to do that I managed to stay busy. It was suggested that I might want to ship most of my stuff home ahead of time, as dragging all of it on a plane would be a lot of work. Good idea, and that was what I started to do.

One of the momentous changes I noticed was that if you left the base with your uniform on, you were asking for trouble. The war had really changed in the eyes of most Californians. It was more than just a little hard for me to swallow what the civilians thought about me. I didn't recall taking any child's life, and certainly I shot at no one that wasn't already shooting at me.

A lot of sailors while on leave would take a ferry from North Island to the downtown San Diego area. There was a USO hotel remarkable close to the waterfront where the ferry landed. The USO of course had rooms for rent, just like any other hotel, and was very inexpensive. The men would rent a room for the day and change their clothes so they would not look quite as military. How incredibly sad this was, but it was the order of the day. Anything military was evil, so even active-duty guys tried as hard as they could to hide the fact that they were part of the infamous machine of war.

On several occasions, I remember doing that myself. I would walk to the USO Hotel and get a room, and then change into civvies. On one occasion, I changed my uniform for civvies to go to the San Diego Zoo. They have one of the finest zoos in the country, and at that time it was free to the military.

I had been there several times before, and always found it a lot of fun. The original part of the zoo had been built in the 1920s with a wonderful art deco flavor. Most of my time at the zoo was spent just sitting and watching the animals in the cages, and the human animals wandering around that were not caged just yet.

On this day, the uncaged humans were there to cause mischief. Their first good target was a group of sailors that had gotten off one of the ships that were constantly coming and going from Southeast Asia. They all had their dress white uniforms on, and of course, became target number one. But these sailors were not having any of it. They quickly formed a square of men around the human animals. All at once, the human animals discovered that they had suddenly been caged themselves. It became a standoff. The sailors were not at all threatening, just firm.

The security guards quickly showed up and the troublesome human animals were removed to their very own cages, made just for troublesome human animals. That was just the way it was, all over the San Diego area at that time.

I just could not put it all together. I wasn't trying to hurt anyone. I was trying, I thought, to protect people that really needed protection, and furthermore, my country asked me to be of service to others. Murder was not on the list of things to do. As far as I can remember, I had never shot at anyone unless provoked. God, was I really so evil?

I began to try and figure out what my place in the world was going to be after leaving the military. What was I going to do with the fact that now I was considered nothing more than a murderer? I didn't think I could live with that, so what to do? It became clear that what I needed to do was going to be very distasteful at least.

What had I done? From high school to now, suddenly, everything had changed. I felt like an old man in many ways.

CHAPTER 12

John Wayne, The Duke

June – July 1970

In any case, I still had a few weeks to go before I had to handle these problems. But I did start to read as many newspapers as I could get my hands on. I felt the need to catch up to society, to be more grounded with what was going on in this country, in business, and in people. I read all the major newspapers up and down the California coast, and I also included the *Wall Street Journal*. It was also the last time I got to attend an event which was covered by the national news media.

This was an event being held at the Hotel Del Coronado. This massive hotel was now almost 100 years old. Originally built to accommodate guests vacationing along the coast, it was very close to a strand of beachfront that eventually extended right through what would become North Island Naval Base. The hotel was old, very famous, very expensive, and very exclusive. The building was absolutely gorgeous, built mostly of wood and covered with white clapboard. You could see it and the estate it sat on from a long way away. As I recall, one of the ballrooms could accommodate more than a thousand people.

The famous actor John Wayne, the Duke, rented the entire hotel for an entire weekend. For his guests, he invited any active-duty service member that wanted to spend the weekend with him and other stars. It was first come, first served, and the hotel was completely booked within hours.

The folks at Combat Camera Group knew enough to be early, very early, and we were. Mr. Wayne asked us to be in attendance and photograph the event. He saw to it that we had access behind stage, even his dressing room.

We of course were tickled to death that he had given us such exclusive access to him. Naturally, this infuriated the national news boys and girls, for they considered themselves to be the special angels of any event. This event made international news. Of course, everyone wanted access to his dressing room.

Only Pacific Fleet Combat Camera Group was given access backstage and to the Duke's dressing room. Everybody in our unit wanted to be in on the backstage photography, especially in his dressing room. It was there that we made the smallest of errors.

You see, by this time in his life, the Duke had lost all his hair. This little fact had been kept secret, and no pictures had ever been taken of him with his hair missing. Well, we didn't know this, and started taking pictures before he had donned his hair piece. This was not good.

Mr. Wayne jumped out of his dressing chair, and grabbed the first camera he came to, and unceremoniously ripped the film out of the camera. We all apologized and told him all our film would be screened and anything not to his liking would be destroyed at once. In the end, the Duke forgave us all, and we all ended up being kidded unceremoniously by Mr. Wayne. He had the absolute best sense of humor.

In fact, he was one of the greatest actors of the day and was responsible for many of the best westerns that had been made at that time. So, the guy was incredibly famous. In addition to his fame, he loved veterans and wanted to give a little back. The place was absolutely packed with military, and everyone anxiously awaiting his speech that evening which was to be given after dinner.

What a speech it was. It was one of the very few times I could remember being praised by a civilian while in the US Navy. His speech wasn't just grounded in patriotism. As it turned out, he was a damn good speechwriter and speaker. He made it clear to all of us, "It was unfair the despicable way you are being treated. Your job was to serve your country, bravely and without question. The blame for the war did not belong at your feet."

Thank God, someone finally told the truth.

This would be one of the last times I heard anyone speak kindly about us. Usually, we did the only thing we could do, keep silent, and talked to no one about our service. We knew to never, ever mention a medal we might have been awarded, as that would always guarantee we would be spit on or worse. It would cost the Vietnam veterans dearly; alcoholism and suicide became prevalent, and among the veterans from Vietnam, at rates that had never been seen before by a returning military force.

Sure, there was a small handful that wore their medals, went out and protested the war, and spat on the military. Happily, I can say that this was indeed a very small number of our soldiers, less than one in forty-five hundred, so I was told, and probably less than even that. Still, there were a few like the man who went into politics, a man sent home in disgrace as far as his boat team was concerned, given medals he didn't earn. He had put his crew in so much peril that finally it was decided to send him home before he had finished his complete term in Vietnam. That was meant to protect his boat crew from a failure to command in combat that could have hurt or killed them.

Unfortunately for him, it was all thoroughly documented by his former boat crew years later. But fortunately, this type of coward was exceedingly rare, thank God. The overwhelming majority of men who served in Vietnam did so with great courage, and never refused to face the enemy. Today, I am proud to be a part of this courageous group of warriors.

SECTION 10

Heading Home

*As a bee gathering nectar does
not harm or disturb the color and
fragrance of the flower; so do the
wise move through the world.*

Buddha

CHAPTER 1

Going Home

S oon my time in the military would be a thing of the past. I'd received orders to release me from active duty on August 8, 1970. In the meantime, I spent every evening in a bar, quietly taking my medicine so I could sleep. It was still working for the most part. Unfortunately, on occasion I would still have awful dreams, very vivid, which without exception left me awake and shaking. I knew I needed to get this under control and tried desperately to find a method that would accomplish this. No one was going to care about, love, or sleep with a guy whacked out, behaving like a little child with night terrors. So, I would wake myself and quietly have a stiff scotch, which usually did the trick.

As my day of separation from active duty approached, I needed to decide. Do I go home in uniform, or do I just put civvies on and avoid any potential problems at the airport? Finally, I decided to defy all of them. I was going home in my dress white uniform, with all ribbons, and my wings on display. I was not going to leave my military brothers by slinking away into the crowds.

When my final day arrived, I dressed as smartly as I could. Frankly, I felt like I could pass inspection. I was ship-shape and squared away. By this time, I was down to one sea bag, as everything else had been already sent home. After checking out of my quarters, I went to the headquarters of Pacific Fleet Combat Camera Group. It took some time to say goodbye to everyone. What a group.

The commander gave me one last chance to change my mind and stay. No, that was all I could say. I was tired, I was burnt out, and I knew if I stayed, I would not come back. Nevertheless, I was grateful for all the kindness he had extended to me and told him so. It was the dream of my life to be a part of this organization, and indeed, I would never forget it.

CHAPTER 2

My God Still Alive

After walking out the base gate for the last time, I took a cab
to San Diego International Airport. As we drove towards
the airfield, I could not help thinking, "My God, I am alive, still
alive, incredible. But why should I have been so fortunate?"

At the airport, I went directly to American Airlines' check-
in counter, got my ticket, gave them my bag, turned, and started
to walk towards the boarding area. I noticed a gaggle of boys
and girls, all dressed in orange robes like Buddhist monks. They
clearly were not, as they were dressed like a cross between a
monk and clown. Most of their robes were incorrectly worn, at
least as far as I tell.

They were just pretending to be monks, but they made me
to think of my dear friend in Thailand. I hoped he was well and
finding peace.

In addition to the 'playing monks,' there were also several groups of college-aged men and women scattered around in
small groups. One of them approached me and stuck a piece
of paper in my hand. I do not remember what he had to say,
but I do remember what his piece of paper said. It was a short

sermon, assuring me that it was not too late to be forgiven. Even though I was a part of Imperialist America, I would be permitted to join them in their fight to remove the generals, the killers, the politicians... blah, blah, blah. I wondered if I really wanted to go to college, to have to live around all of these silly protesters.

I thought better about saying anything and just kept walking towards the gate. When I got there, even though there were a lot of people waiting, I had no problem finding a seat. In fact, I had no problem finding half a row of seats. When I sat down, everyone around me moved away. Damn, I must smell bad or something. It became apparent that it was not cool to talk to me at all.

It was a short flight to San Francisco, where I would take a connecting flight to Indianapolis. The San Francisco Airport brought more of the same, except everyone that said anything to me must have thought I was suffering from a loss of hearing. They all felt it necessary to yell at me when talking, weird.

I expected the treatment, the anger, and the vitriol. This airport was where I had my first run-in with the haters, which I still hadn't quite gotten over. But that wasn't the universal response to me. To my amazement, when I went to check-in, another pilot on the Indianapolis route welcomed me home again. So, the world was not completely mad, thank God.

CHAPTER 3

Another World Home

I had not told anybody when I would be discharged and home-- with one exception. My ever-constant friend Vin said he would pick me up at the airport. He had already told me that I was free to stay with him if I wanted. It didn't take long; I took him up on his offer, and indeed, he had a nice room all ready for me in his house. The beautiful home had been built just a few years ago and was just outside of Noblesville overlooking the White River.

He handed me the keys to his car when we finally made it home. "Go see your family when you are ready. I'm sure they will be happy you are home, and still in one piece. I certainly am."

Yeah, I was home, but being home seemed a lot like being from outer space, looking in at all the humans. Somehow, I just didn't belong, did I? But what could I say? At least I did not have to worry about being shot at. And if I took my medication, I could sleep.

That evening Vin introduced me to Lonnie, a person that was staying with him and slept in a bedroom on the lower level. He seemed like a nice enough bloke, and we hit it off right away.

During the next few weeks, I tried to begin to assimilate back into a place where the military would be completely avoided, and never spoken of any more than necessary, or not at all. Vin's home was built similar to a Swiss chalet. Along one side of the house the windows were placed so that no matter where you were you had a beautiful view of the river.

Although the house had been built for just Vin, it was quite large. He enjoyed having guests stay over for a day or so, and sometimes for much longer. He was a people person, and loved to play his grand piano, which was located in the enormous great room. At this time, I was his only permanent guests. But it was not a lonely home, because he always had a full home full during his long weekends. The party started on Friday afternoon and generally didn't stop until Sunday, and I loved joining in.

It was so odd. Here I was back home, no longer wearing combat boots and green fatigues. But I didn't feel like I was home, it was now all so different. It was like a dream; I just couldn't understand it all. All I knew for sure was that if I got fairly smashed every evening, I could stop thinking, stop dreaming. Fortunately for me, the booze still worked, like a natural on/off switch. The only difference was now I had to be more careful driving at night. But I didn't have a car of my own just yet, so no big deal.

CHAPTER 4

Trying, Failing, Trying, To Get It Right

The first thing I needed to accomplish was get enrolled and set up my schedule for school. At the time, IU had a downtown Indianapolis campus. I figured that it would be best to take at least the first semester there, just in case things did not go as planned. Following the conventional or what I thought was the conventional first-year schedule, I started with Psychology 101, History of the Western World 101, and American Literature 101.

Of course, I had not a clue how difficult would be taking these classes right out of the gate. It was not long before my ship was sinking. I guess I wasn't as smart as I thought. In fact, I was failing.

After giving it a lot of thought, I decided to drop out. As luck would have it, I did not have any idea how you were supposed to leave or resign from school. On Friday afternoon, after one of my classes, I went over to the administration offices to "resign my enrollment."

While I didn't fully understand just yet, at IU like most of the universities at that time, the distaste, and in many cases outright hatred for vets, while under the surface, was no less real. There I stood like I was in the military, asking permission to "resign my admission." Everyone thought that this idiot was just what they needed for Friday afternoon entertainment, a military clown.

Fortunately, one of the people listening as I stumbled and tripped all over myself, was Mrs. House. The stars were all aligned and in my favor that day.

She came to the front and ordered me to her office and told me to sit. Very military-like. I loved it. I finally had someone that understood what I was trying to do. As she sat at her desk, she began by introducing herself.

Next, she wanted to know what I had been doing while in the military. So, I quickly gave her the edited version of my last almost four years. I told her I really wanted to try college, but obviously I was not qualified, and I would like to respectfully resign my admission. Hopefully some other, more qualified person would be able to take my slot.

She asked a few more questions before excusing herself. In a matter of minutes, she reappeared with a pile of papers in her hand, and she asked, "Why are you starting with these courses?"

"Ma'am, I just was told they would be appropriate at this time, so these are the ones I chose."

"I see that that you have not been in a school setting for over four years. And you have not been given any personal advice on what courses you should be taking your first semester?"

"No, ma'am, you are the first person I have had the pleasure of speaking to about this matter."

She tapped the papers on her desk. "Well, Mr. Vincent, according to your military record here, your mental aptitude is way above average. So, I doubt the problem is qualification. You are more than bright enough."

I shook my head. "But Mrs. House, it's not that I'm slacking off. I try to study four to six hours on days I have classes, and much more than that on days when I don't have class."

"I'm sure you do. What's your first name, Mr. Vincent?"

"Oh, sorry, it's Rick."

She made some marks on a course catalog and handed it to me. "Okay, Rick, here is what we are going to do. I am going to have you go home and pick out twelve hours of courses. But notice that I marked some courses, and these are the only ones you can take. These are all courses which a first-year student who has not been in a classroom for over four years should be choosing from."

Obediently I looked at her suggested courses. She recommended replacing English Literature of the Eighteenth Century and European History of the Eighteenth Century and a couple others with courses much less intense. I was relieved. "Okay."

She added, "Then I want you to be here first thing Monday, and we will discuss further your problem. In addition, you should know that your problem can be easily fixed, and I am going to see to it that you get the opportunity to excel."

I replied, "Well, Mrs. House, thank you for all your help. If you think I'm worthy, I certainly will follow your advice. What time is early to you, Mrs. House?"

"I want you here, bright-eyed and bushy-tailed, at 0800 hours." She meant exactly that. The military terminology made me smile. "Yes, ma'am, 0800, Monday, got it."

Finally, I had found someone that was on the same page with me. Mrs. House had reached out and given me that helping hand that made it possible to succeed. She realized that while I was well read, I had been out of a school setting for almost four years. She counseled that I shouldn't jump into the deep end of education headfirst, but rather catch up in a slower, more deliberate way. She gave me time to learn how to learn.

CHAPTER 5

The Weekend

College was very different than my time in the navy. But one thing was the same. My time off was spent with people who wanted to drink and party. Fine with me. Every evening I made sure that I had taken enough medicine to let me just pass out. At the time I thought I was in heaven, no cares, no worries, great music, and plenty of scotch.

While it wasn't the beginning of my deal with the devil, it was the beginning of a drinking ritual that would go on for over thirty more years. Every evening, I drank enough booze to allow me to not dream, to keep it all at bay.

My housemate, Vin, had always been in love with the piano and jazz. One of the constant weekend guests was Al Reeve. Man, this guy could play a piano. He was a professional pianist, and his first love was jazz piano. Now at that time, Vin had just acquired a grand piano, which was centered in the great room. This was nine feet long and what a sound it could put out. The music that came out of that piano when Al was there was absolutely to die for.

Like me, Al liked his alcohol straight and a good joint to go with it. With these supplied, we would all be given a two-hour jazz concert. Sometimes these would go on for several hours more. The jazz that came from him would almost make you cry; it was so beautiful. Among the Indianapolis crowd of musicians, Al was considered the best, and he could have made it on the national scene, he was that good. Most of what he played were his own compositions.

On occasion a bunch of the musicians would get together on Saturday evening at one of the dives on Indiana Avenue, and then come to the house and play together after the bars had closed, usually until the morning sun started to appear on the horizon. Musicians all over town would show up to play with Al. My God, he was the best, and the people that knew jazz would not disagree.

Usually, somebody would volunteer to cook, other than Vin, who was awful in that department. Always the food was magnificent, and the laughter was contagious.

People started showing up on Friday afternoon, and most stayed until late in the afternoon on Sunday. This was definitely not time for me to study. It was party time.

CHAPTER 6

Mrs. House Saves The Day

Despite the wild weekend, come Monday morning I was back in Mrs. House office at 0800 hours, as required. I really liked this elderly woman. She was no bullshit, straight to the point, and obviously smart. Before we got started with my academic problems, I just had to ask her and so I did.

"Mrs. House, I certainly don't mean to pry, and you can just tell me to shut up, if desired. But I was wondering if you had a connection with the military. You certainly know the language, and you have, for the first time made me feel comfortable speaking about my issues."

She nodded, "Well, son, I do have a connection with military culture. You see, my husband worked for years with the Army, in Washington. I have watched the treatment our veterans are getting and find it despicable the treatment you are currently receiving. In your case, we are going to fix that with a little effort on your part."

"Gosh, your husband must be quite the guy. I would love to meet him someday."

"He passed away several years ago, but nevertheless, thank you, he was always my guiding star." She looked down at her papers. "Now, let's take a fresh look at your problem. First, I have looked at not only your current classes, but I've also looked at your military records as applies to your educational situation. Son, you have more than enough smarts. In fact, you have a lot more than most who have recently started college. So, you should not be getting failing grades."

I sighed. "But Mrs. House, I certainly am, and I've studied around the clock in some cases. I cannot explain it, but when I am evaluated, the questions are almost never what I had tried to prepare for."

"Stay calm, Rick. The reason you are struggling I believe, is not for lack of trying. You are taking courses that you're not prepared to take. You see, you should be taking courses that most first-year students find a lot more inviting and will teach you how to play the game."

"What game? When I study, it doesn't seem to do any good at all."

"Because you do not understand the game, and how the system is designed to humble you. Even more, it is designed to enhance your professor's standing in the academic community. So basically, don't focus so much on the readings. Focus more on what has been said by the professor in the classroom. You need to change the way you take notes and always realize that this is simply the way to play *the* game. For example, with a college exam, it will touch on the subject matter, but it will be even more concerned with what the prof said in his lectures."

"So that's the game?"

"Yes. Now tell me. What do you want to get out of college?"

"Well, Mrs. House, I wanted to major in business or economics. It is my understanding that IU has an exceptionally good business school, and I was also thinking I might go on to get a master's as well. Now I'm not so sure."

"Rick, that is all possible. You have the life experience and the will, and that puts you way ahead of most of the others. This is what we need to do first--change your courses."

I protested, "The semester has already started. I can't change now."

"Yes, you can if you have the approval of a counselor, and you do have the approval. Fortunately, you came in here to 'resign' just in the nick of time."

"OK. What do I do first?"

She laughed. "First, lose the word resign. If you were in the military setting, it would work, but not here. Let's change your curriculum to courses that you will need for your major but just aren't quite so hard. This will give you the opportunity to learn how to play the game. I've taken our course curriculum book and circled the courses to choose from. You will notice that they also give you the hours earned on completion. Do you understand how that works?"

"Yes, I do, and that would be fine."

"Notice, we are now on civilian time, no more military. Do not worry, you will catch on. See you at 1:30 PM."

Of course, Mrs. House, my saint, was exactly right. After we made these course changes, my grades went from failing to all A's. After the time spent with Mrs. House, I never had problems maintaining a B+ average and graduated with a 3.8 out of 4 grade point average.

I remember that Dad had taught me to always do the best that I could, and it would always be enough. It took years, decades really, for this simple lesson to have meaning. It was peculiar that Dad was so often right. But the simple lessons he taught were so beneficial to me long after he had passed away. The lesson taught to me by Mrs. House, Indiana University counselor, was the same, only more cynical.

Even as my grades finally improved, my life in general was not improving. Naturally, I had to take my medicine every night in order to sleep. Sure, it worked like a charm, but there were evenings when I wanted to stay sober, like when I was with a girl.

So occasionally I did not drink as much before a date, and usually it was a disaster when that happened. More often than not, I would have to slip out of bed in the middle of the night and take my medicine, increasing amounts of alcohol. No matter what, I needed to keep the devil at bay. This need to drink was beginning to become too large a problem to live with, but I didn't know what else I could do.

CHAPTER 7

What's Wrong With This Picture

By this time, the war was winding down, and the country was slowly starting to return to peace. But there wasn't much peace for vets. We were absolutely despised, and especially on college campuses where there were lots of anti-war groups. This was the period of constant rioting, at the Democratic National Convention in Chicago and elsewhere.

While the VA did offer help for returning Vietnam veterans, at that time the VA Centers were being run by people that had been appointed by left-wing Democrats, who of course despised anything military. To make matters worse, they made the jobs permanent, so these military haters could not be removed easily from the VA.

If you came home with any kind of undiagnosed medical problem, your chances of being properly taken care of were a crapshoot, at best. Even those with problems that had been identified during the war were likely to be treated with disdain.

The only thing I could do, the only thing most of the vets could do, was just keep on keeping on. The smart vet play was to just not say anything, stay silent, grow your hair long, and try to just blend in. Of course, most did just that. Sometimes it just was not possible, and those guys ended up alone. In my case, I learned to play the game, wear long hair, and bib overalls, say nothing, just keep my mouth shut.

I felt this was the only solution, the only choice I could make and stay on a college campus. I even tried to dismiss any lingering thoughts about my service, and to be as close to "'normal" as possible. At one point I even entertained the idea of joining an anti-war group, but this was really a bridge too far. I just couldn't dishonor my fellow vets, no matter what.

Even with much improved grades, I was still feeling lost and like I didn't belong. Hell, the truth was, I just was not ready for regular life, so I just gave up. Gave up on me, gave up on friendships and everything. I decided to leave, to run.

Now instead of trying my best and following Dad's advice to stick with it, I became a runner. It was at the time the easiest thing to do, just run. Running away from myself, however, turned out to be impossible.

SECTION 11

Full Circle

*True love never has a happy ending,
because there is no ending to true love.*

Alexander The Great

CHAPTER 1

Now What

Summer 1971

With the spring of 1971 rapidly approaching, I got a call from my brother David who now lived in Bristol, New Hampshire. He was kind enough to extend me an invitation to visit, and I accepted.

At the time I had just bought a Fiat two-seater. It did get good gas mileage, but that is about all it got. It rarely started if the temperature was below thirty-two degrees. In any case, I filled the back seat with my clothes and headed east with no intention of ever coming back to Indiana.

I must say my brother David was quite generous and allowed me to stay as long as I cared to. Shortly after arriving I purchased a Honda 360 motorcycle; it was cheap but seemed to run fine, and more importantly spring was just coming on.

After catching up with David and his wife, I must have slept for a week. Living in Bristol, New Hampshire was a change I really needed, more than I could have imagined. It was a tiny community but close to a lake that was surrounded by summer homes. With Criss-Craft boats, the finest, and fine cars in the drive, Bristol was a very wealthy summer community.

One of the local amenities was a little ice cream and sandwich stop, located on the road into town. I liked it and soon got into the habit of stopping for an ice cream cone, about every afternoon. There was a cute college-aged girl running the counter. I flirted with her, and she returned that with flirts of her own. Soon we became involved, Lynn was just what I needed. We quickly fell in love and started seeing each other daily.

She lived just down the road and right on the lake. After a short while, I was introduced to her mother, who I very much liked. She had the most beautiful smile and was so easy to like. He husband had a gorgeous Chriss- Craft inboard motorboat, completely restored, her stepdad's favorite toy. As I recall, he was a Wall Street player, and yes, that boat was downright beautiful and unbelievable fast.

We made love like I had never experienced. She was gentle, sweet, and kind. At some point she told me she had a boyfriend at Yale, so I knew our time was limited, but it was the best of the best. I needed to be cared for, I needed to be loved, and Lynn generously gave me her affection.

When she left for school, I once again was like a leaf in the afternoon breeze. But she had her road to follow, and I had to follow mine. By this time, I had decided to attend University of Vermont, but needed to have had a residency in the state for at least one year to afford the tuition. By this time my brother had moved to Vermont, and I became a resident of his home. I had agreed to work for a contractor who lived in Bristol, so that is where I stayed during the week. My thought was I would work until the first snow, then spend the winter in Europe.

CHAPTER 2

Plans Changed-- Do Over

Fall 1971

It was a good plan, I thought, and my first week of work went by uneventfully. When the weekend came, I thought I would take a trip to Concord. It was a bright sunny morning, and my bike started right up, even though I had not started it for days. Off I went down this country road up in the foothills, and the wind felt great.

As I went around the last curve before the highway, I lost it and had a bike out of control. Fortunately, I was not going extremely fast, but slid right into a large boulder. I knew right away that my collarbone was fractured. With a lot of struggles, I got the bike upright and luckily, it started at once. Now all I had to do was ride it back to the house. With only one hand. In a lot of pain, I managed to get back to the house and parked.

Now my workdays were over, my trip to Europe was toast, and I really didn't have enough money to get an apartment for the winter. So, with little or no choice I called Vin in Indiana. He graciously told me my room was still just the way I had left it.

Back in Indiana, I tried to keep myself as busy as possible, and I don't think I complained to anyone. Within a month or so, the cast had been removed. But the doctor warned me to use my arm lightly for at least the next month, so as not to cause the break to open again.

It was at this point I decided to sell all my photo equipment. I had two Haliburton cases full of cameras and lenses. I had reasoned with myself that it was time. Still, it was painful. I didn't know if I would be able to talk about life, if not with pictures. But I knew, or thought I knew, that it was time to abandon my past, to leave it all behind. The war, photography, leave it all behind. Like so many veterans, I was truly struggling with my past. Memory of Vietnam was still there and would rear its ugly head unexpectedly.

In hindsight, it was irrational to do that. But giving up the past would not be as bad as the nightmares, the little black box that kept bringing forth old memories. Would I ever be able to bury the black box? God, I hoped so, someday, somehow.

CHAPTER 3

Now What

Late Fall 1971

Once I was back at Vin's, I needed to get myself enrolled in school, again. Fortunately, I was still considered a resident of Indiana. My past grades were more than satisfactory, and now it was just a matter of going to Bloomington, Indiana University's main campus, and re-enrolling. As soon as I got to Bloomington, I enrolled for the coming spring semester, and then went to campus housing and to find somewhere to park my butt while at school.

By this time, I had acquired a 1963 Chevy, which I had purchased from a good ole boy on the south side of Noblesville. It ran great but had been in a wreck, and the guy I bought it from had replaced the hood, a fender on one side, along with one of the doors. So, it was now a three-color car with all the replacement parts, a fender, door, and hood, coming from a local junk yard.

I didn't care much about its looks as long as it ran well. The person I bought it from was a garage mechanic, and the car ran great. For one hundred and fifty dollars, it was the best car I ever owned, but it was sure ugly.

The day I went looking for campus housing, it was a rainy day, and cold, with a strong northwest wind. Housing was in a small office, with little ads all over one wall. There was only one other person there at the time, and he was looking, too.

As I stood there looking for a place, I realized I should have done this sooner. There was nothing posted. Then the big, heavyset guy standing next to me pointed at one of the remaining ads: "Two-bedroom trailer, Foxe's Trailer Park, call 336-1409."

"Thanks man, for pointing out that lead." Then I introduced myself, "My name's Rick Vincent, would you like to look at it with me?"

"Cool, sure, but I don't have a car."

I was glad to be able to say, "No problem, I do."

"Wow, really cool, let's go, wait, maybe we should call first."

"Absolutely, we should. Wonder if they have a phone around here."

He pointed to the opposite corner of the room, where there was a phone for students to use.

When we got to the trailer park, we found the old two-bedroom trailer, beat all to hell, with a For Rent sign on the door. Interestingly the front door faced a Black church, Brethren Behold. I had never attended service in a Black church but had always been curious about their services. It looked to me as so much more fun than the solemnity of white churches. The trailer was satisfactory for both of our needs, so we gave the owner a deposit, and we each got a key.

Wait, I need to tell you about my new roommate, Blaine Newcomb. He was a big guy, with broad shoulders and a tall meaty body. He was the son of two college professors, both of whom taught at Ball State University, which was about seventy-five miles up the road.

Blaine was incredibly smart but did not have a lick of common sense. There were times when I just had to shake my head in wonder, how in the world did he get this far. What a doofus. He had never cooked a thing, or used a vacuum, or cleaned a sink. Otherwise, he had a brilliant mind.

Man, he was scary smart. He would read a textbook in no time at all, and could then answer questions from the book, proving that he not only read it, but he also understood it.

CHAPTER 4

Blaine Newcomb, Master Chef

Early 1972

Blaine soon became one of the best friends I could hope for. He was kind, and he wanted to get his commonsense skills refined, and I was the man for the job. We both agreed to split all expenses regarding our new home. The first thing we needed to do was fill the refrigerator, and get some of the necessities, like soap and booze. I decided to take him to a local grocery store to stock up. He was amazed that I knew what all the cans and jars were to be used for. At least he did recognize peanut butter and jelly.

I explained to him I had no intention of cooking all the meals for him, so he was going to have to learn, and I would be the teacher. To begin our first lesson, I bought a box of pizza mix, and told him to go pick out some kind of meat to put on it as a topping. Regretfully, I didn't pay any attention to his choice.

When we returned to the trailer, I told him he would be cooking tonight. He was as excited as a little kid being given a piece of candy. First, I explained we would need to use the aluminum disk that looked like a cookie sheet. We had just purchased a new one, although he didn't have a clue what it was

344

for. I told him to wash it before we used it for the first time. He thought this was extremely odd, as it was brand new and looked pretty clean to him.

This led to a discussion of germs, which you couldn't see with the naked eye. Blaine did learn amazingly fast, but he had never had anyone explain to him basic things, like how to make a hot cup of tea. I kid you not.

I told him I would help with his first meal, and to begin he needed to read the instructions on the back of the box, carefully. I helped him mix the dry ingredients for the dough and showed him how to roll it out and get it onto the pizza pan, now washed.

Then I handed him a can of pizza sauce, told him to spread the sauce evenly all over the dough. This he did, without too much help from me. Next, I told him to sprinkle the cheese all over the sauce, and then I told him to get the meat he purchased at the store and place it in small pieces all over the pizza and then put it into the oven which I had just shown him how to use.

In the meantime, I sat down at the kitchen table and started to sort out books I was sure I would soon need. After a brief period, Blaine was jumping around yelling, "I did it, I did it." So, we pulled the newly created pizza out of the oven to cut it up and prepare for dinner. There was a fairly round pizza, cooked about right-- with a topping of baloney. What could I say? This baloney pizza did not look all that bad. When we sat down to eat, I must say, it did not taste that bad. Blaine had just prepared his first meal, fried baloney pizza. Well, it was a start.

As we sat there eating, I thought, I have a great guy to share the trailer with. Blaine was going to work out fine, just fine.

CHAPTER 5

The Job

Summer 1972

The next week was spent running back and forth from home and moving my clothes and school supplies into the trailer. Also, I found a place to put the car during the day while at school. In addition, I walked all over campus, trying to learn where everything was. While walking around, I began to think about finances. I had the GI Bill to use, and if I was a touch frugal, it could be enough for everything. But I began to think I needed just a little more extra cash. So, I walked over to the office that managed the federal student work program.

They needed a short form filled out to qualify for the program, which I immediately did, and qualified on the spot with the use of my dog tags to verify my status with the GI Bill. I was told, all the slots that were then available had been filled. But I filled the forms out anyhow. Man, was I glad I did.

It turned out that the federal program required them to pay you the reasonable value of whatever skill level of work you were applying for, which for me would be photography. I let them know that I took pictures for the government, mostly in

Southeast Asia, mostly as a photojournalist. It turned out that a professional photojournalist was rated at $29 per hour, which at the time was an enormous amount, so that was what they had to pay me.

Wait, it gets even better. They also had to place me in a job commensurate with my skill level. International photojournalists are paid a lot of money, it turns out, so I was placed at the top of the food chain of hourly employees at IU.

To add to my joy about all this loot, as luck would have it the TV station, WTIU, Public Broadcasting, needed a photographer. Was I willing to work for PBS? Yep. I got the job.

The TV department was broken up into two sections, one in which the employees working for PBS were located, and another for students in training for a career in TV journalism. They hired me as a PBS employee, not as a student, and said they would work around my short hours. The station had never gotten their hands on an actual experienced photographer. The fact I had worked on the international stage made it even better as far as they were concerned.

The guy I would be working for, Mel, oversaw the station art department. As luck would have it, we hit it off immediately, and over the next few years we became good friends. He told me they had not even been looking, after the last photographer left. They really could not afford it. He was a little concerned about being able to afford me, in fact, but I was only going to cost them $1.50 per hour. The Federal government would pay the remainder of the salary up to reasonable value. For once in a long time, the stars were all in alignment for me.

When I gave him a quick account of the work, I had been doing for the last several years in the military, he was even happier. The fact that I could do both still and motion pictures work and understood how to blend the two if needed was a very big bonus as far as he was concerned.

Even after all I had been through, I still had no idea the value of my worth. I guess it was those old doubt demons from grade school that I was only going to make a good garage mechanic, never run the garage. But I was starting to blossom, if only just a little bit-- if only I could put Vietnam in the rearview mirror and keep it there.

I was only beginning to realize the past was a problem, and I needed to somehow address it.

CHAPTER 6

The Golden Girl

1972

The students who were interested in becoming an announcer after graduation had their makeup rooms right down the hall from my darkroom. One of the students often getting makeup applied was a beautiful young woman who indeed would go on to the national stage. She would become a major TV announcer for one of the big three in New York and remain on the national stage for years.

Rarely have I met such a pompous ass. She felt her beauty was a valuable asset for the station, and this made her arrogant. She rarely followed orders completely. This was a big no-no, especially as she was still unknown. Naturally, she had a difficult time working with the rest of the crew, in this case students trying to achieve a good grade without the use of good looks. This was an unrecognizable problem for her. She was used to coasting on her looks. But beauty really does only go so far, and she ran out of it with me.

One day, Mel told me they needed still photos of little Ms. Jane P. on the set stage. Could I please go downstairs to the studio and get a few pictures before they went on the air. Sure, no problem, I had done this dozens of times. But Ms. Jane P. was having none of it. Her importance just would not allow a peon, a photographer, to be on the set before airtime.

As all the students working on the set watched, Ms. Jane P. had to endure a serious attitude adjustment, dispensed by me. I simply told our little golden girl that I had collaborated with Presidents and everyday dirt farmers, and as a consequence, I knew the difference between arrogant bullshit and the truth. I finished my tirade with, "Little Ms. Jane, you think your shit doesn't stink, but I assure you it does. And if you want decent photos of you, any of which could end up at PBS in Washington, I suggest you sit down, put a nice expression on your face, and I'll be gone very quickly, got it?" Indeed, she did get it, and not a peep came out of her mouth until airtime.

I followed Ms. Jane's career for a while. She did make it onto the national stage, which was quite an accomplishment. However, I heard she was always at odds with stage and set people and didn't learn a thing.

CHAPTER 7

Summer Dreams

1972

My second attempt at school was everything I dreamed it would be. It was heaven, absolutely heaven. I had a blast that year, and I decided to stay in Bloomington and take summer classes as well. In the summer there were not nearly as many students on campus, and the courses were shorter and consequently a lot easier. I signed up for all the courses I felt would be harder if I'd have to take them in fall semester.

I also discovered that most of the classes were given early in the morning, leaving the rest of the day open. Often the TV station also did not have as much to do with most of the students gone, and Mel let me do most of the work when I wanted to. At night, with nobody around, the studio was always quiet, and he got in the habit of putting anything that was needed in my darkroom to be photographed as I saw fit. I always made sure that everything would be sitting on his desk by morning.

That summer I joined the IU Sailing Club. Each day we would take one of the smaller boats out on Lake Lemon, and sail for hours at a time. I knew little about sailing but took to it quickly. There is nothing quite like sailing. Using just wind to move about is incredible. I became part of the wind, moving slowly around, going into and out of every little crevice. Marvelous, and what joy it would bring to me. The wind would always die down around noon and so we went in.

Sailing brought me the same peace that I had found on Mt. Fuji, quiet, gentle wind. This was life to be lived.

CHAPTER 8

Limestone Pits

Summer 1972

After sailing in the morning, we would often pile into my old car and head for one of the limestone strip mines. Southern Indiana is set on a bed of limestone, so when one mine was played out, the limestone miners would move to another site. The first pit would fill with crystal clear water, almost always from a spring that had broken through deep below the bottom of the pit. Some of these pits were quite large. The favorite of ours at the time was about two hundred yards long by around seventy-five feet wide. The walls on each side were mostly very smooth, as they had used this pit for a long time.

One side had rock close to the surface, but the other side was mostly straight down, to the bottom. Some places it was thirty to forty feet down from the surface, and so the water was often more than thirty feet deep. What fun to drop off a thirty, forty-foot-high wall into crystal-clear, ice-cold water after sunning for an hour or two. It was just the thing to get you refreshed.

Usually, we went to the quarry and just stripped, both male and female. Nobody seemed to care all that much about nudity.

On occasion high school kids would show up and wander off towards the end where they had some privacy and didn't have to look at naked college boys and girls. It was a big quarry, and so we just left each other alone.

This one particular day I had just jumped into the water, swam to the end, and decided to lie on a flat rock which was towards the end where the high schoolers usually hung out. But today, they were not around.

Well, with the cool water, combined with the warm flat rock, this was a perfect place for me to lie down and sun for a bit. I quickly dozed off. During my brief nap, the high schoolers all appeared. I lifted my head just a little and thought, "Well, we will have to just co-habitat for a while, but I should probably swim back down to the other end in just a minute."

As I was lying there, one of the girls jumped off a small rock into the water. She swam about twenty-five yards out. When she went in, I knew right away she was in trouble, cramped and sinking. Without hesitation, I jumped into the water and went to her, got her under one of my arms so she could breathe. Then I started swimming back to shore, but as we were moving towards shore, she began to thrash around just a little. She was resisting. When I finally got her close to shore, I realized what the thrashing was all about.

She was embarrassed by my lack of clothing, but she still needed to be saved. So, she only moved around a small bit, until I got closer to shore. Then she became a whirling dervish. A couple of her girlfriends jumped in to protect her, I guess, from the college kid with no clothes. Nevertheless, I managed to see to it that she made it back up onto one of the large stones before I went back to the gang I had come with.

"Thank you" was not needed for me; it was more than enough that I was able to help. In the end, I just wanted to make sure the girl was back on firm ground and safe. It was a good reminder from Dad, "Be helpful, always, and always try to help your fellow man, if you can. Thanks, are never needed, and never required. But being ready to offer a helping hand was different, always required. It was our duty to do what we could do to help others."

CHAPTER 9

Mike

1973

With the money I was making at the TV station, along with the GI Bill, I had way more than enough. So that summer my brother Mike came to share my apartment. He was now enrolled at IU and needed a place to stay for the fall term, which I was happy to provide. By this time, I had put together a really fun place, furnishing mostly with stuff I bought at auction. The apartment was just down from First Street and Henderson, in a beautiful old brick apartment building.

I really very much enjoyed living with Mike for a time. It was fun to make all kinds of desserts for him and his friends. With someone to cook for, I could also put on much more elaborate feasts, which I must say everybody seemed to enjoy a lot. What can be better than to smoke a few joints and then with plenty of good booze, have an enormous feast. In hindsight, I guess it was such a relief to give back to somebody. It was a clue that not everything had been lost in the war. I could still be kind and enjoy providing for others. At the time, I thought of my desire to cook as just a weird oddity.

As I recall, Mike could still not cook much at all. As a house-warming, I baked him his favorite pie, shoofly pie, a dark sugar cream pie that the Amish were famous for. My high school girl-friend's mother was raised Amish, and we would sometimes go up north for summer family get-togethers in Mishawaka. With a little bit of help from her, I was able to get a good recipe. It turned out to be fairly simple, but man, was that pie delicious.

School was once again everything I had dreamed it would be. For the next two and a half years, I had the time of my life. There were just a couple of hiccups every now and then. On evenings where I didn't get quite drunk enough, sometimes a memory would escape from my little black box. But most of the time, I took my medication and had not much trouble with the memories.

It had now become second nature to have several drinks before bed at night. I kept sensing that this couldn't be good, but I really thought I had no other choice. The devil was in charge, or that's what I believed in the moment. Without my medicine, the memories became worse with time, not better as I had hoped.

CHAPTER 10

My Last Photo Shoot

Late spring 1974

One of the very last jobs Mel asked me to do was take pictures of Bill Monroe, the guy that created bluegrass music, for a documentary that PBS wanted to make about his life. It was supposed to be aired later in the year nationwide on all PBS stations. I couldn't think of anything that would be more an honor, and I was immediately on board. They were going to record some of his music during the festival he put on every year close to his hometown of Bean Blossom, Indiana which was between Bloomington and Nashville, Indiana. His family had lived there for a long time, and he purchased a sizeable piece of land in order to have the festival every year.

What a terrific event it turned out to be. There were individual bluegrass artists and entire bands from all over the world. The cool thing was the preponderance of them seemed to be from Nashville, Tennessee, or Memphis, but there were also a lot of people from all over the place. I photographed a band from Japan and several others from other countries.

They all wandered from one camp site to another, playing their instruments, singing, and of course, drinking. It was marvelous. Everyone was having the time of their lives, including me.

This event was put on by Monroe for the players of bluegrass music, and for those of us who just wanted to listen. He had been putting this affair together for many years, and as I understood it, every year it got better and better. Now he had in attendance the best of the best from all over the world.

In the end it was a way for him to get every group, every player in the world together, just to play a little bluegrass and enjoy each other's music.

Usually at an event of this kind, you must be careful of just who you are shooting, because most artists were worried about proprietary rights when somebody was playing one of their creations. But I did not once have someone tell me not to take their picture. It seemed that the only thing they cared about was getting a few licks in with Bill Monroe, and a lot of them did just that.

When Bill showed up early in the evening, he introduced himself to me. A big man, he was dressed in a fancy embroidered western-style coat with a western hat and boots, and a beautiful guitar over his shoulder. He was just "down home," that is the only way to describe him, and he kindly asked me if I would need anything. Without hesitation, I told him, "Do not let me get in anybody's way." I assured him that the pictures would be as good as possible, and that I had done this for a good while and thought it would work out just fine. Also, I mentioned that the film would all be going to Washington for editing and use in the upcoming documentary about bluegrass, and how it all began with him in the late 1930s.

There was a nice stage set up, and I asked him if he intended to play on stage today. He said, "We will be putting together some informal bands in a while, and then we'll all head for the stage and entertain these folks until the sun comes up in the morning, I suspect."

To keep all his musical guests safe, he had a few guys set up in front of the stage where it had been roped off for about six feet, so there wouldn't be too many fans get too close. He introduced me to his facilities manager and told him I could go anywhere I wanted without asking.

That day, I shot well over a hundred rolls of thirty-six image film. Now that is a heck of a lot of film, but I was having such an enjoyable time, and the pictures I could visualize were everywhere. That was the day I fell in love with bluegrass music and have enjoyed it ever since.

This would be Bill Monroe's last big event. He died not too long after. And it would be the last time I shot a story of any consequence. Shortly after this, I turned my cameras back in to the TV station and left for home.

Filming that bluegrass event was the end of a big part of my life. Without my cameras or reason to shoot, over time I began to not see pictures. Now movement was just movement, the sky was just the sky. But back inside me, somehow, I knew I wasn't finished just yet. It never occurred to me that it might be over thirty years before I even looked at a decent camera.

CHAPTER 11

Baby Killer

There was only one time when I had a problem about the war while at school. After a couple of semesters at IU, I had found a nice apartment on Henderson and First Street. It was only a few blocks from campus, but it was a long hike to the TV station. On this day, I was running behind and decided to use my bike to speed things up.

The night before I'd had an awful dream from the black box buried deep inside me. So, I was not in a good mood to start with. It was a beautiful fall day, with a gorgeous afternoon sun beating down. As I crossed the last main street into campus, the street with a lot of the fraternities' houses, someone from one of the fraternity houses right on the corner yelled at me a disparaging remark.

At that time, I was wearing my leather flight jacket, which had been given to me when I was awarded my aircrew wings. These jackets are now somewhat of a cherished item on E-Bay today, and can cost a lot, but at that time not so much.

This little turd sitting on his frat house front porch yelled at me something about my being a "Fucking Baby Killer." I just snapped. It was the only time I had ever lost control, but I did. The bike and I came to a complete stop in the middle of their yard. I slowly put down the kickstand to the bike, and very slowly walked to the frat house porch. The little shit was sitting with three or four others in old metal chairs, drinking beer. When I got to them, I just stood for a minute looking at them. Then everything just exploded inside me in a terrific rage. I pulled the guy who was yelling at me right out of his chair, gave him a crushing slap across the face, and then pitched him headfirst off the porch into the bushes that bordered the porch. He was clearly pretty shaken up, and at first did not move at all. After a brief period, however, he did come around. It made me feel a little bit disgusted with myself, but on the other hand, he certainly had earned it.

The only thing I said was. "No good soldier wanted to kill anybody, least of all a child. If you would take the time to find the facts, instead of sitting there like the giant turd you are, you would know that the North Vietnamese were responsible for tens of thousands of women, children, and old folks being slaughtered. In Hue, during the Tet Offensive, we discovered mass graves, created by the NVA when they slaughtered whole neighborhoods, for simply not giving praise to their foolish cause."

I continued, "It amounted to tens of thousands of innocent people put to death, murdered, sometimes children, babies, slaughtered. Have you ever seen a mother and father hacked to death, with their little baby disemboweled lying all together? Well, I have, you little turd. That's what we were fighting against, to stop the slaughter of innocent human beings. So, asshole, you don't have a clue. Maybe you should learn. First, learn to keep your slimy little mouth shut unless you are sure you know what you are talking about. Maybe learn to accept the facts, which wouldn't hurt as well."

I couldn't stop myself at this point. "Yes, of course there were atrocities committed by us, but it was a rarity, because men snap in the intensity of war. When it happened the men responsible were court-martialed and sent to Leavenworth to spend a long time behind bars, then thrown out of the military in disgrace. The NVA openly praised their soldiers for killing innocent men, women, and children. They thought their actions were entirely appropriate. Anyone that didn't believe blindly in their cause did not deserve to live. They also killed strictly for the terror it would bring to the countryside if they were not obeyed."

I finally managed to finish up. "You little ass, why don't you put your actions into motion, go over there and volunteer to spend some time helping in one of the villages, then if you come back alive, a very big if, let me know how you feel. No, better stay here, where mommy can take care of whipping your ass."

By the time I arrived at the TV station, WTIU, it was over. My rage seemed to just disappear, thank God. It was the only time I ever just completely lost it since my time in the military. Everything just exploded.

After that I paid a lot more attention to what was going on inside of me. At any cost, I needed to keep the little black box buried deep. There was no room to let it out. That was the only time, thank God, that I allowed my inner self to grab hold of the situation at hand.

It scared me. The anger was still there even after all this time. I wanted desperately to put it all behind, to allow me to live in peace. I really hated the self-loathing; the devil was certainly at work. I needed to figure a way to forgive myself, but how to even begin?

CHAPTER 12

Going Round And Round With The Devil

School was just about done, and my first intention was to move back to Vermont. But my old friend Vin suggested I stay in Noblesville for just a while before I made the move. In the meantime, he asked me to work as an interior designer for his furniture store. At first, I was not interested in that at all, but as time went on, I was getting excited about the prospect of this new job.

Those three years at Indiana University Bloomington were some of the best of my life. I loved it all and even today have fond memories of those times. But in the end, I realized that there were more adventures out there. I just needed to go find them.

After accepting that position as interior designer with Noblesville Furniture, I did begin to feel that things were going to be all right after all was said and done. With this new job, I put the past away, told myself it was time to put even the war back in the rearview mirror as well. Unfortunately, along with the past, photography also began to fall into the background.

I forced myself not to think about what I had lost, and tried as best I could to put everything into interior design. Fortunately, a lot of the creativity I always had was able to be fed with this new adventure of interior design,

To this day, I regret leaving photography behind. But I learned my new craft of interior design, and as I did, I realized that we all make mistakes, sometimes pretty big ones. The trick was to keep moving forward, try to learn from mistakes, but at all costs keep moving.

CHAPTER 13

Marriage

My first child Tyler was born in 1984, just as my marriage was falling apart. The marriage failure had nothing to do with Tyler's mother, Anne. Really it was just more unfinished business. No matter how I tried to dispose of it, that little black box buried deep inside of me just kept reappearing. By now drinking to try to control it didn't help either. Still, I told no one about the trauma, and just hoped it would eventually go away.

But until I got control of it, I knew I was not going to stay married, that I would do something to harm the marriage, and I did. In hindsight, it seems quite obvious. There was going to be only one ruler. Either I could let that all go and spend all those energies on marriage. Otherwise, my drinking and almost daily thoughts about the war were going to control me.

Without dealing with Vietnam, I felt doomed to continue to drink. It had been the only method I could find in the moment to keep a lid on the memories. I realized later that I had become a functioning alcoholic. Get shitfaced every night, get up and go to work every morning. While it still worked to keep the bad memories from the war stuffed deep inside me, it was also taking a toll. The devil was cheerfully guiding me down a long, slow road of pain. The drinking really wasn't working nearly as well as I thought it was. Eventually a very steep price was going to be due one of these days.

We tried to keep the marriage alive and sought therapy and marriage counseling. But with all my problems that I wouldn't even acknowledge, recovery was hopeless. Consequently, she divorced me, and rightly so. Really, I wasn't worth the effort.

It would be the beginning of a long period of failing as the effort to keep everything under control slowly began to ebb.

CHAPTER 14

On My Own

It didn't take Anne long to move on with her life, thankfully. But for me, everything was different after the divorce. I had brought a child into the world, and needed to be as responsible as I could when he was with me. Shortly, I got into a routine of having Tyler over to stay with me every other weekend, and life started to rebound a little.

By this time, I had established my own design firm and was doing more commercial design work. I was continuing to see a therapist even after the divorce, and she introduced me to a really delightful woman, another therapist, in the office next door.

As luck would have it, Susan S. was a wonderful person, and I enjoyed her company enormously. Before I knew it, I found myself married once again. This time, we had two children together. They were both the love of my life, and the business was running along smoothly.

Ben was born in 1991, and Susan and I this time had at least a fighting chance to make everything work but still my little black box was still there, and demanding I take even more booze to keep it at bay.

Quite predictably, I ruined this marriage as well. It really wasn't, when it came down to it, Susan's fault. My drinking steadily increased, although I did try and never have a drink until evening. By this time, I had become a functioning alcoholic, staying sober during the daytime, and getting drunk every night. It was no longer just to keep my memories from Vietnam at bay. Now I was hooked. The devil now had me in his charge, and I was going to do as he wanted me to do.

After all these years, finally the war, the memories, and all the nightmares came roaring into the front of my life. No longer did I have a chance to keep any of it at bay. I was in trouble, and I knew it. While I did seek help from the VA, they quickly denied me again. It was still being run by political appointees from the Department of Veterans Affairs. These were always political appointments, and often not for the benefit of the veterans. These appointments were political payoffs in many cases.

Many of these lifetime appointments were not interested in the veterans at all. In many cases, they openly expressed their disdain for the vet, or even worse used their time to just ignore the needs of the veterans. During the 1980s and 1990s, dealing with a veteran's hospital was a horrible experience. The agency didn't really get a thorough housecleaning until President Trump came on the scene and fired all of them, then replaced these people with ones that truly cared about the veteran's needs.

It was another act in the tragedy of the way Vietnam veterans were treated after coming home.

SECTION 12

Demons to Rest

From every wound there is a scar, and every scar tells a story. A story that says, "I Survived".

Father Craig Scott

CHAPTER 1

Help Please Help

While I was still married to Susan, my dear friend from grade school, the one I'd gone to camp with, stopped by to visit one night out of the blue. Sergio Kornov and I had always remained close, but the last couple of years, we hadn't seen much of each other. So, it was good to see my dear friend. When he came by, he wouldn't come in, so we sat on chairs in front of my house, each drinking a beer. I could tell he had been suffering a lot.

By this time, I knew that Vietnam could be a big issue for some of us. Sergio and I were in the same bucket, suffering in both our own ways. We talked for hours, way into the next day.

We reminisced about our school days, our games together, and of course Sister Concepta, and finally the war that had changed both of us in so many ways. We were both quiet, gentle souls, and as kids had been taught to always be kind to others and respect the elderly. It was what our moms and dads expected of us both. There was never any question. You must always be kind to other people.

Killing was never brought into our vocabulary. It was just something the bible said was a mortal sin, period. But then we went to war. We both felt we had crossed some imaginary line, killing, and could never go back, never.

So, I took my medication every evening, and Sergio took his. But Sergio needed to start earlier in the day in order to keep his little black box buried.

As we talked, we realized we were both suffering from the same symptoms because of Vietnam. Sergio's case was even worse, though. He used booze and often other drugs to control his demons, morning, noon, and night. I could tell he was really strung out and needed help desperately, but he would never get the help he needed.

Sergio told me he had been a door gunner on a Huey, the main helicopter in the war. A door gunner was incredibly important to all our missions. The door gunner would usually see ground fire first, and it was his job to keep the pilot informed. He would also use his gun to suppress live enemy fire, especially if the Huey was dropping troops in the field or into a village. It was extremely dangerous and took a great deal of courage for him to continue while the enemy tried its best to shoot him dead.

He asked what I did in the war, and I told him I just held a camera and took pictures of guys like him as they were being shot at. Not as tough as his job, I told him, he told me to stop lying. He knew it was just as bad. Some of our experiences were almost identical, and we chuckled at the craziness of it all.

But even as we laughed, I knew, somehow, I felt in my heart Sergio was slipping away. There seemed to be nothing I could say or do to hold him.

A few days later, he gave up the fight. He took an overdose and died, I never was sure if it was deliberate or accidental. No more pain for Sergio. Thank God for that at least, no more pain.

It caused me to wonder if that would also work for me. But maybe you would have to take all the pain with you when you died. I didn't know, I couldn't figure it out, but I sensed it would only get worse for me after Sergio died. And I was right. It did.

CHAPTER 2

Reunion

In 2004, after being kept secret for over thirty-five years, the squadron that I had flown in, VO-67, was finally declassified. Almost immediately one of the guys began trying to find as many of us as he could. We all kicked in, and before long we had managed to find out about everyone. We decided to get together in Los Vegas and catch up. I remember that reunion like it was just yesterday. I remember that as I looked around, I could hardly identify anybody. Over the last thirty-five years, we had all indeed changed. My nineteen-year-old body then was now the body of a fifty-six-year-old man. So much had changed, but we had survived, and that was something, I suppose.

Here we were, all of us standing together for a group shot. It felt so odd to me. What happened to the other guys, the guys we left behind? Where were they standing just now? In a good place, I would hope. Really, I didn't know, and I guess nobody really knew. Nevertheless, I prayed. I prayed for Sergio, I prayed for all the guys I had seen killed, I prayed for my squadron buddies that didn't make it. But I couldn't pray for me. What I had done was to join the evil that is so often felt in battle. The funny thing was, I still thought that I would be forgiven, somehow, someday.

By this time, I was realizing I had to figure out how to live with my demons or they were going to kill me. Drinking more alcohol was always the only satisfactory solution available. I could still sleep, and the demons weren't as much of a problem during the day, as long as I kept busy.

That meant I always had to keep busy, never stopping for even a minute. Now, back from the reunion, I was starting to worry about it all. I worried that staying busy every minute of the day would no longer be effective. Was my drinking really out of control? That's what my gut was telling me. I was in big trouble.

But I was tired, so very tired of dealing with it all. After all these years, why couldn't I just figure out a way to make it all stop?

CHAPTER 3

This Is The End, My Friend, The End

Finally, I met Susan Smith in 2005, we just clicked. For a few years, we stayed extremely cautious, but finally we both felt the same and took a chance. We married in 2008.

This time, marriage was different. This time, Susan confronted me about my drinking during the evening hours, every night. She told me it wasn't normal. She suggested I seek help. No, she did more than suggest. She ordered me to see somebody that could help, and she was right. I knew she was right.

There was no denying the truth. She was shoving it in my face. So finally, after forty years of fighting with the little black box deep inside of me, I knew I needed at least to try something, to finally fight back, to somehow get the little black box somewhere that I could be in control.

Before our marriage, a couple of times I had seen a therapist, Dr. Judy, that I always liked. I gave some thought to asking her to help me find someone that could help me with my drinking. You see, to my way of thinking, what I needed to do was not stop, but just to find a way to control the amount I was drinking. Good idea, I thought at the time.

I finally broke down and gave her a call, and she agreed to see me about a week later. What luck this turned out to be. She was just right for my situation, almost perfect. She had also suffered as I had with trying to treat alcoholism. Also, she knew how stubborn I could be, and how to get around it

She was exactly the right person to go to, and I liked and trusted Judy to give me good advice. It was surprising to me that she knew exactly what my problems were, and what should be done first. At first, I refused to hear it. But in her kind sweet way, she listened to my problem, and made me repeat myself, "Judy, I need to figure out how to not drink as much."

She asked, "Well how much are you drinking?"

"Well, it seems to be a little much, at least my wife thinks so, almost a fifth of scotch every evening. Never a full fifth, however, I always leave a little in the bottle. But rarely do I drink during the day."

You see to my way of thinking, I had just lost control of my drinking, and I just needed to figure out how to put it to better use. That way it would keep me from the nightmares and hearing what the little black box had to say. It had gotten control and was soon going to wreck my life. I thought of how my best friend from grade school, Sergio, had lost control, and the outcome for him still gave me great sadness.

To avoid what had happened to Sergio, I felt that not using booze at all was a fence I could never get over. The predicament I found myself in was the most fearful thing I had ever experienced.

Finally, after a month or so I got the courage to tell Judy exactly what I thought would happen if I stopped drinking entirely.

I did not want to become another casualty of the war. I had managed to keep the war stuffed deep inside me for an awfully long time. With the help of booze, I could sleep, and the war stayed in the little box and could not get out. At least I thought it could not get out.

Little did I know just how cunning and evil booze really was. It was not helping me sleep at all. It was just delaying me for an even bigger crash, which had to happen, or at least that's how I felt. It never occurred to me there could be any other outcome, that I had a chance of winning this battle.

I didn't realize that if I let my demons loose, I didn't have to face defeat, I could even win the battle. But first I needed to admit to myself this evil was dragging me around, and it didn't have to be this way.

One day, while Judy and I were discussing what should happen next, she asked me a favor. She knew that I didn't consider that booze itself was not only part of the problem, but it was also the problem. Also, she knew that to my way of thinking, it wasn't booze that was the enemy, it was something else.

"Rick, I want you to do something for me. Before you shake your stubborn head no, let me ask what I want from you. There is an Alcoholics Anonymous meeting in Zionsville on Thursday evening, and I want you to attend it and then again on Saturday." That was all she wanted, just to go and come back and sit in this chair and tell her what the meetings were all about.

This was nuts. What in the world did she expect me to get out of this? But because she had been, up to this point, really helpful, I agreed. "Okay, Judy, I'll go for two meetings. But after that we need to work on a strategy that will let me continue to drink, just drink with more impact so I can get my demons back under control."

Judy nodded. "Fair enough, I'll settle for two meetings, but they must be this Thursday and then again on Saturday. Also, I want you to go to the same group for both meetings. Because it's Zionsville, you probably won't run across anybody you know. You don't have to speak at these meetings if you don't want to. If they ask if you want to say something, just say pass."

I replied, "I can do that, and I'm pretty sure that I can do Thursday and Saturday."

"Good, let's meet the first of the week, and look at what you have found. Does Monday, say at 1:30 PM work for you?"

"Yea, that's just fine with me. I'll rejigger my schedule so I can be in town all next week."

Well, the Thursday meeting went off without a hitch. In fact, I really enjoyed it. Nobody seemed to care if I spoke or not, and some of the talk was interesting. They all had a place they could go and yak about their problems.

The whole idea of the program was I thought, pretty clever. Somebody had created a place for all the drunks to hang out and feel sorry about all the shit they had created for others. I thought it was a very clever system to keep track of all the drunks in town.

Naturally, I was totally misreading everything. I wasn't ready to see the trees in the forest just yet.

On my way home Thursday evening, I stopped in Westfield, a little town not far from home and purchased myself a fresh bottle of scotch. By the time I got home I thought it would be fun if I could just look at the bottle and not open it for one day, so I set it on my desk in my office. Good idea, I thought. I could take it or leave it at will. This would at least convince Dr. Judy that the purpose of drinking for me was just to work as my medicine.

Well, that Saturday, the meeting was held at 9 AM, and there was a far larger crowd. At the earlier meeting, I had already met a few of this group, and I have to say they looked normal to me. But what did I know.

They had a little short prayer they all recited before they began. It was something like, "God grant me the serenity to accept the things I cannot change and the courage to..." It was pretty cool, but I didn't participate, just sat there and quietly let them do their thing. Somebody had brought in a humongous box of doughnuts. I've often thought that God in his infinite sense of humor was going to have me reincarnated as a doughnut as sort of my purgatory.

They started off by asking if anybody needed a start-over token. This was a coin about the size of a silver dollar, and it interested me. After a bit, I figured out how the coin deal worked. If you were a drunk and took a drink between meetings, they gave you a start-over token. Then they gave you a different color if you made it for a week, two weeks, one month, up to six months. Then if you wanted, I guess, you got nicer coins. If you stayed off the sauce for a year, they gave you a brass coin with the Roman numeral I in the middle of it. I hadn't noticed that the first meeting, or I just wasn't paying attention. In any case, this kind of start-over tactic was intriguing.

Then they would ask if anybody had a subject they wanted to discuss. Now this all went fairly quickly, and then we were off to the races. They let everyone talk who wanted to, and after an hour they cut the meeting off. That was it, except about everyone stayed after the meeting was over.

A bunch of them put the chairs away and folded the tables up. Then I couldn't believe it, but it must have been a dozen or more came up to me with offerings of doughnuts and a moment of chit-chat. They were all very nice, I must say, and most of them were professionals of one kind or another.

There were a couple lawyers, a pediatric doctor, and several executives. There were even a couple nurses, one an emergency room gal and another a surgery room specialist of some kind. They all seemed to be interested in me, which I had a hard time believing. But it was true-- we must have stood around talking for a half hour or more.

Actually, I got a good referral out of the deal. One of them had a wife who couldn't make her mind up how she wanted to re-do their family room. He actually asked me if I could help him out. Of course, I could, that was what I did for a living.

They did ask what caused me to come to this meeting, and I let them know it was to satisfy a therapist's desire for me to attend two meetings. At the time I thought, "Uh-oh, now they will begin their little preachy song and try to convert me."

But that didn't happen. They all just said about the same thing, something like, "Oh, that's wonderful, we hope you got something out of it, and come back. We would love to have you back for another meeting if you want to come back."

Of course, I damn sure didn't want to come back.

But one of the guys, Frank, let me know they usually all went somewhere for breakfast after this meeting. He laughingly said it was just a giant bullshit session with good breakfast food and fun. If I wanted, I was welcome to come along.

For some reason, as I stood there laughing with these folks, I thought, "What the hell, they look completely harmless, and one of them gave me some design work, so why not."

The breakfast was as advertised, damn good, and their company was full of laughter, and a good time was had by all. On my way home, I thought about my drinking. I realized it was worse than I thought. Was it possible, was I a drunk like they all used to be? Dear Lord, please tell me it isn't true. I didn't need this to add to my growing list of problems. The devil had worked me over for thirty-five years. I damn sure didn't need another problem added to the list.

CHAPTER 4

Start Over and Put It To bed

These thoughts were troubling to me. Most importantly, I wondered if I really was a drunk, and had to give up drinking, how would I manage the flashbacks, the nightmares? I was sure the devil had me firmly in his grip, and I didn't think he was going to open that box buried deep inside me without destroying me.

I felt in danger the way I did back there in Nam. Only now I could lose everything—not just my life, but my family and my business. Sergio was right all along. This was too much. How was I going to sidestep all of this? Death was certainly a working proposition.

God, I really wanted this all in my rear-view mirror, please.

That weekend, I did manage to stay sober. It was a first in almost forty years. I had relied on the booze to stuff all the bad into my little black box at night, as during the day I could fight back much better. At night, they would come for me, the demons, the killing, the blood, and I was defenseless.

But that weekend, I was strong. I faced it all without my medicine.

With Monday's morning sun, I hopped out of bed and told Susan I wouldn't be home until early evening. Even with Judy's help, I wasn't sure if I could stay on the course. It was so much to ask.

Our appointment was for 1:30 PM and that gave me a few hours to kill. I felt like I should think over everything before seeing Judy, but I needed to eat first. Now breakfast has always been the meal that I love most. I knew all the best breakfast restaurants around town. One of them catered to a lot of business folks, they served terrific food, and they were close to Judy's office. I knew the hostess well and asked if I could have a slow, really slow breakfast. "Well, of course you can, Rick. Just give me a minute."

I had been coming into this joint for quite a long time, and she was always the best. She fixed me up with a corner booth that was perfect. She also delivered to the table a stack of their special waffles with a fruit sauce that was to die for. Not bad for starters.

Now I had lots of time to reflect on the situation I had boxed myself into. I thought I had no hope, no way out. It was impossible after all this time to defeat this devil inside me. To make it even loosen its grip a tiny little bit seemed like asking for the moon.

At least I could report to Dr. Judy that I did more than just go to the meetings. I also stayed sober for three days. Cut right to the chase, I was scared shitless, just plain scared out of my wits. The only thing I did have going for me that day was that Dr. Judy had never lied to me, and always shot straight with me. I figured the least I could do was give her a chance to speak and let the chips fall where they may.

Unfortunately, the "chips" included my family. By this time in my life, there was not much left in the way of trust from my children. Sure, they knew Daddy was in the habit of drinking a bit much from time to time. But they didn't know it all.

It was still not firm in my head that I was sure about much of anything, except drinking. It was the most important tool I had to keep things on an even keel during the day.

I just wanted to close my eyes and know that when I opened them, it would all be gone, the devil, the little black box buried deep inside me, all of it gone.

Sometimes, it just seemed like I always must choose the most difficult road. There was no way I can make the destination easy or simple. It always must be hard. Now I thought, man, this sure as hell looks mighty, mighty hard. It kept occurring to me over and over, could I do this? Could I really conquer this demon? I just didn't know what the outcome was going to be. I just knew I couldn't go much further without trying.

At least, I told myself, trying something different could not make things any worse than they had already become. Could they? I just didn't know. I just wanted the pain to end, however it had to. It just had to end.

After my sumptuous breakfast, I made it over to Judy's office. I was way too early and had to wait. This was fine with me. During my wait, I couldn't help rehashing the issue over and over. Now I truly understood the torture Sergio had been going through. Was this the only way to conquer this demon that had taken residence during the war we had left behind? Maybe there just wasn't a satisfactory way out.

Dr. Judy was right on time, as usual. I swear you could set your watch by that woman's schedule. Once it got started, our meeting seemed to move along well, as we rehashed everything that had transpired the last couple of days.

Then it seemed like we slid right into the meat of the weekend. Did the participants get something out of the meeting, she asked? She wanted to know if I had participated in the meeting at all, but she knew the answer before I had a chance to respond.

I remember we both just sat there for a few minutes. Then she looked up and said, "Well, it appears to me that you didn't get too much out of the first meeting, but by the second meeting, you seemed to have gotten quite a lot."

I nodded slowly. "Yeah, I think that's about right. During the second meeting, I began to think that maybe they all weren't quite as kooky as I thought at first." I laughed. "There was even a substantial percentage of the people there that were quite well educated. Let's see, there was a pediatric doctor, a couple of nurses, and a couple of lawyers, and several business executives. Oh yeah, there was a guy there that wrote science fiction, and apparently had been published. What a story he had. Holy shit, you think I have problems; this guy was a mess."

Dr. Judy replied calmly. "That's very interesting. Sounds like it was a crowd you could listen to. Tell me, did you pick up any advice or thoughts from the meeting?"

I gave this question some consideration. "Yeah, a couple, I guess. They seemed like they all were driven by a purpose, they wanted to be there, and most had stayed sober for a good long time. What they said seemed to be the truth. Well, maybe, except for the writer." I chuckled. "He told me his pen-name and I'm going to check it out at a couple of libraries and bookstores. He had been living in the west, around Vegas, I think. He said his agent made him come to Vegas every few months, put him in a pleasant hotel suite, furnished him with a bottle of vodka, and ordered him to finish the draft he had been working on. Apparently, he couldn't leave until he had it finished. I guess this guy stayed drunk all the time, except when he ran out of money and was forced to write so he could keep drinking."

Dr. Judy looked interested, so I continued, "He said he always did as asked, but this time, he went somewhere in town, bought a shotgun, and decided to blow his head off. Said he was trying to be considerate of the hotel staff and decided to end it all in the closet of his room so they wouldn't have much to clean up. Well, he did manage to get the gun loaded, but before that, he had decided to finish off a bottle of vodka and apparently, it caused him to pass out this time before he was able to perform his task."

I continued, "When he came to, he was so frightened that he just got up, left the loaded gun, his clothes, everything. He bought a plane ticket to Indy with what money he had left, and then took a cab to a second cousin's house in Zionsville. According to his story, his cousin paid for the cab and put him up for the night. But he didn't want him to stay longer, and so he took him to downtown Indy to the Salvation Army. They have been providing him a place to stay since that time. He's been sober for several months now and has just recently started to write again."

Well, Dr. Judy was really listening to my story. "OK, here's what I want you to do next. The Zionsville meetings are populated with people you can identify with, so let's start there. What I think you should do is try meetings for a month, but just one month is all you must do. Then let's decide what to do next. Because your nightmares are a significant issue, I'll give you a prescription that will help with this problem, for thirty days. After that, let's see where we are and what we need to do."

I nodded.

She continued, "Eventually, I think we can get you to a place where you will be able to sleep on your own without the use of alcohol or any kind of drug. But let's do this one step at a time."

I took a deep breath. "Okay, I think I can do this-- but only because I trust you to not let me go off the diving board. At least not without a life preserver. If that is workable to you."

Judy smiled. "Of course, it is. Just remember to call me if you believe it isn't working. Your days of conquering problems like this on your own need to come to a stop. Also, let's try one additional thing. As you go along, you're going to find that AA has a very specific program for guys exactly like yourself. It is a program that they have been using a long time and is a proven program. Why not give it a try? It's not too hard."

"Okay."

"Just go slow, and I think you just might be made for it. Also, once you get out of the starting gate, I'm pretty sure the VA has an AA program at the downtown VA Center. If for some reason, it doesn't seem to be right for you, just let me know, and we'll figure it out together."

CHAPTER 5

Start Of The End

That was the start of the end of the war for me. I made it with the help of a lot of people from my wife Susan to my AA sponsor Frank, and to everyone that believed I was willing to take on the challenge. We were all be part of the miracle.

The Alcoholics Anonymous program turned out to be just about perfect for me. There is no bullshitting around in these meetings. If you try to evade the truth, someone will almost always call you out. They'll tell you straight up to cut the bullshit and tell the truth or shut up and say nothing. Of course, this is exactly what I needed and wanted.

While these meetings could be rather brutal, they also were truthful, and the folks in the meeting were always there to encourage me to keep moving forward. After a while, I began to see the logic in the meetings and that they certainly were not designed for the faint at heart. If you went to a meeting and had remained sober for several years, great. If you went to a meeting and had stumbled off track, even though you might have had a two-year token, you were never ridiculed. They simply gave you a start-over token and you began again. No ridicule, no castigation, no admonishments were given. Just "welcome back" and start all over again. Nobody said a disparaging word. After all, we all knew that it was only by the grace of God that it wasn't us relapsing.

It was indeed exactly what I needed, a no-bullshit method, along with honesty. After a couple of months, I began to realize they had an almost perfect twelve-step program for folks like me. All I really needed to do was go to the meetings, and with a sponsor's help, work the steps. This was not a new program, as it was started in the 1930's, and while it had evolved a bit over the years, the core of the program had always stayed constant. Eventually I would be able to confront the devil that had been crushing my soul all these years.

Now I had a place to go where I could truly express my desire to stay sober and defeat the devil that I carried around all these years. I know now that everyone around me believed that there was good to come from this journey. Now I firmly believe that everyone felt me capable of defeating the evil that stirred my soul in turmoil. With all the belief and encouragement given to me by these wonderful friends, I won the challenge. This taught me we all can be a part of the miracle, if only we learn to believe.

With the help of a sponsor from the meetings, eventually I was able to confront the evil that had stayed with me from Vietnam. This was a slow process for me, but I knew the changes taking place in me were real.

One day, almost a year into the AA program, I asked my sponsor if he could meet me to talk over some stuff. Of course, he readily agreed to meet that same day. I guess he was pretty good at judging me at this point.

When we finally got together, latter that day, at first, we had a friendly chat, like guys do. We just had a cup of coffee, and both shared our day. Then all of a sudden, I started to tell him all about Vietnam, and the little black box that helped me keep the devil at bay, or so I thought. Before I was done, I told him everything, every detail of the war, the things I did, the things I saw, everything, including the little black box deep inside me where I thought the devil controlled everything.

When I was finished, I felt mentally and physically exhausted. I didn't even realize that for the last half hour or so, I had been crying without stop. The tears just poured out of me, along with the whole story. I had finally got it all out, into the open light of day, and it was glorious, just glorious.

That was the beginning of the end of the little black box and the devil's punishment. My sponsor at the time, Terry, suggested that perhaps I should consider giving the monthly speech the Zionsville AA had on Saturday.

At first, I wasn't keen on that idea. But as time went on, I decided to go ahead and do it. Normally meetings are for only men and women in recovery. However, when they had a meeting with a speech, they allowed anyone to attend. So, I invited my wife Susan to attend and hear my talk.

Well, it went well. It felt so good to now be able to talk openly about it, and now I knew the devil didn't have a chance.

It still took me several more years to defeat the evil that had resided in my heart. But now I knew I had a chance. Finally, after quite the struggle, I did defeat it all. No longer do I have to fear my days at war. Now I can keep all that ugly stuff at bay, look at it, and know that none of it was my fault.

This was my beginning. I could acknowledge now that it hadn't been all bad, my military years. I had really accomplished something. I got to meet wonderful people along the way, some very famous people, and some that really knew life and weren't afraid to teach me. I've followed my dream from the beginning.

But then, beginnings are what life is all about, and so I reminded myself, each day, each moment in a day is a new beginning.

The End, Naw, Just The Beginning

It took a while to ferret out all the bad stuff living inside me. But with the help of a lot of kindhearted folks that really cared, I've now got all those demons under control. They no longer control me, I control them.

In retrospect, I don't blame anybody for what happened to me in Vietnam. It really was nobody's fault. War is full of evil, sometimes demons, sometimes lesser things, and everyone that goes into war has to face it on their own. There is no doubt that the horror of war is real. Some have the ability to just let it all slide away into distant horror that no longer is oppressive. But some are doomed to deal with it for a long time.

In my case, it took a little longer. In the end, in the aftermath of it all, my journey turned out for the better. So, I don't regret much of anything. My country asked me to serve, and I did so as honorably as I possibly could. Eventually they got around to hanging a bunch of medals on my chest, which meant nothing

much to me, except for one, which was given to me at our first
VO-67 reunion.

Because the entire squadron participated in helping our
Marine brothers at Khe Shan, the President of the United
States, George Bush, awarded us the Presidential Citation for
our actions there. But with the medal came a letter from the
Commanding Officer of Khe Shan. That letter was truly special. He told us that he was sure the base was going to be over-
run, but with our placement of the sensors, they were able to
know exactly what the enemy was up to and defend the base.
The result was that the North Vietnamese decided to retreat,
all 26,000 of them.

Of course, I do have a certain pride in doing for my country
what I could. But I ask myself, if I had it to do again, would I?
Yes, I probably would. After all, we only have one country to
live in, and I felt that the alternatives in the moment would be
a transgression of my duties as a citizen. So, I chose not to run
away to Canada, or some other country where I couldn't be
caught.

At one point, after returning to civilian life, I was asked to
participate in demonstrations against the war and my country. While I did begin to question the war, for me to have put
my medals on and paraded around in the antiwar movement
was just not acceptable. Those that did should be ashamed of
themselves. I feel like doing so would be much like trampling
on brave men's graves. Fortunately, of the men that served in
combat, less than one percent did that sort of performance, and
only one or two of them used their service for political gain.
There is surely a special place in hell for these cowards.

My only big regret is not having dealt with the pain inside of
me from the war sooner. It was booze that became my crutch,

and it nearly destroyed me, and in many ways, it harmed my children. They did not deserve this, and for that I shall always remain deeply ashamed.

Fortunately for me, I was able to take a path that led to forgiveness. When I think of my dear friend Sergio Kornov, it still brings on a deep sadness. He didn't deserve what he was forced into, and I hope that we never allow men returning from the service of their country to feel that despair is the only path possible.

Now I'm in the autumn of my life and trying to do for others what I can. I am thankful that now I have the chance to do what Father Gilman and Dad always wanted of me: To do good, live each moment, and before taking, give back, always.

Acknowledgments

M y wife, who encouraged me to write this book for my children. As I began, I quickly realized that I needed help, or at least encouragement, and soon found myself looking for an author living close by. I stumbled upon a national known author of many books, most best sellers, and asked if I might buy her breakfast and ask a few questions. At that point, God blessed me with Susan Crandall, not only a published, well known author, but she was raised in my hometown. Without her help, encouragement, and enthusiasm for this book, it would never have made it farther than a rough draft. She spent many hours reading what I had written, giving me advice on how to make it better, taking time from her own writing schedule to encourage me. Without her there is no question the book would not have crossed the finish line. Then, I discovered my brother-in-law, Rick Ranucci, a former attorney working as an legal editor for one of the largest publishers in New York, graciously offered to help review the rough draft and gave me a lot of very needed advice.

Of course, my brother Joe and his beautiful bride Claudette, who also gave a lot of very good advice, and kept me moving in a straight line. Last but not least, Alicia Rasley my very steady handed editor, and Danna Mathias-Steele, a really great cover designer and interior book designer as well.

9 798987 873038